ANNUIT: "He Agrees" (favors)

COEPTIS: "With the Cause which has Started"

NOVUS: New

ORDO: Order

SECLORUM: of the Ages

Under the ALL-SEEING EYE of Lucifer (Satan)!

(please see page 257)

THE WORLD'S LAST DICTATOR

By Dwight L. Kinman

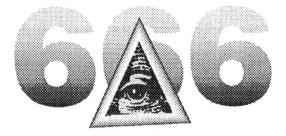

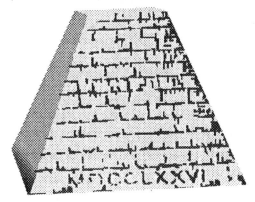

Solid Rock Books, Inc.

979 Young Street, Suite E
Woodburn, Oregon 97071

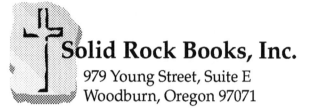

". . . Fear not: for they who are with us are more than they who are with them. And Elisha prayed, and said, 'Lord, I pray thee, open his eyes, that he may see.' And the Lord opened the eyes of the young man, and he saw; and, behold, the mountain was full of horses and chariots of fire round about Elisha."

2 Kings 6:16, 17

"Be strong and courageous, be not afraid nor dismayed for the king of Assyria, nor for all the multitude who are with him; for there are more with us than with him. With him is an arm of flesh; but with us is the Lord, our God, to help us, and to fight our battles . . ."

2 Chronicles 32:7-8

"And they overcame him by the blood of the Lamb, and by the word of their testimony; and they loved not their lives unto the death."

Revelation 12:11

"What shall we then say to these things? If God be for us, who can be against us?"

Romans 8:31

". . . For He hath said, 'I will never leave thee, nor forsake thee.' So that we may boldly say, 'The Lord is my helper, and I will not fear what man shall do unto me.'"

Hebrews 13:5-6

Content

Foreword

This book is about hope: a hope that burns like an inextinguishable flame in the heart of every believer in Jesus Christ. This hope of which I write is described in the Holy Bible in Titus 2:13:

> Looking for that blessed hope, and the glorious appearing of the great God and our Savior, Jesus Christ.

There were two men who lived in the 20th century. Each of these men wrote about hope. One was an avowed atheist. His name was Bertrand Russell. He was one of the world's most eminent philosophers of his time. Before his death he analyzed the impending world's crisis. He wrote these words: "Mankind is on a spiral downward to despair: I have given up all hope."

The second man was one of the great psychiatrists of Europe. He was a humble follower of Jesus Christ and was thoroughly convinced that the Bible was the Word of God. His name was Paul Tournier. Toward the close of his life, he too wrote about hope. These are his poignant words: "The only hope for the redemption of mankind is a personal confrontation with the Lord Jesus Christ."

In the following chapters we are going to analyze some of the great prophecies of the book of Daniel, written twenty-six centuries ago, and the book of the Revelation written almost 2000 years ago.

It is astounding to see these prophecies being fulfilled before our eyes in this last decade, of the 20th century A.D. These prophecies are leaping out of our television screens and literally screaming for our attention.

These men dared write history in advance. That is exactly what Bible prophecy is — history pre-written. No other book in all the ages has ever been able to do anything like this. It has never missed. It has a 1000% batting average! Its relevancy and up-to-dateness is startling!!

The fulfillment of these Biblical prophecies, alone, incontrovertibly establishes the credibility of this book of books and proves that it is the inspired, inerrant, infallible Word of God.

It is my sincere prayer, as you read the pages of this book that you will have the same personal confrontation of which Paul Tournier wrote, a confrontation with Jesus Christ and that you will come to know Him as your Savior and Lord.

Dwight L. Kinman
P.O. Box 386
Canby, Oregon 97013

ONE

New World Order

*By the end of this decade (2000 A.D.)
we will live under the first One World
Government that has ever existed in the
society of nations.*
One World Government is inevitable.
— **Pope John Paul II**
from the book *Keys of this Blood*,
Malachi Martin

"**I**f you do not stop this alert we will kill you!"

The voice of a man who identified himself as a Satanist came over the telephone while I was on the air – live – in a Salem, Oregon, television studio. My life had never been threatened before. I did not take the threat seriously.

Later that evening I walked out of the studio at about 10:30 P.M. I stepped into my compact car, pulled away from the curb, and entered the first intersection. Madison Street is dimly lit but I could see for several blocks in either direction. As I entered the intersection, for one fleeting instant, I caught a glimpse of a huge motor car flashing on his head lights. He had been waiting in the darkness and had timed it almost perfectly. He was upon me at high speed. I was blinded by the glare of his lights and deafened by the roar of the motor. I did not have even a split second to hit the brakes or the gas pedal. Then suddenly, I was through the intersection. He had missed me by a hairsbreadth.

The engineers at the television station told me later, "There was no possible way he could have missed you, but for divine intervention." I now believe that it was the hand of God that came in between that night.

About three days later an anonymous letter came to our post office box. It read, "If you do not stop this alert we will kill you. There is no power on earth that can stop us. Stop now while you can."

It was the most vicious letter I had ever received. I took it to my wife. We read it together. We had just celebrated our 42nd wedding anniversary. "Honey," I said, "I love you and our boys and our daughters-in-law and grand-children very much. What shall I do? Shall I quit?"

"We will never quit!" was her instantaneous response.

The letter read "We will kill you. There is no power on earth that can stop us." What they did not know was that there is a far greater power that is not of this world. They did not realize that I have protection in high places — very high.

> He that dwelleth in the secret place of the most high shall abide under the shadow of the Almighty. I will say of the Lord He is my refuge, my fortress . . . in Him will I trust (Psalm 91:1).

They did not know that I carry a heavy life insurance policy. I am fully covered at all times. It is John 3:16. They were also unaware that long ago the CIA had moved in to protect me twenty-four hours a day. No, not the government CIA, but the heavenly one — Christ's Innumerable Angels. "For He shall give His angels charge over you to keep you in all your ways" (Psalm 91:11).

For a few brief moments I felt afraid. Then my mind flashed to one of the great promises of the Word; one that had long ago become my life verse.

> According to my earnest expectation and my hope, that in nothing I shall be ashamed, but with all boldness, as always, so now also Christ shall be magnified in my body, whether it be by life or by death (Philippians 1:20).

Fear left me, and from that moment until now God has preserved me. I have been enabled by His grace to continue to be a watchman on the wall giving a clear, clarion sound of the trumpet. My goal now is as Paul the great apostle wrote in Acts 20:24,

> But none of these things move me, neither count I my life dear unto myself, so that I might finish my course with joy, and the ministry, which I have received of the Lord Jesus, to testify the gospel of the grace of God.

The Coming New World Order (One World Government)

There is a plan to bring America into a New World Order which is the secret code phrase for a one world government. It is gathering momentum and accelerating with the speed of a runaway freight train.

Behind this plan are powerful, global, mega forces that are on an inexorable, relentless drive to establish, on planet earth, a super world government by the year 2000 A.D. They believe they have it almost within their grasp, and they are about to make a dash to the finish line. It is that plan that we wish to analyze in this book.

New World Order in Microcosm

The plan for a New World Order in Microcosm is this: All nations, states of the earth, yield their separate national sovereignties to a World Central Authority — thus all of the political, economic, military and ecclesiastical power of the entire world would be brought under that central authority — the United Nations (a fearful master). All nuclear weaponry to be brought under the total control of the United Nations.

If Americans allow this to happen, our Constitution will be gone, our Bill of Rights will be gone forever. Our guns will be confiscated, never to be returned, and the free citizens of this nation will descend into slavery of a One World Government – super totalitarian state.

World Leaders Calling for the New World Order

For the first time in American history a president of the United States, George Herbert Walker Bush, called for a New World Order (the secret esoteric code phrase for the One World Government).

> We stand at a unique and extraordinary moment. This crisis in the Persian Gulf, as grave as it is, also offers us a rare opportunity to move toward an historic period of cooperation. Out of these troubled times, our objective — a New World Order — can emerge . . . A hundred generations have searched for this elusive path to peace, while a thousand wars raged across the span of human endeavor. Today, that New World Order is struggling to be born. A world quite different from the one we've known.[1]

On the eve of the Gulf War, General Brent Skowcroft, National Security Advisor to the President said, "A colossal event is upon us, the birth of a New World Order."[2]

In his book, *The Keys of this Blood*, Malachi Martin, a Roman priest, relates a statement by Pope John Paul II:

> By the end of this decade (2000 A.D.) we will live under the first One World Government that has ever existed in the society of nations . . . a government with absolute authority to decide the basic issues of human survival.[3]

He speaks about forces that are propelling us toward a One World Government. Then he added, "A One World Government is inevitable."[4] This book was highly endorsed by the Vatican.

Senator Mark O. Hatfield of Oregon, on the eve of the Gulf War wrote to President Bush,

> I want to be sure you know of my full support for you and the young men and women under your command. I look forward to joining with you in forging a New World Order.[5]

Norman Cousins stated in 1985, "World government is coming. In fact it is inevitable. No arguments for or against it can change that fact."[6]

The purpose of this chapter is to analyze that plan. First, let's trace it to its fountain-head.

The Fountain Head

It began with Adam Weishaupt, a professor of Cannon Law, in Ingolstadt, Germany. This apostle of Lucifer was an ex-Jesuit priest of Rome; a man involved in free masonry and witchcraft, in which he became an expert and founded the sect called the Illuminati on May 1, 1776.

Weishaupt's goal was to hide the sciences of witchcraft behind philanthropy, destroy Christianity, then set up a One World Government.[7] The men of the order have in mind for us a seventh millennium in which a superior race of god-men will take charge and guide the planet to a golden age. The vast majority (of people) are misfits, ignorant and unworthy of divinity. These will be destroyed or else reduced to surf status.[8]

The Illuminati

Like Free Masonry, the Illuminati is a Luciferian movement to preserve and promote the ancient black arts of Babylonian and Druid witchcraft. Its goal is the destruction of Christianity and all world governments and then to unite them under a One World Government whose ruler will be Lucifer. It wreaked havoc in Europe: masterminded the French Revolution where two to five million people were killed — hundreds of thousands via the guillotine. It leaped the Atlantic and came to America in the late 1770s. (Because of lack of space we will begin to trace its clandestine operation in America beginning in 1913.)

It Leaped Across the Atlantic

In 1913, there was a powerful man associated with Woodrow Wilson, the president of the United States. His name was Colonel Mandell House. He was one of the most powerful men controlling the government of the United States. He was one of the illumined ones. His ingenuity rushed through the United States Congress, the Federal Reserve Act, which actually culminated in 1922. The goal was to establish a New World Order, a One World Government. Through Colonel House and powerful men around him, they organized the Council on Foreign Relations. After Woodrow Wilson had signed the document that established the Federal Reserve, he realized what he had done, and then he said, "I have unwittingly ruined my government."[9]

The Council on Foreign Relations

The Council on Foreign Relations was established and it is one of the most powerful organizations in America. They make our foreign policy. The infrastructure is made up of men and women of the highest positions of power in the United States: banking, congress, education, and even religion. It is controlled by super mega-banker David Rockefeller. The Rockefellers and the Rothschilds of London are deeply involved in the craft — Free Masonry, the Masonic Order. Free Masonry is the hidden catalyst behind many of these secret organizations, but more on this later. The Rothschild and Rockefeller financial empires are almost too fantastic to calculate. Rothschild is strong into the Luciferian doctrine. We have information that he often places a chair at the dinner hour at his mansion in England where he invites Lucifer to come and sit with him at the meal.

Some "key" Members of the Council on Foreign Relations

Some of the members (and there are two thousand of them) are household names.

- Cyrus Vance, the man who is now working to establish peace in Somalia. Watch him on television.
- Paul Voelker introduced the new money. He's a powerful member of the Council on Foreign Relations, and former chairman of the Federal Reserve Board.
- Henry Kissinger, former secretary of state under Richard Nixon.
- James Baker, former secretary of state under Ronald Reagan and George Bush.
- George Bush, a 33rd degree Mason.
- Richard Cheney
- David Rockefeller
- Alan Greenspan, currently chairman of the Federal Reserve.
- General Brent Skowcroft, security advisor to President Bush.
- Ross Perot. Ross Perot didn't suddenly appear. He was groomed to be the spoiler. Be on your guard about Ross Perot, the man who said he would change the system ("it needs fixing" – our Constitution). He is also an advocate of gun confiscation.
- Jesse Jackson

There are almost two thousand others and they hold the highest echelons of power in the United States. Their priority is to establish a One World Government under the secret code – New World Order.

Some are members of the media, all powerful communicators. We have dozens of their names. To name just a few who are members of the Council on Foreign Relations, Trilateral Commission and some even members of the Skull and Bones: Dan Rather; Bill Moyers; Ted Koppel; Irving R. Levine; Barbara Walters; and David Brinkley.

One of the chief members, Richard Gardner, made no bones about their goal not long ago. He wrote,

> The House of the World Order will have to be built
> from the bottom up rather than from the top down . . . an
> end run around national sovereignty, eroding it piece by

piece, will accomplish much more than an old fashioned assault.[10]

He's talking about eroding our Bill of Rights and the Constitution and the sovereignty of the nation that you and I love and the flag we proudly salute.

The Rider on the White Horse

The Foreign Affairs magazine is the official relations magazine put out quarterly by the Council on Foreign Affairs. Recently a strange symbol began to appear on the cover. It is a mysterious logo of a rider on a white horse. The rider stretches his hand upward in defiance of the God of Heaven and he is making a mysterious hand gesture, the sign of Satan (diabolus).

> And I saw when the Lamb opened one of the seals, and I heard, as it were, the noise of thunder, one of the four living creatures saying, Come. And I saw and, behold, a white horse, and he that sat on him had a bow; and a crown was given unto him, and he went forth conquering, and to conquer (Revelation 6:1-2).

The goal is to bring about the surrender of the sovereignty of the United States of America. Rear Admiral Chester Ward, former judge advocate, general in theU.S. navy, and member of the Council of Foreign Relations for sixteen years, wrote:

> Submergence of the U.S. sovereignty and national independence into an all powerful One World Government . . . this lust to surrender the sovereignty and independence of the U.S. is pervasive throughout most of the membership.[11]

Look on the Back of Your $1.00 Bill

Where does the insignia or the actual phraseology of the New World Order come from? Look at a dollar bill. The great seal of the United States is on the dollar bill. On the back of the dollar bill you will find the insignia, the symbol of the triangle, the supreme symbol of Free Masonry which can be traced back to Egypt where Satan established the symbol of his three satanic deities. Yet it was not only Egypt's symbol but also that of ancient Babylon which was satanic to the core. It represents the three satanic deities, a mockery of the triune God of Heaven. Under the pyramid you'll see the words NOVUS ORDO SECLORUM meaning "new order of the ages."

Look above the triangle. You'll see the all-seeing eye of Lucifer and the words in Latin ANNUIT COEPTIS meaning "he agrees with the cause which has started."

That seal was designed in the late 1780s by five Free Masons. Two of them were Benjamin Franklin and Thomas Jefferson. The triangle in Egypt represented the religion of the three deities of ancient Babylon. And Benjamin Creme, the North American director of the New Age Satanic New World Religion, has revealed that the point within the triangle represents to the New Agers the coming world leader. Their cosmic Christ is none other than the Antichrist.

The Tri-Lateral Commission

The second secret organization –– the Tri-lateral Commission — was established in 1973 by David Rockefeller. He chose a Columbia University professor by the name of Zbigniew Brzezinski, security advisor to President Carter, to be the director. The Tri-lateral Commission is the executive arm of the Council on Foreign Relations. It has about 200 members. The Tri-lateral Commission of 1993 is comprised of the twelve nations of Europe, Canada, America, Mexico, and Japan. The Tri-lateral sphere in conjunction with the Club of Rome, the Tri-lateral Commission, divided the planet into ten bio-regions. The United States is region one; Europe is region two; and Japan is region three. That is designed to be the power center of a ten nation, one world transnational one world government in the New World Order. These nations, the G7, are to be the political and financial power of the world. Their driving goal is to make the United States a region in a global community of nations, a New World Order.

Senator Barry Goldwater wrote:

> David Rockefeller's newest international cable . . . is
> intended to be the vehicle for multi-national consolidation
> of the commercial and banking interests, by seizing
> control of the political government of the United States.[12]

The Tri-lateralist movement is unwittingly setting the stage for the political-economic One World system the Bible predicts for the last days. What the Tri-lateralists are trying to establish will soon be controlled by the coming world leader, the Antichrist himself.

Let me list just a few names you will recognize of the members of this commission: George Bush; Zbigniew Brzezinski; Henry Kissinger; David Rockefeller; Brent Skowcroft; Jimmy Carter; and many more.

The Skull and Bones

From Yale University, came one of the most powerful, secret organizations now driving toward a New World Order. The members in this organization hold powerful positions in the world: David Rockefeller, George Bush, William Buckley, General Brent Skowcroft, and Averill Harriman, etc.

Anthony Sutton, a teaching fellow at Stanford University, wrote the book *America's Secret Establishment — An Introduction to the Order of Skull & Bones*. The Skull and Bones Society is centered in Yale University. Each year fifteen graduates are chosen and inducted into the Society. They lie in a coffin; they drink blood from a human skull, surrounded by Nazi swastikas – the eternal sign of the Babylonian sun god; they rise as reborn man-gods. I will summarize the 280 page book in one sentence:

> We're going to use the Hegelian Dialectic process to
> bring about a society in which the state is in absolute and
> total powerful control, a new world order where the state
> is absolute and the individual can only find freedom in
> blind obedience to the state.[13]

This describes a total occultic socialist one world dictatorship!

According to the oath George Bush took when initiated years ago in the Skull and Bones this oath would absolve him and take precedent over any other oath, even the oath to protect and defend and uphold the constitution of the United States of America.

United Nations

Another organization, the United Nations, forty-five years ago formulated the charter and by gradual process of regionalization, in fact in the charter of the United Nations, they outlined the eventual regionalization of the planet. They would move the nations through regionalization into a "one world government." Already the planet is divided into those ten magna regions.

Foreign Troops Now Training on American Soil for the Global Police Force

I want to reveal something else to you about the United Nations. Troops from foreign governments are now on American soil. United Nations' troops are now on American soil. We have evidence that there are perhaps a 1/2 million. The president of the United States is calling for an international police force to operate under the United Nations. Perhaps with 100,000 American troops integrated with hundreds of thousands of United Nations troops from various nations, America will be the police force of the world integrated with the soldiers of other nations. They are known as the multi-national jurisdictional task force. I am not paranoid but they are now operating on American soil. They travel in black helicopters, in black uniforms with blue helmets.

I was recently in Medford, Oregon. A security guard who is a warm, personal friend of mine revealed to me that in October of 1992, when Air Force One touched down in Medford and George Bush was in the last few days of campaigning for the presidency, the security guard said:

> I approached that plane and when it was opened, I and other security guards saw twelve blue helmeted, black suited United Nations soldiers. They looked as

though they may be from Czechoslovakia and East Germany. Our security people in Medford asked them, "Who are you?" One of their spokesmen replied, "It's none of your business, get out of here." And the local guard had to withdraw.

We have a letter from the office of Dick Cheney, formerly Secretary of Defense. He revealed in that letter to a man in Oregon, that Fort Dix was being set aside to train United Nations' troops right now. President George Bush addressed the world leaders of the United Nations some months ago, and he said, "It is the sacred principles enshrined in the United Nations Charter to which we will henceforth pledge our allegiance."

World Police Force

The plan is to integrate American troops with foreign troops to be trained on American soil — a multi-national jurisdictional task force (MJTF) — a world police force of 100,000 troops. (PLEASE READ WITH ALL THE ALERTNESS OF YOUR BEING IF YOU LOVE FREEDOM!) Under the direct command of the United Nations we will be brought one step closer to world government.

I have a letter dated November 5, 1992, from the Office of Secretary of Defense. It states that President George Bush (then President of the United States) in a speech to the United Nations authorized U.N. troops to train on American soil. Fort Dix was designated as one of the main centers for this operation. President Bush stated: "We will achieve the great objective of the U.N. Charter."

Remember a part of that charter states, "The regionalization of the nations of earth into a One World Government."

House Bill 2616 the Oregon State Legislature 1993 regular session:

> While engaged in law enforcement activity within the state, an officer of the national police corps has all the powers, authority and immunity from liability as a peace officer.

This is frightening!!

Surrender Our Arms

A world constitution has already been framed. In its preamble are these words:

> The age of nations must end . . . the governments of the nations have decided to order their separate governments in one government of justice to which they surrender their arms.

This will be the Federal Republic of the World. The U.S. State Department Publication 7277 calls for complete disarmament of the United States.

John Rankin was a loyal American. As a U.S. Representative, he stood on the floor of the House of Representatives and made this statement:

> The United Nations is the greatest fraud in all history. Its purpose is to destroy the United States.

There was a wise man who once held the office of President of the U.S. He warned the American people:

> No free man shall ever be barred the use of arms. The strongest reason for the people to retain their right to keep and bear arms is, as a last resort to protect themselves against the tyranny of government.   *Thomas Jefferson*

In 1990, a female student from Beijing, China, described her parents' last words to her:

> Tell the American people never to lose their guns. As long as they keep their guns in their hands, what happened here will never happen there.

History reveals that for those people who surrender their guns — the next step is slavery.

How Close Are We to the New World Order?

May, 1992, at an ultra secret Bilderberger meeting, held in Evian, France, Henry Kissinger said that the U.N. needs to be the cornerstone of the New World Order. Then he made this incredible statement:

Today Americans would be outraged if U.N. troops entered L.A. to restore order — tomorrow they will be grateful.

Brace yourselves for this next statement:

When presented with this scenario, individual rights will be relinquished for their well-being **granted to them by their world government.**

There is a new book out that is one of the most popular books in the world. Hundreds of thousands of copies are being sold. It is called *Planethood*. This book reveals that the U.S. Constitution is to be superseded by a World Constitution.

A World Constitution

They intend to have:

1. A Bill of Rights for 167 nations — each nation would have one vote (that means America could be outvoted in the U.N. 166-1).
2. They plan a civilian executive branch to enforce world laws directly upon individuals. (Translation: our Bill of Rights would be transcended by U.N. world government law.)
3. The world body would control all weapons of mass destruction –– they would disarm all nations under careful inspection down to the level of internal policing.

Massive Media Hype

The American people are being conditioned on a massive scale by a Rockefeller controlled media for the New World Order. One poll showed that fifty percent of the people believe it would be a "good idea" to live under the rule of the United Nations. Gradually, like the frog in the pot, we are being conditioned for the day the New World Order crowd will pull the cord — the trap will snap shut and we will find ourselves in a One World Government.

Adam Weishaupt, upon establishing the order of the Illuminati, smugly reflected on how he "conned" the "gullible Christians" of his day, saying:

> The most wonderful thing of all is that the distinguished Lutheran and Calvinist theologians who belong to our Order really believe that they see in it (Illuminati) the true and genuine sense of the Christian religion. Oh, mortal man, is there any thing you cannot be made to believe?

Jesus said, "He would deceive the very elect if it were possible."

The Bilderbergers

The next secret organization is the Bilderbergers of Europe — "The Fourth Reich of the super rich" — a powerful group of 100 men and women in Europe and the United States. It is interlocked with the Council on Foreign Relations. Some of the members in America are: Henry Kissinger; Zbigniew Brezinski; David Rockefeller; Robert MacNamara; Gerald Ford; William Buckley; Catherine Graham, editor in chief of the Washington Post; and Lloyd Bentson, attendee.

They are powerful. They are unbelievably powerful. It is the Bilderberger group who designed the fusion of the United States of Europe, the European community. Actually, it was the catalyst to fulfill the prophecy for the last days world empire — the ten toes of Daniel's image — a Revived Roman Empire.

Some of those who attend the Bilderberger's meetings (which are ultra secret meetings) in Europe are: Baron Edmund D. Rothschild of London, who controls almost all of the oil in the eastern world, sets the gold standard of the world, and is deeply involved in the Luciferian doctrinism of the Illuminati and Free Masonry; Helmut Kohl of Germany; Prince Barnhardt of the Netherlands; Prince Charles of Great Britain; Lloyd Bentson, an attendee; and Gerald Ford and Wm. Buckley of the United States.

Bill Clinton

The Bilderbergers had an ultra secret meeting in Germany at the Black Forest in mid-1992. David Rockefeller was the key-note speaker and this was the text of his opening remarks:

> We are grateful to the *New York Times,* the *Washington Post, Time Magazine,* and to many others whose directors have attended our meetings and respected our promise of discretion for almost forty years.[14]

The translation is "Thank you for the forty year cover-up." The left wing and the Illuminati looked the other way and hid it from the American people.

Thus one of the top gurus of the Bilderbergers in America, David Rockefeller, gave credit to the newspapers and these magazines for covering up a plan to dissolve the sovereignty of the United States and our constitution and our Bill of Rights.

They invited a man from America, a man whom the New World Order elite had groomed for twenty years: a man who was closely associated with George McGovern (Mr. McGovern is on the Board of the ACLU — an organization that is seeking to delete the name of God from all American life). This man of whom I write is a Rhodes scholar. The Rhodes scholarship was established at Oxford University in England, to train outstanding young men in England and America to become leaders in the coming New World Order. It has been described by one researcher — an authority on the New World Order — as induction into the Illuminati. He attended Georgetown University, a Jesuit school, where his chief professor and mentor was Carrol Quiggley, one of the main advocates for the New World Order. He moved on to Yale University, the home and global base and training center of the Skull and Bones secret organization.

There at the ultra secret Bilderberger meeting in Baden, Germany, he was auditioned and screened. He passed with flying colors. He is the man who placed his hand on the Bible, on January 20, 1993, and solemnly swore to uphold, protect and defend the constitution of the United States of America.

"Earth in the Balance" the Vice President

The Vice-President wrote in his book *Earth in the Balance,* "Our religious heritage is based on a single earth goddess who is assumed to be the fountain of all life."[15] This is the ancient religion of Babylon. Earth was their mother goddess and her Satanic number was 666. The Vice-President says that we should embrace the eastern religions. "All men have a god within. Each man has a god within because creation is god. Nature in its fullness is god." He has embraced the lie of Eden described in Romans 1:25:

> Who changed the truth of God into a lie, and worshiped and served the creature earth more than the creator who is God blessed forever.

He writes that the fundamental Christians who teach Bible prophecy are "heretical." I think he is saying that we are heretics.

As a United States senator he led the American delegation to the Rio Conference in 1992. This conference was backed by the full power of the New Age religion.

He writes about the mother goddess. This great senator, "the darling of the New Age," calls for all Americans to embrace the great eastern religions. Hinduism is the religion that says we are evolving into gods and by reincarnation we will never die.

Rev. James Parks Morton is closely associated with the man of whom I write. They are planning through Global Forum, a parliamentary gathering of all religions, a gala event set in Chicago for August 1993, and from all information we've gathered, it is alleged the senator will be there, sitting down with the leaders of all the great false religions of the earth. This man is pro-gay, pro-abortion, and pro-mother earth religion, the darling of the New Age.

He placed his hand on the Bible in 1993, on January 20th, and pledged as Vice President of the United States of America that he would uphold, protect and defend the constitution. His name is Al Gore. Could it be that the man of whom I first spoke, the man who sits in the Oval Office, the man who is backed by the full power of the secret organizations, the Council of Foreign Relations, the

Bilderbergers, controlled by the Free Masons and the Illuminati, could he be the catalyst under the controlling, permissive hand of God to bring America into a New World Order?

The Secret Known Only to God

I do not know. That's a secret known only to God. Could it be that the second man, who is just a heartbeat away from the presidency of the United States, Al Gore, deeply involved in the New Age religion, could it be that the man who believes that we have a god within, the man who has embraced the lie of the serpent of Eden, the man who believes that we should worship nature, the darling of the New Age, could be the catalyst to lead America into a One World church and a One World government?

It was Mr. Gore who led the American delegation to the Rio Summit in June, 1992. Mr. Don McAlvany makes this incisive observation:

> The environmental crisis is the vehicle upon which the New Age movement and the New World Order plans to move the world to global government before the close of the 1990's.[16]

How close are we to the New World order?

Special Report

"Elitist Insiders Dominate Clinton's Appointees"

(Key: CFR – Council on Foreign Relations; TLC – Tri-lateral Commission)[17]

Bill Clinton is a member of the CFR, TLC, Bilderberger Attendee and was inducted into the DeMolay (Masonic) International Hall of Fame in 1988.

High level appointments:

- Warren Christopher, Secretary of State, CFR.
- Johnetta Cole, appointed to head the transition team. She has been a supporter of Castro's Communist Cuba.
- Lloyd Bentson, Secretary of Treasurer, former CFR, Bilderberger Attendee.
- Roger Altman, Deputy Secretary of Treasurer, CFR.
- Donna Shalala, Health and Human Services, CFR, TLC.
- Robert Reich, Labor Secretary, Rhodes Scholar.
- James Woolsey, CIA Director, CFR, Rhodes Scholar.
- William Crowe, Jr., Foreign Intelligence Advisory Head, CFR Director, and TLC.
- Strobe Talbot, Ambassador at large and special advisor to Secretary of State on now independent states of Russia, CFR director, TLC, Rhodes Scholar.
- Winston Lord, Assistant Secretary of East Asian Affairs, CFR, former CFR president, TLC.
- Bruce Babbitt, Interior Secretary, CFR, former TLC.
- Joycelyn Elders, Surgeon General who has served on the Rhodes Scholarship Selection Committee.
- Madeline Albright, United Nations Ambassador, CFR.
- Les Aspin, Defense Secretary, CFR.
- Anthony Lake, National Security Advisor, CFR.
- Stephen Oxman, Assistant Secretary of State for European Affairs, CFR, Rhodes Scholar.

Rhodes Scholarships was established by Cecil Rhodes as a part of his plan for world domination. Cecil Rhodes set up the scholarship fund to train the intellectual cream of America and Great Britain and indoctrinate them in the plan for a New World Order (One World Government).

Fritz Springmeir's research in his book *Be Wise As Serpents* reveals that a Rhodes Scholarship is an induction into the secret society of the Illuminati.

More High Level Presidential Appointees[18]

- Attorney-General Janet ("Johnny") Reno — shocking proof that she's a hardened lesbian. Discover the real reason why she wickedly burned to death the innocent women and children at the Branch Davidian compound in Waco. (See Murder at Waco appendage.)
- Surgeon-General Dr. Joycelyn Elders — she'll make sure that pre-schoolers and elementary school children are given condoms and told about all the "benefits" of abortion.
- Judge Ruth Bader Ginsburg — for seven years she was a radical feminist lawyer for the ACLU, an organization that has fought to ban Jesus, prayer, and the Ten Commandments from our schools. Ginsburg just loves abortion rights. Now she's Hillary's choice for the Supreme Court.
- Donna Shalala — the lesbian community claims she is the Amazon "love sister." As Secretary of Health and Human Services, Shalala is indisputedly the meanest Christian hater who's ever held a top cabinet post. She's also a member of the Council of Foreign Relations and the Tri-lateral Commission.
- Laura Tyson — a former Berkley professor, Tyson is Clinton's "Economic High Priestess." A member of both the CFR and the Tri-lateral Commission, Tyson is an avowed Marxist who wants to transform America into a Communist paradise.
- Roberta ("Bob") Achtenberg — Hillary's put this lesbo crazy in charge of all federal housing policies. Proudly marching in a Gay Rights parade, the video cameras captured Achtenberg passionately kissing her lesbian lover. She once led a vicious hate campaign against the Boy Scouts.

Hillary Rodham Clinton was reported to be communicating with the dead spirit of Eleanor Roosevelt. This was stated on the Rush Limbaugh radio program via 600 stations coast to coast in June 1993. This is necromancy and is forbidden in the Word of God. This is communication with demons who masquerade as spirits of important dead personages. God's Word warns us in Leviticus 20:6:

> And the soul that turneth after such as have familiar spirits . . . I will even set my face against that soul and will cut him (her) off from among his people.

The evidence points to the stark reality that the American government, in the highest echelons of power, is now in the hands of a clique whose primary goal is to bring about the surrender of the sovereignty of this nation to a One World central authority (their New World Order) and unless we Americans realize this, and quickly, it will be too late. Their trap will snap shut and we will be in a One World government.

Only One Piece of Paper Stands in Their Way

But there is only one piece of paper that does stand in their way of reaching their goal and that is the Constitution of the United States and our Bill of Rights.

If you love liberty and freedom and our flag please read this very carefully, because I bring you the truth!!! I have an unimpeachable documentation or I would not report this. It happened on April 2, 1992. I have an eye-witness account; one newspaper, the Spot Light, was represented there in the United States Senate. That newspaper was not afraid to tell the truth in an exclusive article *Senate Ratifies U.N. Treaty* by James P. Tucker, Jr.

> The United States Senate, with little debate and no recorded vote, and while the controlled media looked the other way has ratified the treaty permitting U.N. police to enter this country and charge you with a crime if your words are perceived to be politically incorrect.

> Senators fearful of public outrage ratified the international U.N. Covenant of civil and political rights, the human rights treaty with a voice vote on April 2. It came on a Thursday when no other significant action was pending because Congress was leaving town for its usual four day weekend. No Senator demanded a recall vote to

get his colleagues on the record. Nobody questioned whether a quorum was present. It was simply announced that 2/3 had approved the matter by a voice vote.[19]

This is the comment that is made in that article, "A sneaky surrender of the United States sovereignty by the U.S. Senate and its ratification of the U.N. Covenant on civil rights, political rights is an act of treason comparable to a coup d'etat."

The Constitution, Article II, Section II, on the President of the United States:

> He shall have the power by and with the advice and consent of the senate to make treaties provided 2/3 of the senators concur.

Article VI, Section II states in part:

> . . . that this constitution and the laws of the United States which shall be made in pursuance thereof that all treaties made shall be the supreme law of the land, the judges in every state shall be bound thereby.

Secretary of State John Foster Dulles wrote in 1952:

> The treaty making power is an extraordinary power by the United States Senate and it's liable to abuse. Treaties make international law and also domestic law. Under our constitution, treaties become the supreme law of the land. Treaties can override our constitution. They can cut across the Bill of Rights, given to the people by the Constitution and the Bill of Rights.[20]

U.N. Covenant

If the U.N. Covenant on human rights should receive the support of two-thirds of the United States Senate in its treaty making power, whether they realize it or not, our whole Bill of Rights will be automatically and immediately repealed. It will be transcended by the charter and the laws of the United Nations.

It is just that simple. I have the Congressional Record, April 2, 1992, Article II. There were two powerful U.S.

Senators that pushed that treaty ratification through. They rushed it through with a voice vote and Senator Mitchell banged down the gavel and said, "So ordered." Who were those Senators?

    1. A powerful New Age United States Senator by the name of Claibourne Pell.
    2. Senator Al Gore.

You can find it in the congressional record April 2, 1992.[21]

The only way this could be reversed would be by a majority vote of the Supreme Court of the United States. This information has been withheld from the American people by the Illuminati, Rockefeller, Bilderberger controlled media — it is a complete cover-up!

The New World Order has shifted into high gear and the time bomb is ticking off the seconds where the power elite secret societies will make their move and Americans will find themselves in a One World government under the control of a fearful master — the United Nations.

The President and "New Politics of Meaning"

Insider Report by Larry Abraham, July, 1993

The next Clinton/Rodham revelation comes from the British Press *The Sunday Telegraph* of June 20, 1993. Headlined "White House gets cult fever," subtitled "Bill and Hillary's guru in a yarmulke preaches Moses mixed with Marx." This lengthy item is by-lined by Ambrose-Evans-Pritchard in Washington, D.C. It begins thusly:

> The full story is beginning to come out. The President and First Lady of the United States are followers of an eccentric cult, a Jewish heresy no less, that mixes the Old Testament with a dash of medieval cabbala mysticism and a good deal of 1960s campus Marxism.

The significance of this article, especially in light of what we have revealed in the past about the First Persons, must be taken very seriously. I've therefore excerpted at length from this piece. Here are some of Mr. Evans-Pritchard's more salient points (with British spelling and punctuation intact).

> We knew something was amiss when Hillary Clinton departed from her health care script in April and began calling for a "new politics of meaning", a spiritual revival to cure the "sleeping sickness of the soul" that ails America. But now we learn that both she and her husband have been drawing their philosophical inspiration for the past five years from Tikkun, an obscure left-wing Jewish magazine.

> The Tikkunistas — there are 40,000 subscribers — meet in cells around the country. Once a month they gather for a Tikkun Sallon, during which they share a vegetarian potluck meal and then discuss some deep political theme. They may drink, but they do not smoke.

Then we learn where Bill Clinton got the term, "New Covenant," which so upset many religious leaders with its borderline blasphemy. Mr. Evans-Pritchard writes:

> The editor of *Tikkun*, Max Lerner, scarcely looks the part of a guru-in-chief to the Clinton White House. A dishevelled, chubby man of fifty, brimming with nervous Jewish charm, wears a beaded yarmulke and walks with a heavy-footed clumsiness.

> It came as a bolt out of the blue when Bill Clinton wrote him a letter in 1988 saying: **"You have helped me clarify my own thinking."** Hillary was converted a little later, but she is now a true believer in Tikkun's plan to "feminize" America, and to achieve the **"New Covenant"** by means of the paradigm shift. (And in case you don't know what that means, I don't either.)

> "Man," says Mr. Lerner, "is naturally caring and sensitive. **It is capitalism that has turned him into a brute, therefore the system must be totally reformed."**

> As to Lerner's background, we find: In the early 1970s, as a junior professor, he led the Seattle Liberation Front, an ultra-left organization described at the time by the state

attorney-general as **"totally indistinguishable from fascism and Nazism."** His many adventures led to an indictment for a violent assault on a U.S. federal courthouse in Seattle.

His earlier relationships include a non-legal "marriage" with one of his students, with whom he had a child. At their cohabitation ceremony, the wedding cake was decorated with the words "Smash Monogamy."

The breakdown of families, the deep trouble people are having in finding and sustaining relationships are rooted in the psychodynamics of the capitalist marketplace.

Tikkun fuses Left-wing politics with religiosity. It promotes a Jewish variant of **"liberation theology"** — the Catholic-Marxist hybrid adopted by guerrilla priests in Latin America. The word Tikkun means to "mend, repair, and transform the world." It is inspired by the Zohar manuscript, a late medieval work that posits the primordial perfection of man. Orthodox rabbis regard it as borderline heresy, believing that man is inherently flawed and sinful.

At root, the Tikkun craze is about the middle-aged crisis of meaning for a coterie of Yale Law School graduates and their confused friends. Culturally adrift, they are trying to create a new designer religion for themselves out of the fetishes of modern life — a bit of ecology here, a bit of psychobabble there — **a cult without faith, without God, without transcendental purpose, doomed to failure.**

What are we to make of a Presidential couple, a Baptist and a Methodist, dipping into the heresies of other religions? It seems they have no fixed sense of themselves, no moral anchor, no bottom.

As I stated above, this type of insight to the Clinton/Rodham co-presidency is extremely significant in that it helps to explain what for many has heretofore been inexplicable — why they do what they do.

Considering that this administration has either been in or preparing for office almost nine months now, one nagging aspect of their conduct and attitude seems to be emerging. It could best be summarized as "They are not one of us." Without actually using this phrase (it's more a feeling than a remark), the majority of Americans, regardless of age or political affiliation, are starting to feel that there is something about this administration which is just not right.

Here's the bottom line. **Bill Clinton and Hillary Rodham do not share our cultural beliefs.** They are, in fact, powerful representatives of a counter-culture. What Michael Lerner is preaching and they are buying into flies directly in the face of Judeo-Christian civilization. It isn't just about Marxian economics or libertine sexual license, **it's about power — dark power — and it challenges the very tenets of our civilization.**

How can these people talk about "preserving the family" and then propose every possible move and measure which works to undermine the very definition of same?

How can these people talk about "defending children" when every policy and program put forth ultimately places our children's fate in the hands of the State and in some cases, deviants, i.e., Roberta Achtenberg?

How can these people talk about "making America strong" when every administration dictum is designed to weaken those who can best provide that strength — the middle class?

And finally, how can these people talk about "leading the West" when their core beliefs conflict with the very philosophies and theologies which make "The West" what it really is — a civilization incorporating the Judeo-Christian ethic?

Make no mistake about it — the White House guru's Tikkun is no more Jewish than Hillary's Methodism is Christian. And neither will mankind provide the means to "repair and transform the world." **Believing as they do in the "primordial perfection of man" can only lead to chaos, confusion, or worse.**

In thirty years of studying, writing, and speaking about the problems and issues facing our world, our nation, and ourselves, I have come to believe that the single most difficult idea for basically decent people to grasp is that there are some among us who consciously and willfully choose to do evil. By "choose to do evil," I do not mean the normal process of providing a rationale to evil actions or the development of what is called a lax conscience. What I mean is exactly what I said: A premeditated act of the will which is by its very nature knowingly and willfully evil.

The very "coming to grips" with this awful and terrifying reality is the one thing which most of us will avoid at every turn — it's just too terrible to contemplate.

And while you (I hope not briefly) reflectively explore this horrifying possibility, let me leave you with one more undeniable fact. While some among us may purposefully choose evil and act upon it, very few have the wherewithal to destroy the lives, property, or way of life of millions of people. **Only heads-of-state are that powerful. And most examples of such devastation in history feature 20th Century heads-of-state. Contemplate that as you watch the Clinton-Rodham Administration work its will and exercise its power.**[22]

TWO

Ten Magna Regions
Executive Order 11490

*We are on the verge of a global
transformation. All we need is the right
major crisis and the nations will accept
the New World Order.*

— David Rockefeller
Council on Foreign Relations

*The financial system of the free world
is on the verge of a major catastrophe. In
fact it almost collapsed in the summer of
1983.*

— John Zajack
Delicate Balance

What could be the catalyst to bring about a paradigm shift (a sudden change in the global consciousness of the peoples of America and the world) that might cause them to desire to surrender the sovereignty of their nations to a New World Order (One World government)?

We can discover what that catalyst will be by monitoring these elitist global leaders and what they are saying, because little by little they are giving us a glimpse of their plans as they drive to usher in the New World Order. Willis Harmon of the Stanford Research Institute and president of Noetic

Sciences is quoted by Dr. Dennis Cuddy, Ph.D., in his book *Dawning of the New World Order,*

> The oppressive debt structure could induce a partial breakdown of the world's economic system.[1]

This could provide the crisis needed to usher in the managed New World Order desired.

David Rockefeller, the powerful leader of the Council of Foreign Relations, said,

> "We are on the verge of a global transformation. All we need is the right major crisis, and the nations will accept the New World Order."

In his book *Toward a New World Order,* Don McAlvany quotes from the Club of Rome: "Only a revolution, the substitution of a New World Economic Order can save us." The Club of Rome intends to control international trade, world food, world minerals, and ocean management.[2]

The book *Microelectronics and Society,* a report to the Club of Rome, edited by Friedrichs and Schaff states,

> The move to a cashless society seems inevitable; given the technological push provided by microelectronics and significant cost advantages associated with the transfer of funds electronically.[3]

On April 18, 1980, the *Calgary Albertan* carried the following article entitled "Club of Rome Says, 'Messiah Needed.'" Its founder Aurelio Peccei stated,

> A charismatic leader — scientific, political or religious — would be the world's only salvation from the social and economic upheavals that threaten to destroy civilization. Such a leader would have to override national and international interests as well as political and economic structures in order to lead humanity away from maladies that affect it.[4]

The Club of Rome

The Club of Rome, founded by Aurelio Peccei of the Fiat Corporation, is comprised of approximately 100 of the most prestigious leaders of earth. These interlock with the powerful Bilderbergers of Europe and with the Council on Foreign Relations and the Tri-lateral Commission in America, including the Rockefeller Family.

The Club of Rome issued a report in 1973, which revealed the planet has now been divided into ten political and economic regions which are referred to as kingdoms.[5]

To the student of Bible prophecy, Revelation 13:1; 17:3, 12, 13 are literally leaping out of the pages right before our eyes.

Ten Magna Regions

The Club of Rome and the Tri-lateral Commission have already divided the planet into ten magnum regions.

- Region #1: The United States, Canada, and Mexico
- Region #2: Western Europe
- Region #3: Japan
- Region #4: Australia and New Zealand
- Region #5: Eastern Europe
- Region #6: Latin America
- Region #7: North Africa and the Middle East
- Region #8: Main Africa
- Region #9: South and Southeast Asia
- Region #10: Central Asia

The first three regions are known as the Tri-lateral Sphere and have been designated as the power center of the earth, economically, politically and militarily. The famous G-7 represent the Tri-lateral regions. There is another phase in their plans.

Executive Order #11490

In some future economic, political, or military crisis, total dictatorial powers have already been granted to the president of the United States, under Executive Order #11490. Des Griffin, in his splendid book *The Fourth Reich of the Rich states,*

Total dictatorial control over America can be exerted instantaneously with **one stroke of the pen**. The measures stand as executive orders waiting to be evoked by whatever the President decides is a major crisis. These decisions give the President, through a bureaucracy of unelected officials in the office of the Federal Emergency Management Act (FEMA) — unlimited powers. You will have no recourse but to submit to their wisdom and judgment. This governmental total control over your life becomes effective (according to the language of the Executive Order) in times of increased international tension or economic financial crisis.

The following are the executive orders combined under Executive Order #11490. In one single hour the President (government) could take over:

- All communications
  (all media — radio, television, etc.)
- All electric power — petroleum, gas, fuel, etc.
- All farms and food reserves
- All transportation, highways, railroads, etc.
- All citizens to be drafted into a governmental work force
- Entire population centers could be moved
- All health education and welfare taken over
- All citizens, nation-wide, to be registered by the Postmaster General
- Seize all airports and aircraft
- All housing financing
- All railways, in-land waterways, and all public storage facilities

Under Richard Nixon, the orders were grouped into a single Executive Order #11490. This was signed into law by James R. Carter on July 20th, 1979. All it takes to push the button on this bone-crushing machinery is for the President of the United States to declare an emergency.

John F. Kennedy is purported to have made a speech at Columbia University in mid-November, 1963, in which he said,

> The high office of the President has been used to
> foment a plot to destroy Americans' freedom, and before I
> leave office I must inform the citizens of their plight.

Ten days later, in Dallas, Texas, JFK was assassinated.

There is another piece that fits into this giant
international power play for the New World Order take over
— the Federal Reserve Board, also known as the FED. The
Federal Reserve Board has absolutely nothing to do with the
federal government of the United States. It is controlled by a
group of international bankers, most of whom are not even
citizens of the United States. The FED has a strangle hold on
the American economy. There is much evidence that
President Kennedy had plans to abolish the Federal Reserve.
He went against the tide and for that he was killed.

Many years ago, United States congressman Louis T.
McFadden, who was chairman of the House Banking
Committee, stated:

> When the Federal Reserve Acts were passed, the
> people of these United States did not perceive that a
> world banking system was being set up here.

> A super state controlled by international bankers, and
> international industrialists acting together to enslave the
> world for their own pleasures. Every effort has been
> made by the FED to to conceal its powers **but the truth is
> the FED has usurped the government.**[7]

Three Giant Federal Reserve Banks

These power hungry men plan a massive financial
squeeze play to phase down the banking system of the world
into three major banks which will control the world's
currencies and direct the entire world's economy.

Three giant federal reserve banks will then be in
operation:

- The Federal Reserve Bank of the United States
- The Federal Reserve Bank of Europe
- The Federal Reserve Bank of Japan

Charles Lindberg Sr., father of Charles Lindberg (first to fly from New York to Paris), at the time the Federal Reserve Act was passed, said,

> This act establishes the most gigantic trust on earth; when the president (Wilson) signs this bill, the invisible government of the monetary power will be legalized . . . the worst legislative crime of the ages is perpetrated by this banking and currency bill.[8]

Thomas Jefferson warned the American people:

> If the American people ever allow private banks to control the issue of their currency, first by inflation and then by deflation, the banks . . . will deprive the people of all their property until their children wake up homeless on the continent their fathers conquered.[9]

> Very few Americans realize that the Federal Reserve is not a government agency and neither the Congress or the president has one iota of control over it . . . the chilling truth is that the Federal Reserve, America's central bank, is simply one component of an interlocking international banking cartel that now controls the wealth of this planet.[10]

I have discovered that most of the members of the Federal Reserve Bank of the U.S. are not even citizens of this country. Since its inception in 1913, it now has a vice grip on the American economy.

Mr. Wally Wood, Jr., author of *Cashless Society; World Without Money* published an article in 1981 entitled "New Money for A New World." He wrote:

> Our present system of economics is on precipice of total collapse. The depression that is just ahead promises to be more overwhelming than the one in the thirties. It will not be an accidental depression. It will occur by design. Its purpose will be to bring the world, especially America, to its knees crying out for something or someone to alleviate the pain. That something will be a New World Order and that someone will be a New World leader of inestimable charisma and power and the whole world will be deceived.[11]

The machinery is all ready to set in motion, by design. Their plan is to bring about a world-wide financial collapse of the present monetary system. The Order has determined that their goal of ruling the world **can only be achieved by a cataclysmic financial crisis.** They know those who control the money of the world, control the power of the world.

Get Ready for a World Currency

A few years ago I received a copy of the *Economist* Magazine that is published in London and New York City. The *Economist* is one of Great Britain's elite financial magazines. It is read as the virtual "blue book" by the financial leaders of the world. The caption of the article read, "Get Ready for a World Currency."

Let me now quote from Texe Marrs, former professor of the University of Texas in the fields of political science and international affairs. In his book *Millennium* he writes:

> On the front cover of the Economist was a picture of a Phoenix bird rising from the burning ashes of all the world currencies. About the Phoenix bird's neck was a chain on which hung a gold coin, printed with the words *Ten Phoenix.*

The article in the *Economist* concludes, "It will not be long until the dollar collapses — it will collapse . . . then, pencil in the Phoenix and welcome it when it comes."[12]

Mr. Marrs explains,

> The Phoenix was an ancient symbol in Egypt and Phoenicia and it represented Lucifer. It is the bird that rose to heaven in the form of a morning star. Lucifer, Satan, masquerades as the morning star (the counterfeit). **JESUS DECLARES IN REVELATION 22:16, "I AM . . . THE BRIGHT AND MORNING STAR."**

It is startling: the symbol that the World Order has chosen for the New International Economic Order is the ancient symbol of the "god of this world" — Lucifer. The impact is even more revealing for those who know the Word of God. Such a New World Economy is described in Revelation 13. The New International Economic Order, the

Bible tells us, is to be a total cashless society with a mark in the right hand or in the forehead and all the people's of the earth will worship Lucifer (Satan), the "god of this world."

In my own personal research over the years, I have discovered the leaders of the New Age religion and the internationalists in the economic and political area have a secret networking language. It is the language of occultic symbolism.

Could it be that the *Economist* magazine, one of the giant financial publications of the world, was signaling that when the economic melt-down took place it would be at that point they would offer their designed and pre-planned solution: The N.I.E.O. (New International Economic Order)? Their New World Order (the One World Government), comprised of the ten magna regions of earth, is to be under the control of a supreme world leader — a satanically controlled (Luciferian) world dictator.

And so the global stage is almost set. The Tri-lateral sphere of nations will control the planet and the Order has decreed that the E.C. (the United States of Europe) will become the seat of the One World Government and from its capital the supreme leader of the world will rule. They are in perfect alignment with God's Word pre-written in the book of Daniel, twenty-six centuries ago.

Their intention? In the midst of the coming financial crisis, the peoples of earth will literally be crying out for a leader to bring them out of their chaos and morass caused by the financial crash. At this point the Order will announce the ten regions of earth will become Federation Earth in the New World Order — the One World government.

The former newspaper correspondent and noted researcher Salem Kirban in his report *The Coming One World Currency* says,

> Their first priority is to shut down the smaller banks and develop a conglomerate of a few huge banks . . . all eventually under one central bank. Thus a World Central Bank.[13]

How close are we to a world central bank?

Would you be surprised to know that the super world bank has already been formed and is now in operation?

THREE

The Super World Bank

Surely the Lord God will do nothing,
but He revealeth His secret unto His
servants, the prophets.

Amos 3:7

The Super World Bank has already been formed. It is called the *Magna Charta World Bank*. I have complete documentation on how it was formed and where it was formed. We have the names of some of the elite international bankers and environmental leaders of the world who were there. We have even some of the plans (with their voices on tape) — David Rockefeller, director of Council on Foreign Relations; Baron Edmund De Rothschild of London (the man who sets the gold standard of the world).

Always, when God's people are in danger, he raises up a watchman on the wall — a storm warning voice. Now enter Mr. George Hunt of Boulder, Colorado. He is a warm, personal friend of this writer. We have spent hours together pouring over the Word of God and the plan of the Order for their One World government. For nineteen years Mr. George Hunt was on the faculty of the University of Colorado as professor of Accounting. The following is his amazing story.

Mr. George Hunt tells the story of his quest for God, during which he lined up with the Ashrams of India (those who follow the Hindu religion in the area of Colorado — the New Age religion). He became deeply involved in that

religion but it left his soul empty and searching. One day he
made this prayer as his heart cried out to the God of heaven.

> Oh, God, if Hinduism is the way, would you show
> me? If Zen Buddhism is the way, would you reveal that
> to me? If Jesus Christ is the way, would you reveal that
> which is the truth?

The true and living God will always answer a heart cry
like that. This sounds like the book of Acts, but it is all true.
A precious little saint of God living in the city of Boulder,
Colorado, saw him in a vision. God revealed to her that she
would meet that man. That when she met him, she was to
tell him how the Lord Jesus Christ had given His own divine
blood on Calvary's cross as the full payment for his sin; how
Jesus rose from the dead; and how by repentance and faith
he could invite Jesus Christ into his life and know that he
found peace with God and that his name was written in the
Lamb's Book of Life. Within three.days she met George
Hunt, the New Ager, who was searching for God. She told
him what God had revealed to her, and soon after, George
Hunt knelt at the foot of the cross and received the Lord
Jesus Christ into his life as his own personal Savior.

But soon after that, his son was killed in New Zealand.
Thereafter, becoming extremely interested in the
environment, an announcement for the "Fourth World
Wilderness Congress," 1987, caught his attention. It was to
be held in Estes Park, Colorado. However the cover price
was beyond his pocket book. How the Holy Spirit divinely
guided him is a miracle.

One day he called a business friend who, to his
amazement, said, "George, I have been chosen to be the co-
host for the World Wilderness Congress, but I'm terribly ill
with the flu. Would you take my place?" That's how George
Hunt, the former New Age devotee, just a new Christian,
came to be on the staff as the co-host of a meeting comprised
of the international bankers in the top levels of global
finance. At that meeting, September, 1987, in Estes Park near
Denver, Colorado, he found himself sitting down with the
international bankers of the world. This also gave him
recourse to the elite persons involved at the top level.

Mr. Hunt stated that he was given a card with high priority and access to the press room at all times, and to the elite persons involved at the top level. The emissaries of divine light were his fellow co-host. These "emissaries" go about talking about Jesus, but it is a different Jesus than he knew. It was not the Jesus of the Bible. Paul, by the Holy Spirit, tells us that there will be those who will proclaim another Jesus. They are very sly. They talk about a Luciferian light, and this is a false Jesus.

The opening party was given in downtown Denver by the mayor of the city of Denver. David Rockefeller of the Chase Manhattan Bank was there. His empire is almost too fantastic to describe. He chairs the most powerful arm that's driving toward the New World Order — the Council on Foreign Relations. He founded the Tri-lateral Commission. Associated with David Rockefeller are the members of the Club of Rome and the powerful Bilderbergers of Europe. Other representatives were there; the World Bank and the United Nations. The secretary of the United States treasury James Baker III was there and made the keynote address. The Prime Minister of Norway, who was chosen to put all of their plans forward in what they call the "Common Cause" was there. Those very plans were presented a month later to the United Nations, where they were approved and accepted by the World Body.

William Ruckleshouse, director of the Environmental Protection Agency was there. Edmond D. Rothschild, who sets the gold standard of the world, was there. Fifty-two nations of the world were represented. The Fourth World Wilderness Congress was not reported by the media because the international banking cartels did not want you to know what was taking place. The plan they drew up was for the World Conservation Bank — a federal reserve bank of the world. David Rockefeller said virtually that **the super, super world bank will be the financial 'Savior' of mankind.**

The plan that they developed is to "debt-swap" wilderness lands of the nations by forgiving their huge debts. In doing this, they will say to the debtor nations (such as Brazil, where it has already been implemented), "We will forgive your six billion dollar loan if you will give us your wilderness lands" (and in some cases, your mineral rights,

also). And this scam (actually, one of the greatest hoaxes of
all times) is to lock up forever one-third of the surface of the
earth by the power elite and the international bankers.

As stated before, they also plan to collapse the monetary
system of the world. Here is the plan! In **the coming
financial crisis**, the farmer down in Iowa is going under.
The small business man in Oregon is floundering. The S&L
in Texas is in trouble. The bankers will say, "This super,
super world bank has already been set up. We anticipated
this crisis. It has unlimited capital — trillions of dollars. We
will offer you all that you need at 3% interest, no payments
for five years."

What will happen? The nations, the small and large
businesses, and the S&Ls that may be in trouble, are going to
buy into this — lock, stock, and barrel. Then, at a given
time, the international bankers will call in those mortgages,
and when they can't be met, **the trap will snap shut, and the
super cartel will virtually control the wealth of the world.**

George Hunt has placed his life in jeopardy for you and
me to have this information. He is often shadowed. He was
on a radio station in Texas, and a voice came over the
telephone to the manager, "Do not have this man on again,
or it will go hard for you." The manager had him on the
following week. The third week, that station was bought out
by Rockefeller money and began to play hard-rock Mexican
music.

Let me give you the very words of Edmond D.
Rothschild, as he set this all in motion. Remember, this is the
man who controls almost all of the oil in the East, and whose
financial empire is so fabulous that it's almost hard to
imagine. This is a capsule version of what he stated. (We
have his words on audio tape.)

> Recognizing the need to protect our ecology and
> environmental heritage within the concept of the Fourth
> World Wilderness Congress for the preservation of the
> wildlife on our planet, we ask the Prime Minister of
> Norway to be the promoter of this International
> Conservation Bank.

The World Wilderness Congress set in motion a One
World Economic System, with the United Nations to be the
Legislative Congress, the Royal Bank of Canada being the

banker (the Federal Reserve of the world), and the dictators of the world being the hub of the people of London. Michael Sweetman was chosen to be the director of that world bank. George Hunt's analysis of the Congress is:

The Gaia Hypothesis

The World Conservation Bank will be pushed as **helping Mother Earth.** (Does that sound familiar? "Gaia" – Mother Earth.) The New Agers believe, and many of the top environmentalists, that earth is a living, breathing entity. This is actually the ancient religion of Babylon. They are tying it in by helping Mother Earth. The New Age religion is involved. You're either going to be dependent, when the crash comes, on the World Conservation Bank to provide you the living you need to sustain your life, or you're going to trust in the Lord Jesus Christ to sustain you. **That is going to be your decision.** This is a spiritual dilemma that all peoples are going to be put to.

Date Line — October 25, 1993

Mr. Hunt has just published an alert that this Trojan Horse, the World Conservation Bank, under the play of environmentalism is moving into high gear via NAFTA — North American Free Trade Agreement.

The following is a verbatim from Mr. Hunt's report to the nation (used by permission).

The United States Will Get
the Shaft (A) From NAFTA

The Mexican and U.S. tories are moving a Trojan Horse into NAFTA. A seed of the World Conservation Bank will be planted into the NAFTA super-country agreements. Some may find it exciting to see a brave new "super country" formed out of chaos — the Club of Rome has already numbered the vast new expanse as "#1" out of the ten world super states presently being chiseled from the nations of the world.

LET THERE BE NO MISTAKE ABOUT IT. IF THE TREATY IS PASSED BY CONGRESS AND IMPLEMENTED, THE UNITED STATES WILL GET THE SHAFT (A) FROM NAFTA!

No one escapes when freedom fails. The best men rot in filthy jails, and those who cried, "Appease, Appease," are hanged by those they tried to please.

Des Griffin, editor of the *Midnight Messenger* writes:

NAFTA (the North American Fraud and Theft Agreement) . . . has nothing to do with improving the standard of living for folks south of the border. Mexico owes the International Monetary Fund $300 Billion in bad loans, and another $100 Billion to Chase Manhattan — the same roster as the 'Fed' banker boys. The only way Rockefeller and Co. will realize any payback on these loans is to start vacuuming out America's economy. NAFTA isn't fair trade or creation of jobs.

The real bottom line was revealed by Henry Kissinger in a special article he wrote for the Los Angeles Times this past summer. Writing of NAFTA, Kissinger stated: "It will represent the most creative step forward toward the creation of a New World Order taken by any group of nations since the end of the Cold War. But the stakes are too high to wait much longer . . . "

NAFTA isn't a question of jobs, it's a matter of loyalty to the sovereign Republic of the United States. Those who pledge allegiance to NAFTA are pledging their allegiance to foreign power.

Wall Street Journal

In its October 19 issue, The *Wall Street Journal* revealed to the public for the first time the creation of an Environmental Bank that is part of the NAFTA treaty. This bank (funded by the international bankers) would allegedly "fund environmental cleanups" along the US-Mexico border. According to the *Journal*, Mickey Kantor, Clinton's U.S. trade representative, "expects the total border funding to reach $7 billion to $8 billion. This would include roughly $2 billion from a new development bank set up by the two countries. About $3.5 billion to $4 billion would be made available to Mexico from the World Bank.

Mr. Griffin continues:

"Rothschild was personally conducting the monetary matters and the creation of this World Conservation Bank." What emerged — albeit in code — from the speeches and in the various forums during the days that followed was the outline of a plan that would eventually result in the natural resources of the entire world ending up in the hands of the international bankers, whom Congressman Louis T. McFadden, former head of the House Banking Committee once described as a "dark crew of financial pirates."

The plan outlined was as simple as it was diabolical. Basically, it was the application of the Hegelian Principle (Thesis, Antithesis and Synthesis) on an international level. Pressure from above and pressure from below, all in the glorious name of the Environmental Movement, would result in nations being forced to surrender both their sovereignty and their natural resources into the hands of the international banksters through ultimate default.

This, of course, is perfectly in line with the long-range plans of the international bankers. In this regard, it is important that we remember the clear statement of Dr. Carroll Quigley, Bill Clinton's mentor during his years at Georgetown University in Washington, D.C.: "[T]he powers of financial capitalism [have] a . . . far reaching aim, nothing less than to create a world system of financial control in private hands able to dominate the political system of each country and the economy of the world as a whole. This system was to be controlled in a feudal fashion by the central banks [owned and controlled, of course, by the international bankers] of the world acting in concert, by secret agreements arrived at in frequent private meetings and conferences" [such as the one in Denver in 1987] (Tragedy and Hope, McMillian 1966, p. 324).

Make no mistake about it. The World Conservation Bank (the Super World Bank) that was crafted by the International Bankers in 1987 (George Hunt was there and has it all on audio tape — even the inflection of their voices) is alive and well and is now accelerating, full throttle, via NAFTA.

The goal: A giant central world bank (a super Federal Reserve Bank of the world) and a New World Order and a One World government. Dr. Kissinger let the cat out of the bag. "It will represent the most creative step forward toward the creation of a New World Order. But the stakes are too high to wait much longer . . ."

He means the people of America are "waking up."

FOUR

New Money

The End of American Sovereignty

*Frightening changes are coming in
U.S. currency. Bar codes on U.S. currency
are a certainty. The FED is working
feverishly to impose radical currency
changes which will forever alter your
way of life.*

— James Bejoria, Chief Executive Office
Numismatics Ltd.

*The new money will be a way station
to a cashless society.*

— Harvey Watchman
American Association of Liability Attorneys
writing in *New York Times*

In the last chapter we looked at eight clandestine, global organizations — mega forces that are driving to bring all the nation states of our planet into a New World Order (One World Government).

But behind these esoteric, secret organizations there is a power, a hidden aristocracy, a power elite, "A fourth reich of the super rich," "the lords of the money", "the brotherhood", or the "order". Dr. John Coleman has written a book *The 300 Men Who Rule the World*. But many believe there is an even smaller group — "The power elite — of thirteen old line families who control the wealth of the planet and thus they control the power of the planet."

The Thirteen Men Who Rule the World

These are hard-core, super mega international bankers. They direct huge banking dynasties, powerful interlocking cartels. They sit as chairmen of mega banks. They prefer to remain anonymous and to be known simply as the Brotherhood. This is the power behind the Bilderbergers of Europe, the Council on Foreign Relations, Tri-lateral Commission, the Society known as Skull and Bones (America's secret establishment), the Club of Rome, etc. They are the king makers and nation breakers. Their combined wealth is staggering. They control the largest banks on earth and supervise giant corporate empires. The order is a giant serpentine monster and its highest priority is to bring in a New World Order — a One World Government.

This is not something I have conjured up. Winston Churchill wrote of the order in his memoirs. Woodrow Wilson knew of the order. He wrote:

> Since I entered politics, I have chiefly had men's views confided to me privately. Some of the biggest men in the United States, in the field of commerce and manufacturing, are afraid of somebody, are afraid of something. They know there is a power somewhere so organized, so subtle, so watchful, so interlocked, so complete, so persuasive, that they had better not speak of them above their breath when they speak in condemnation of it.[1]

Winston Churchill wrote of this global esoteric organization.

> From the days of Spartacus, (Weishaupt, the founder of the Illuminati, used the name Spartacus as a secret code name) to those of Karl Marx . . . this world-wide conspiracy for the overthrow of civilization and reconstruction of society . . . has been steadily growing. It has been the main spring of every subversive movement during the 19th century, and now, at last, this band of

extraordinary personalities from the underworld of the great cities of Europe and America have gripped the Russian people by the hair of their heads and have become the undisputed masters of that enormous empire.[2]

Six Global Goals

These men have power — unbelievable power!! Like Adolph Hitler, in Mein Kampf, they have spelled out their agenda in advance. That Global Agenda is constructed around six goals. We now know what those goals are. As you read them you will be dumbfounded because they are following the exact script, with uncanny precision, that the Spirit of God wrote in the Bible almost 2000 years ago.

GOAL #1) The establishment of a new international economic order unified and under the direct command of the unelected elite on the highest level board of The Order.

GOAL #2) The establishment of what will appear to be a democratic One World Government, which will actually be controlled behind the scenes by The Order.

GOAL #3) The conquest and subjugation by economic, financial and spiritual means of the two super powers, the United States of America and Russia, also (formerly known) as the Union of Socialist Republics (USSR). Their goal for America is to bring her to her to her knees by a massive depression. Then out of the chaos and panic the American people will be begging for the New World Order.

GOAL #4) The ascension of the coming United States of Europe as the dominant nation in a confederated One World Government.

GOAL #5) The ushering in of a supreme world leader to preside over the New Unified One World Government.

GOAL #6) The establishment of a One World religion which will coordinate all the world's religions, cults, faith groups, and spiritual beliefs under the guidance of a Supreme Pontiff, the spiritual equivalent of the Supreme World Leader.[3]

New International Economic Order

Let's remember the first goal was to establish a New International World Order. I made note in 1988 that the two leaders of the two great super powers on earth, President Ronald Reagan and Mikhail Gorbachev called, within the same month, for a New International Order (financial world order). The *Oregonian*, Oregon's leading newspaper, quoted George Shultz when he spoke to a prestigious group of government leaders in Washington, D.C., "We are already in the New Age and a new Financial World Order is fast taking shape."[4] He literally astonished the audience.

Previously, Richard Gardiner, of the Aspen Institute for Humanistic Studies, had called for a New International Economic Order. This was presented in the official magazine of the Council on Foreign Relations *Foreign Affairs*.

> An end run-around national sovereignty, eroding it piece by piece, will accomplish much more than the old-fashioned frontal assault.[5]

What was the first global goal of the order? To establish a New International Economic Order!!

A Carefully Contrived Plan

In the ensuing years we have discovered their ultimate goal (the bottom line): They have carefully crafted and contrived a plan to condition the peoples of earth, step by step, into a **total cashless society**. They have designed it in three phases. The three prongs of their esoteric plan are:

(1) The issuance of new money to be followed by a call-in of all the old bills.

(2) To issue all citizens in America a debit card and via the use of the debit card system to gradually condition the people to use the debit system, thus there would be the gradual phasing out of coin and bills.

(3) A **micro chip** — a silicon chip to be placed in the right hand or forehead of all peoples in the industrial world and eventually all buying and selling on earth would be done

via the electronic funds transfer system. All currency, coin and checks would become obsolete and all commerce on earth would be carried on by a total cashless society.

Now enter Ron Paul, former Congressman from Texas, a medical doctor. He rose to chair a powerful financial committee in the U.S. House of Representatives. He began to hear rumors of the issuance of new money by the Federal Reserve. He began to probe, but he could find no answers. By virtue of his office, he subpoenaed the Federal Reserve office and put them under oath. They revealed that there was a plan to print and issue new money. We now know the U.S. Mint was built in Fort Worth, Texas, and that President Bush toured the plant on April 9, 1991, and gave them the "green light" and the presses began to roll. Could it be by coincidence that its symbol is an occultic pyramid which is the symbol on the back of your one dollar bill (*NOVUS ORDO SECLORUM*) the New World Order, under the all-seeing eye of Lucifer? The presses are rolling twenty-four hours per day.

New Money is Here

A recent press report reveals that Harvey Watchman, the Executive Director of the American Association of Liability Attorneys is stumping the nation calling for the new money and for a cashless society!

At first the FED hinted the new money would be colored. Then they threw us a "curve ball." It began to be circulated in 1990, first in one hundred dollar bills. It was green exactly like our old money, but with a fibre optic strip from the top of the bill to the bottom about one inch over from left to right. This is a security thread (fiber optics) and it cannot be copied. If you examine a one hundred bill closely you will see inside one of the two lines, which surround the portrait of Benjamin Franklin, hundreds of markings. These are micro-printed with magnetic ink. With cellular scanners along the freeways of the nation they can now tell where the money is and how much you have with you. The plan behind it is *Total Surveillance*. Folks, with total surveillance eventually comes total control. The cellular scanners are now in place across

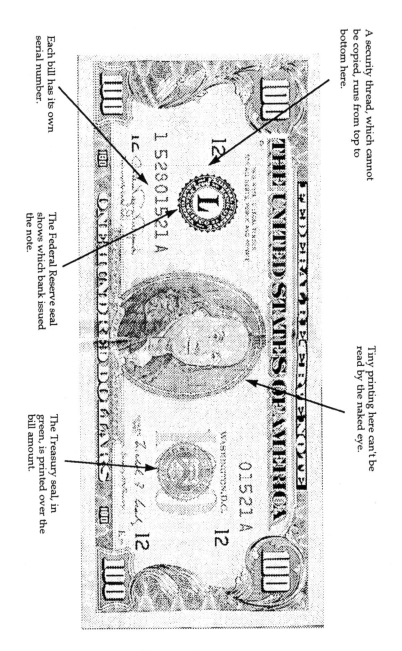

A security thread, which cannot be copied, runs from top to bottom here.

Each bill has its own serial number.

The Federal Reserve seal shows which bank issued the note.

Tiny printing here can't be read by the naked eye.

The Treasury seal, in green, is printed over the bill amount.

The Federal Reserve Note

total control. The cellular scanners are now in place across the freeways of America.

When the mint turns out enough new money to fuel the economy of 250,000,000 Americans (the new money is now out in the banks in hundreds, fifties, twenties, and tens) Ron Paul reveals that there will be a call-in of all the old bills. The old bills will be declared obsolete. We cannot be sure about the ratio of exchange the old bills will be for the new. Some believe it will be on a one-to-one basis.

Former Congressman Ron Paul has alerted us that "The new money is electronically traceable and what they are after is total surveillance, and that is why the money is electronically traceable." He warns that when you go to the bank to exchange your old cash, if you have more than a thousand dollars in old bills, you will be put high on the suspicion list of the IRS.

Goal: Total Surveillance

At the present time black boxes are being installed on the trucks in America. As the truck passes through the cellular scanner, it will instantaneously record the type of truck, the number of the truck, its license number, its weight and its speed. If it is exceeding the speed limit, a citation will be issued and that citation will come up on the screen. Soon these surveillance devices will be installed in all cars in America. The new money is magnetized and electronically traceable. With the new money the IRS will be able to keep an accounting of all your financial transactions.

The new money will be a stepping stone to a global currency, a central bank, and ultimately to a computerized cashless society which is intrinsic to the New World Order (One World Government). The government's ultimate goal, as they move us toward a cashless society is not new money ultimately, but to a cashless society where every dime of our money can be traced and taxed.

Stepping Stone to a Cashless Society

The establishment lawyer Harvey Watchman wrote in the *New York Times,* "The new money is a way station to a cashless society."[6] The new money is now in most of the nations of the world. I have observed that on most of the new money in foreign countries, there is a blank space in the upper left hand corner of these new bills. Why is it there? Some believe it will be to soon identify it as global money in a global economy. Texe Marrs, former professor of hi-tech science at the University of Texas, an astute researcher in the field of Biblical prophecy, believes that it could be for the portrait of the coming leader of the New World Order. But of that we are not sure.

Mr. Paul issued the following report:

> This group, elite, headed by David Rockefeller, seeks the new money, the cashless society, the end of American independence in a New World Order, the crushing of our liberties, the shackling of our economy, the raising of our taxes through a world IRS and ultimately a world central bank and a world electronic currency.

Mr. Paul writes in his *Ron Paul Report* on January 15, 1993,

> President Clinton will escalate the war on cash to unprecedented levels. There will be an effort to initiate a sudden recall of existing currency, to be replaced with new, and more sophisticated currency will be revisited. The past two presidents have been unsuccessful at doing this but Clinton has vowed to succeed where others have failed. Clinton may have the reputation as a moderate, but when it comes to violating the financial privacy of Americans he will be ruthless.[7]

And so this seems to be the plan: First the government will eliminate all old cash and require all old money to be exchanged. Then we will move to Phase II. After the new money has done its work we will be issued a debit card bio-chemically imprinted with the owner's own hand and retina (eye) prints. Watchman says this will smash the underground economy and enable the government to collect up to one hundred billion dollars more in taxes.

Debit Card "Smart Card"

Your debit card will be the smart card. It will give an instantaneous profile on all citizens of America. It is being tested now on the Paris Island Marine Base in South Carolina. Every marine is issued a smart card. His pay is electronically entered into it. He must use the card for everything he purchases. The government can thus trace every cent and know where it was spent and for what it was spent.

A very close, personal friend of mine called me from Arlington, Virginia, recently. He said, "All of Arlington is rapidly moving to the debit system. They don't even want my cash any more."

In late 1992, a Christian wrote to me from Seattle. He is on the staff of one of the giant corporations in Seattle, Washington. He wrote, "On November 1, 1992, this company will inaugurate a total cashless society."

Debit System to Begin in the Military

This is being rapidly introduced into the military. We have a pastor friend in Alabama. In late 1992, one of the young men in his church was inducted into the military. He began to receive all of his pay via the electronic funds transfer system. He wrote to his pastor requesting him to write a letter to his commanding officer, and request that he receive his pay by cash or check. Here is a part of that letter and the subsequent result:

> We, an interdenominational church of the United States of America, conscientiously object to the government of the United States of America forcing citizens, including members of the United States armed forces, to take part in the cashless monetary system.
>
> We realize that the governments of this world will one day in our near future enforce a bar code mark or a number to be placed upon each citizen or inserted by a micro-chip into their body. We object to this system, and all the preliminary procedures that are paving the way for

this system to be put into operation. Our reason for
conscientious objection is because the Bible clearly states
that the government will enforce upon its citizens a
cashless monetary system, whereby a mark or a number
will be placed in the hand or forehead of each person, as a
means of identification and giving one the right to buy
and sell. The Bible forbids Christians to take part in this
system.

The following are portions of Scripture regarding this
system: "And he causeth all, both small and great, rich
and poor, free and bond, to receive a mark in their right
hand, or in their foreheads: and that no man might buy or
sell, save he that had the mark, or the name of the Beast,
or the number of his name" (Revelation 13:16-17).

"And there fell a noisome and grievous sore upon the
men which had the mark of the Beast, and upon them
which worshiped his image" (Revelation 16:2).

"If any man receive his mark in his forehead, or in his
hand, the same shall drink of the wine of the wrath of
God, which is poured out without mixture into the cup of
his indignation; and he shall be tormented with fire and
brimstone in the presence of the holy angels, and in the
presence of the Lamb: and the smoke of their torment
ascendeth up for ever and ever; and they have no rest day
nor night, who worship the Beast and his image, and
whosoever receiveth the mark of his name.

"Here is the patience of the saints: here are they that
keep the commandments of God, and the faith of Jesus"
(Revelation 14:9-12).

We request simply a freedom of choice, concerning
automatic transfer of our funds. We believe each citizen
should have the option to refrain from taking part in this
method of deposits and withdrawals, and should be free
to receive their salaries by check or bank draft, while we
still remain under our present monetary system.

After the letter was given to his commanding officer, this
young man was escorted, not on his own will, to see a

psychiatrist; thinking him crazy, he was psycho-analyzed in the mental department and then released.

McAlvany Alert

The McAlvany Intelligence Advisor, edited by Don McAlvany, goes into fifty-seven nations of the world. Mr. McAlvany is a Christian and I have found his information extremely accurate. The report is read by senators, representatives, and world leaders. The following appeared in the MIA in July, 1993:

> Just as in George Orwell's *1984*, "Big Brother's" machinery for tracking and monitoring every American citizen continues to grow. The FDIC is about to implement a system for tracking the deposits of all Americans in all financial institutions. If you have deposits in several banks and/or S&Ls, they will be completely tracked at all times by the FDIC (and hence by the government). Once installed, a major part of your financial privacy will be almost totally eliminated.

> One of the most dangerous aspects of the Clinton administration is its hatred of privacy. The national identification card being pushed by the Clintonistas is a classic example. Under the pretense of national health care reform, the Clintons are moving to implement what Clinton and Gore talked about in their campaign book *Putting People First*: "Smart cards for everyone coded with personal medical information."[8]

The new card will be the size of a credit card; it will be issued at birth; it will have imbedded in it a powerful computer with a memory chip and microprocessor with up to 1,600 pages of personal information on its owner implanted on it, which will be sufficient for a complete dossier on the entire lives of most American citizens. No one will get "official" medical care unless he presents the card.

Martin Anderson, a former official with the Reagan White House (on the President's economic policy advisory board) wrote on April 4, 1993, in *The Washington Times*:

When I worked in the west wing as President
Reagan's domestic policy advisor, I was surprised by the
ardent desire of government bureaucrats, many of them
Reagan appointees, for a national identity card. Brushing
aside any concerns about personal privacy, a powerful
array of government agencies (i.e., the Immigration and
Naturalization Service, the State Department, the FBI, the
IRS, the CIA, etc.), each with its own special reasons,
lusted after a law to force every American to carry a
national identity card. Such a law was within a whisker
of being endorsed by Mr. Reagan's cabinet in 1981, and
was stopped only when the President personally vetoed
the idea on the grounds that it was a massive invasion of
privacy.

End of Privacy in America

Today, twelve years later, there is virtually no resistance
to the card. Ira Magaziner, Hillary's socialized medicine
Czar, a socialist who wrote a book on the glories of socialism
called *Minding America's Business,* is spearheading the drive
for a national computerized ID card. It will eventually
include your tax history; how many cars you own; the
number and kind of guns you own; data on your children;
your history addresses and phone numbers; any dealings
with any federal agency; your electronic photo; your
fingerprints; and, of course, your medical history and much
more. The FBI has already signed a contract with Harris
Corporation of Melbourne, Florida, to give the government
the electronic fingerprint capacity.[9]
As Martin Anderson recently wrote:

> Unless this national ID card is stopped quickly, we
> may live to see the end of privacy in the U.S., all of us
> tagged like so many fish. Of course, the argument goes,
> "If you have nothing to hide, you should not be
> concerned." And, hey, you don't have anything to hide,
> do you?

Part of the Clintonista push for the ID card will also be:

> Don't you want better health care at a lower cost?
> Then you have to have computerized medical records.

A major push is about to be launched by the establishment to persuade the American public to forego their cash and begin using the so-called "Smart Card." The "Smart Card" is a vital part of moving Americans (and the peoples around the world) towards a cashless society, which is in turn a major element of the coming New World Order/New Age era. "Smart Cards" have been pushed hard for the past few years, with very little acceptance by the public. Now another media blitz is about to be launched by the establishment emphasizing convenience, safety from loss or theft, and the versatility of these cards (i.e., the same card can be used to unlock a door, to get into a parking lot, to punch a time clock, to pay for food in the cafeteria, and to buy goods at local stores).

Martin Anderson continues:

Health Security Card Would Kill Privacy

President Clinton's health care plan is beguiling, but buried in the 215 page preliminary draft of the radical changes he has proposed are numerous nuggets of danger to our health and to our privacy . . .

There is something else in the plan that may be far worse than the new taxes that will be heaped upon us, or the increased physical pain and suffering we will endure as a result of the endless waiting lines for health care.

That something else is a device that will invade our privacy as it has never been invaded before.

Clinton held it in his hand, when he addressed the nation, proudly waving it like a small American flag, only it wasn't a flag. It was the health care security card — his slick name for a national identity card.

Under his plan, a national health board would establish **a national, unique identifier number for every single one of us**. Every time we visit a doctor or get a prescription or go to the hospital, the records would be captured, retained, and transmitted via the identity card.

*The President's health care card
mandated for every American citizen.*

Those records would feed into electronic networks, and
the federal government would set up national standards
for electronic data transmission.

A national computer data bank, holding all our most
personal medical records would be open to the prying
eyes of government bureaucrats and other authorized
people, and of course, any unauthorized snoopers who
figure out how to crack the system. What makes this
privacy nightmare possible are striking advances in
technology; that pretty red, white, and blue card the
President was waving around is called a **SMART CARD**.

Some cards contain computer chips, some have optical
storage devices. That kind of card is capable of holding
thousands of pages of personal data, computerized finger
prints, a mug shot and even your voice. Once in place, the
card will be impossible to get rid of. It is just the card we
need — another plastic card to carry in our wallets and
purses. **And make no mistake about this one. You will
carry it. For the possession of that identity card will be
necessary for you to receive medical care of any kind.
If Clinton's so-called health security card becomes a
reality, we can kiss our privacy as we now know it
good-bye.**[10]

The picture of the Phoenix bird on the President's health care card is a Phoenix (not an eagle). Is it coincidental that the ancient Phoenix bird (also spelled *Fenex*) has been Lucifer's (Satan's) symbol from the very birth of witchcraft? Barbara Walker wrote in *Woman's Encyclopedia of Myths and Secrets,* "The Egyptians and Phoenicians taught the god represented by the Phoenix bird rose to heaven in the form of the Morning Star, Lucifer."[11]

Is it pure chance that the ancient spelling of Phoenix was *Fenex*? In Greek transliterations *like the name Lucifer, Fenex means Shining One.* The Greek value of the letters *Fenex* is *666.*[12]

Cash to Become Obsolete

Cash is to be phased out, and a 100% computerized paper trail is to be phased in. If the establishment is successful, all privacy (financial and otherwise) will disappear and a major element of people control will have been installed.

Watch Out for Hillary's New Health Care Plan

President Clinton has promised a total restructuring of the health care plan which has been placed in charge of Hillary Clinton because the present health care system is outdated and buried under a mountain of ever-changing regulations. President Clinton wants every citizen in the U.S. to have a debit card. In his book *Putting People First* he calls for the issuance of a smart card.[13] It is designed to replace your wallet-full of credit cards, as well as cash. Remember the plan is to phase out all cash as soon as possible and move us toward a total cashless society. With the debit card (smart card) your Social Security number could thus be your universal account number to buy and sell into tomorrow's cashless society. Folks, it's coming quickly!

Startling News From England

We received the following newspaper clipping from a friend in Sussex, England, stating that one of the large department stores is moving into a new debit system.

Smart Store Threat to Girls on the Checkouts

The supermarket checkout girl is under threat. She is likely to be trampled out of existence in big stores by the march of science, another victim of the bar code.

Something else will vanish with her — the queue to pay when the shopping is done, according to a look at stores in the year 2001 revealed by leading business consultants yesterday.

Stores would save on paying staff by making the customers total the cost of items as they walked along the shelves.

"Shoppers would run a wand scanner over the product bar code as they put it into the trolley," said International Business Advisers Andersen Consulting.

When it comes to paying, the wand would be slotted into a console and the total owed displayed.

The customer would then wipe a plastic credit or debit card through the same console to complete the purchase.

"There's no need to worry about people using stolen cards because technology already exists for individuals to be identified by **placing a finger or palm on a scanner**," said an Andersen spokesman.[14]

The Final Step

It is coming very soon to America. In his book *Putting People First* President Clinton is calling for the debit card system (the Smart Card).

President Clinton said in his book, "Smart Cards for everyone coded with personal medical information." It is coming quickly now and the bottom line — to phase out cash, and ultimately move all Americans into a total cashless society.

The ultimate goal, the cashless society — all buying and selling will be carried on via the electronic funds transfer system.

The ploy of the media hype (as they condition the masses for the cashless society via a mark in the hand or forehead) will be: Money (cash, coin) has caused all the ills of mankind for thousands of years — muggings, stealing, murders. Our scientists have developed the most ingenious innovative plan. It will be the answer to all the ills of mankind. With this new technology, we can virtually wipe out crime and bring the peoples of America and the world to affluence and utopia as they have never known. Our technology is so far advanced, we are ready now to implement our plan: a micro-chip (silicon chip) in the right hand or forehead and all buying and selling of earth will be carried on via this electronic transfer system.

Larry Burkett is rated as one of America's foremost financial advisors. He writes in the *Christian American Newspaper*, January, 1994, page 8:

> I think we will come out with electronic currency. We will use no money. It is the only way we can recover. You've got to somehow devise a method to suddenly stop what is going on; take control and devise a brand new currency that you can stabilize. The only way you can do it is electronically.

He states,

> It will occur when the economy can no longer sustain interest payments on the national debt. Then the President takes control under the Omnibus Act of 1975.

According to Burkett's scenario,

> The President will take 100% control of the economy; stop all currency flowing; stop all banking transactions for a period of time. When the banks reopen, he will say, "If

you have dollars, turn them in; they are no longer good. For every dollar we will give you a digit." **From this point on, all transactions will be done via the electronic funds transfer system (EFTS). We will enter the cashless society.**

In the final chapter of this book we reveal how fantastic technology is now ready to place a micro chip in the right hand or forehead of every person in the industrial world, and soon all the commerce of earth will be carried on by the electronic funds transfer system in a total cashless society. **The book of Revelation is unfolding before our eyes with amazing precision.** These words were written almost 2000 years ago:

> And he causeth all, both small and great, rich and poor, free and bond to receive a mark in their right hand or in their forehead (Revelation 13:16).

FIVE

The Coming Money Crash

17 Steps of Preparation for Crisis Days

*And the children of Issachar, which
were men who had understanding of the
times, to know what Israel ought to do.*
— 1 Chronicles 12:32

*The prudent (wise person) sees the
trouble coming and prepares for it; the
foolish pass on, and are punished.*
— Proverbs 27:12

This chapter is about money — The Coming Financial Collapse and How to Prepare for it. The Bible tells us in 1 Chronicles 12:32, "And the children of Issachar which were men who had an understanding of the times, to know WHAT ISRAEL OUGHT TO DO..."

And in the book of Wisdom, Proverbs 27:12, "The prudent (wise) person sees the trouble coming and prepares for it; the foolish pass on and are punished."

Now the Bible speaks much about money. One verse in ten in the New Testament deals with your possessions. There are 500 verses on prayer, fewer than 500 on faith, but over 2,000 verses on how to handle your money. Jesus actually spoke more about money than He did about Heaven.

The Bible tells us, "It is the Lord who gives us power to get wealth. And if riches increase set not your heart upon them." In Colossians 3, "Set your affections on things above, not on things that are upon the earth." Our Lord gave us this promise in Matthew 6:33, "But seek ye first the kingdom of God and His righteousness and all these things shall be added unto you."

But it is not wrong to have wealth. Abraham (the friend of God) was given great wealth. Job had great riches. But also God wants us to be good stewards of that which He has entrusted to us.

Now let's explore the projected coming financial crisis and the steps of preparation:

Recently I was reading a report by John Hagee, who is an expert in the field of finance. This was his statement, "Ten years ago America was the wealthiest nation on earth. Today we are the greatest debtor nation on earth. America," he says, "is racing toward economic destruction."

Our budget debt is almost 4 trillion dollars. If you add the off-budget debt, America's national debt stands today at nearly 12 trillion dollars. That staggers the imagination! How many dollars do you think are in a trillion? It is almost impossible to grasp with one's mind the figure *one trillion*. How many days or weeks or months or years do you think are in a trillion seconds? — 30,000 years!!!

On August the 13th, 1990, Mortimer Zuckerman, editor and chief of U.S. News and World Report wrote in the magazine, "America's financial institutions are stretched thin and the resulting turmoil threatens a serious recession."[1] He says the entire credit and capital system of the United States is now at risk. Well, folks, all our money system is at risk.

Listen to former Congressman Ron Paul, the congressman from Texas who chaired a powerful financial committee in the House of Representatives in the United States banking and currency system. This man is a Christian. He is seeking to urgently prepare us for the coming financial crunch. This man is your friend. I have a copy of a letter he wrote to some intimate friends not long ago, and I want to quote from that letter. "Dear Fellow Americans," he says, "You may not have much time left. The coming new money could wipe you out, destroy everything you work for and save for and leave your family destitute. I don't mind telling you I'm scared for myself, for my family, for my friends, and for my country." He says, "We've seen a lot of financial tyranny from Washington in this century, but this one takes the cake and popping out of the cake with a big surprise will be an I.R.S. agent."

Ron Paul revealed in another report, and folks, this man who chaired at the very powerful committee knows exactly what he's talking about. He says, "I believe in a technical sense every bank is in trouble. None of them are solvent. The FDIC is the only thing that is propping them up, and it has only enough money to protect 1% of all the deposits." Folks, do you realize what he is saying? Only one cent on the dollar could be propped up by the FDIC.

John Hagee reveals,

> It is a historical fact that no nation in our condition has ever escaped hyper-inflation, and hyper-inflation always leads to an economic crash. How will hyper-inflation affect you? Well, you will lose your retirement funds when it hits. The Social Security system will default. There will be no money for payments. Your insurance policies will probably be worthless. Inflation will wipe out your savings and destroy the value of everything you own. Millions of people will lose their jobs and there will be massive unemployment.

The following headlines were in the October 1992 *Time Magazine*:

- THE FDIC IS BROKE AND THE GOVERNMENT HAS CLOSED YOUR BANK
- YOUR PARENTS' SOCIAL SECURITY FUNDS HAVE DRIED UP
- YOUR EMPLOYER IS ASKING YOU TO TAKE A CUT IN PAY
- INFLATION HAS REACHED 200% PER DAY!
- ALL CONSUMER CREDIT HAS BEEN CANCELLED
- WELCOME TO AMERICA IN 1995[2]

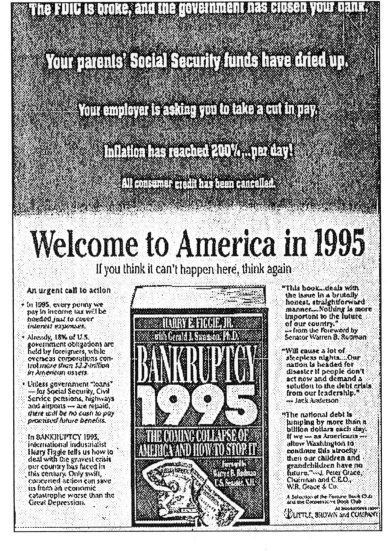
From an ad in Time Magazine, *October, 1992*

Time showed the picture of a new book written by a top financial expert, Harry E. Figgie, Jr. The foreword was written by Senator Warren B. Rudman, U.S. Senator N.H. The title of the book is *Bankruptcy 1995 — The Coming Collapse of America and How to Stop It.* Here is a quote from that book by Mr. Peter Grace, Chairman and C.E.O. of W.R. Grace & Co.:

> The national debt is jumping by more than a billion dollars per day. If we Americans allow Washington to continue this atrocity then our children and grandchildren will have no future.[3]

Mr. Figgie says, "Only with swift concerted action can we save the U.S. from an economic catastrophe worse than the Great Depression."

Texe Marrs, an astute researcher and former professor at the University of Texas warns, and he too, by the way, is a Christian and knows Bible prophecy in depth, "We're on the threshold of a horrible crisis. It has been engineered and orchestrated behind the scenes by an elite group of ruthless men – international bankers, a power elite. A money crash will give them their opportunity to usher in their planned New World Order, the secret esoteric code word for the One World Government."

Make no mistake about it. Their carefully crafted and contrived plan is well advanced. This new money has already been issued, which is the forerunner of a cashless society. Yes, they planned a day to take your money away. They planned it in three phases. First of all the new money is now in the bank in hundred and fifty dollar denominations. They will issue twenty's, ten's, and five's, and when they can fuel the economy of 250 million people there will be a call-in of all old money. We've been using it since 1991.

The Cashless Society is Almost Here

The Bible tells us in Revelation 13 there is coming a day when no one can buy or sell unless he has a number in his right hand or in his forehead. That number would be 666, the Satanic number of the world's coming super dictator.

Let's read about that in the book of Revelation. God the Holy Spirit warned us who would be living in the last days, the end times, that there would arise a super, Satanic world dictator, a false christ. He would institute a new international economic order – a cashless society. In Revelation 13, verses 16-19 we have the Word of God pre-written nearly twenty centuries ago.

> And He causeth all, both small and great, rich and poor, free and bond, to receive a mark (*an emblem* is the Greek word) in their right hand, or in their foreheads, and that no man might buy or sell, save he that had the mark . . .the number of the beast; for it is the number of a man; and his number is 666.

I believe the catalyst to bring in the New World Order, the One World Government will be by design — the collapse of the present monetary system; and out of the pain and anguish and confusion, the Lords of the money, the hidden aristocracy, the Fourth Reich of the super rich, the world order, will pull off their plans for what they call the New World Order, a One World Government and a New International Economic Order of which the bottom line will be a cashless society.

These people call themselves Globalists. They have been working night and day through organizations such as the Illuminati, which was founded in Germany in 1776. The Council on Foreign Relations is an arm of the Illuminati, and most of these organizations are arms of the Illuminati: the Trilateral Commission; the Club of Rome; the Skull and Bones Society (America's Brotherhood of Death); the Masonic Order, yes, the Masonic Order; and many, many more are clandestine organizations such as the Bilderbergers of Europe; Rothchilds; Rockefellers, international bankers, super mega-bankers with their interlocking cartels. Their plan is for a New World Order through the collapse of the American economy. That is one of their six global goals — the collapse of America's economy to create a world economy under a powerful One World central bank.

The book of Revelation tells us they will succeed. They will pull it off. But these men are not even remotely aware that they are fulfilling the Word of God. The Word of God preempted them by nearly 2000 years. I love that verse in

Revelation 17:17: "For God hath put in their hearts to fulfill His will . . . until the words of God shall be fulfilled." They are on God's agenda. They are on God's timetable and they are not even aware of it. They are digging a black hole. They are manipulating themselves into the hands of a super world dictator, whom the Bible calls the Beast, the Man of Sin, the Anti-christ, the false Christ, the man who will be incarnate by Lucifer himself. Lucifer will walk this earth as a man, and that man will have the Satanic number of 666.

This is one of the most amazing prophecies in the entire Bible. In Revelation 13 the world dictator will institute a New International Economic Order, a cashless society in which all coin, cash, credit cards will be obsolete and all the business in the world will be carried on by marks and codes and numbers. By fantastic scientific super computerization, the technical system is now ready to implement that financial world order. The global leaders are calling for a New International Economic Order. The bottom line is to move all nations into a 100% Electronic Funds Transfer System. The technical machinery is ready now to inaugurate that system and all commerce of earth will be carried on without cash or coin or check. It will be by an Electronic Funds Transfer System.

The Cashless Society — How Close?

I have discovered that there is a global marking system— — an electronic, on-line, twenty-four hour a day system in which money is transferred by trillions all over the planet every twenty-four hours. The code number for every transaction is a three digit number. That three digit number is 666. I've had my ear to the ground. The power elite are giving us a clue to what the catalyst would be to bring about a sudden paradigm shift of the global thinking of entire nations, of billions of people, and cause them to be crying out for a One World Government or a New World Order.

Listen to mega-banker David Rockefeller. "One major crisis and man will make the quantum leap into the One World Order." I believe we pretty well know what that major crisis will be. Let's listen to some of the most astute monetary experts in America and the world.

Julian Snyder is one of the world's outstanding financial investment advisors. He said,

> We have a rendezvous with a world dictator, and his appearance may be soon. Always with a collapse of a nation's economy a man arises who restores the currency value. Hitler did that. Mao Tse tung did that! He emerges to become a dictator of the nation. With the coming global monetary collapse the man who restores the currency value will be the dictator of the entire world.

John ZaJack, a top financial advisor to giant corporations in America, says in his book *The Coming Catastrophic Changes of Planet Earth*, I quote him now,

> The financial system of the free world is on the verge of a major catastrophe. It almost collapsed in 1987. The United States government printing office was ready to print new money in case of that collapse.[4]

Yes, the leading monetary advisors of America are warning that we've been on the edge of total collapse, and only the world bank and the international bankers have thus far been able to save it.[5]

In the Christian world there is a man by the name of Larry Burkett. He is a highly rated financial advisor. In his latest book *The Coming Financial Earthquake* he draws a graphic picture. He calls the last chapter of his book a fictional scenario. But somehow I believe, between the lines, he means that it is not just fictional. This is his general synopsis.

> The nation comes to another financial melt-down, as in the summer of 1987. Banks are closing. S&L's are going under. Life insurance companies are failing. A massive depression is eminent. The President of the United States calls for a summit conference with the mega bankers and the great multi-lateral corporation executives of the nation. Verbal battles ensue, and then the President speaks, "Gentlemen, I am the executive officer of America. There is only one possible solution. There is only one hope for our nation. We must move quickly into a cashless society."[6]

I've found uncontestable evidence that the machinery and the technology is ready to implement that cashless society almost overnight. Willard Cantelon, the great Christian financial expert, a superb Christian, revealed even twenty-five years ago that he had sat down in Switzerland, Geneva, with the international bankers of the planet. He watched as they had planned for this very hour that they would restructure the entire financial system of the world. In his book *The Day the Dollar Died* he explains how this was all pre-planned in the highest echelons of financial power over a quarter of a century ago.

Jesus Warned Us of These Days

They must move on God's time table. I believe that when it comes it will come very suddenly. Our Lord spoke about this sudden booby trap in the gospel of Luke. He warned about the Last Days. Let's read in Luke's gospel, chapter 21. He speaks there of the sea and the waves roaring; men's hearts failing them for fear; signs in the sun and in the moon and in the stars; the fig tree shooting forth her buds, I believe that that is Israel returning to her land. He said when you see all of these things beginning to come to pass then lift up your heads and look up for your redemption draweth nigh. But in verse 34 he gave us a clue as to how and how suddenly it would come to pass. Let's read verses 34 through 36,

> And take heed to yourselves, lest at any time your hearts be overcharged with surfeiting, and drunkenness, and so that day come upon you unawares.

"For like a snare shall it come on all them that dwell on the face of the whole earth (like a booby trap, without warning the trap will snap shut). Watch ye, therefore, and pray always, that ye may be accounted worthy to escape all these things that shall come to pass, and to stand before the Son of man."

What should we as Christians in this hour be doing to prepare for those crisis days?

Let me give you seventeen steps that we should be taking now to prepare for coming days of financial crisis.

1) Move toward being out of debt.

All of the best monetary analysts are saying, "Move now toward being out of debt." In other words, get out of debt as soon as you can, or reduce your debt as quickly as possible. The *McAlvany Intelligence Advisor* is one of the finest in the nation if not the world. It is read in fifty-seven nations of earth. It is read by senators, by presidents, and prime ministers. Don McAlvany gives us two ways to move toward being debt-free. I quote,

> You can sell off some of your assets and pay down your debt. Or you can begin to budget and save money on a monthly basis and accelerate your mortgage payments.

There are 600,000-700,000 people filing for bankruptcy every year in the United States, with 1.2 million in bankruptcy court today. The Bible says the borrower is subject to the lender. So the prudent way to go is to begin to pay down your debt and assume no new debt. Now I've been surprised to find all the top financial advisors are saying four words, "get out of debt." If we sink into a major recession or depression we can survive if we are out of debt. Begin to move now toward that goal and then start building an emergency reserve. Begin to save, if you can, up to 10% of your income and have a reserve savings.[7]

The God of Heaven is in charge. They cannot move unless He gives them the green light. But the Bible reveals there is coming a day (and I don't believe that that day is very far down the road) God will allow them to bring in their New World Order and their new financial order – a One World Government – and move all the peoples of the planet to the cashless society – the Mark. God's Word tells us that that is the Mark of the Beast described in the verses we read in Revelation chapter 13. So I would suggest that you ask God for wisdom to show you how to get out of debt as soon as possible and move toward that goal.

2) Stock up on some food reserves.

I'm not alone in this. I've discovered that almost all of the financial experts are saying we should have a six month to one year food reserve. Now I don't mean to spend thousands and thousands of dollars and run off to a mountain hide-a-way cabin and live off the land. Not at all. But lay by a little non-perishable food reserve. As you go through the supermarket on your weekly shopping, lay aside a can of salmon, a can of tuna, maybe a can of beans, and gradually (you will hardly notice the financial outlay) build up a six month to a year food reserve. Then if we move into an economic crunch you can fall back on those reserves. The Don McAlvany *Intelligence Advisory Report* recently told us,

> A grave concern is that there are almost no United States food reserves left. In its 'infinite wisdom' our government has sold or given most of our food reserves to the Russians. The United States food reserve is dangerously low. We have thirty to forty-five days left. That's all. The Russians have a three year reserve supply. Food shortage in the 1990's in America is a real possibility.

Let me share something that I discovered in May of 1992. A man called me from Seattle – a financial expert. He gives an alert to the people of God on a fifty thousand watt Seattle radio station. It has been my privilege to be on that radio station with him. He is a warm, personal friend and has the confidence of the people of Seattle, both Christian and non-Christian. He is a wonderful Christian gentleman.

He stated to me that within the last few days a very close friend of his in the Seattle area, a highly knowledgeable Christian woman of great integrity, had just returned from Wyoming. She attended an educational seminar. She revealed that at that time a Wyoming senator attending the seminar, and with whom she was acquainted, approached her and with tears in his eyes said to her, "When you go back to your state of Washington, begin to gather survival things quickly because we will soon be moving into very troubled financial waters."

This is not "wolf, wolf." This is documented evidence. You must be aware of this. The President of the United States was recently given the executive power by the executive order called EBR #1 — Emergency Banking Regulation Number One. What is it about? Well, he can freeze all assets over night by one stroke of his pen. Also, in that EBR, if you then try to purchase emergency reserves of food, or transmitters, or short wave radios, you would be considered a hoarder and subject to immediate arrest. That is an absolute fact. The wise and prudent person should also begin to purchase survivable equipment – the best that you can purchase — tools, etc.

3) Don't invest in risky enterprises.

The stock market is shaky. The stock market is only for speculators. It may hit new highs or it could plummet overnight to an all time low. Remember the day in 1929, when the Stock Market hit its all time high? That next day it collapsed. One top researcher in this area of finance said, "I would not put one dime in the stock market at this time."

4) Have some reserve cash at home.

It is prudent to have a little cash at home for tough times. Or if there is a banking holiday try to budget to save 10% of your income for this purpose.

5) Don't put your money in tax shelters or corporate bonds.

They are shakey at this time.

6) Avoid all municipal bonds and corporate bonds.

Many cities are on the verge of insolvency. Avoid all municipal and corporate bonds.

7) Don't deposit your money in risky institutions.

If it is not insured by the United States Government don't put your money in it unless the Government has insured it up to at least $100,000. Be careful of grandiose offers of high returns on your money. If people say, "We have a place where your money can get you 20 or 25% (they may tell you your bank is only giving you 3 or up to 7%) and we can get you 25% ..." Watch out! Don't fall for grandiose schemes. You may say, "It sounds too good to be true." It is probably not true.

8) Have some silver and gold coins but keep it yourself.

Don't let someone else keep it for you. You keep that yourself.

9) Treasury Bills are fairly safe routes to go, but don't buy them through a money fund or a money market fund.

Buy them yourself and hold on to them yourself. These are guaranteed by the United States Government. You could not lose on them unless the Government itself would go under.

10) Monitor your bank or your S&L.

Even your life insurance company. It would be well to monitor every six months. Last year four hundred banks went under. Scores of life insurance companies went under in 1991.

11) Monitor your life insurance company.

Often there are hidden loopholes in the policy. Sometimes the big print gives it to you and then the little print takes it away. Have your financial or legal advisor examine it. Often there are hidden clauses in the policy. The cost of complacency can hurt you very dearly. Last year the large Executive Life Insurance Company of California went under suddenly with no warning.

Martin Weiss, in his *Weiss Report*, a very highly esteemed financial report, gave testimony before the United States Senate not long ago, and I want to quote him. This was before the Banking Committee in the Senate of the United States of America.

> We are on the brink of a disaster which could shake the insurance industry to its very foundation. The cause of this disaster is not limited to a handful of junk bonds. Its consequences are not limited to the failure of a few weak companies. The disaster we see ahead stems from many years of high-risk investing. It could result in many decades of hardship for millions of Americans.

He says, if you think you have plenty of time to act, listen to what one widow recently told me.

> I put all my savings in Executive Life. Then I saw the low rating you gave it, but I waited too long. When I finally asked the company to cancel and give me back my money I got a letter from the president telling me there was nothing to worry about. Before I could respond the Commissioner declared a moratorium and now all my money is frozen and I doubt that I will ever get a penny back.

12) Reduce your real estate holdings.

The trend is down because of over-building and over-pricing.

13) Do not have over one thousand dollars stashed away in old bills — the old paper money.

The New Money is now in the banks in one hundred dollar and also fifty dollar denominations. When the Fort Worth Printing and Engraving plant cranks out the money and places it in the bank in twenty's, ten's, and five's, there will be a call-in of all the old bills. If you have over a thousand dollars in old money you will immediately raise the suspicion level of the IRS. You could be fined. You will be required to fill out a number of papers. Do not have over a thousand dollars of old bills in your home.

14) Begin to phase out all credit cards now.

Have plastic surgery. That is, cut up your credit cards. If you use credit cards, discipline yourself to use them only for business purposes, not for personal consumption. I have an article written by a professor of finance at a major university. This is his advice to the Ann Landers column. I do not base my financial projections on Ann Landers but the man who wrote it is a professor of finance at a major United States university. Here is his advice. He gives it in these steps.

a) Pay off the full amount owed every month of that credit card.

Never let a balance remain on which you will be charged interest. Even 14% is too high for most consumers. If you don't have enough monthly income to do this, select the next option.

b) Get your scissors out.

Cut up all your credit cards and cancel all your charge accounts.

c) Then pay cash for all your purchases except homes and cars.

If you can't pay cash, don't buy it. Use your head. If you charge something you still have to pay for it or stretch out the payments and get stuck with high interest charges. Paying cash would do the following things: Speed up your interest repayments by one month; delay retailer's sales by one month; decrease interest revenues to lenders, banks, finance companies, and department stores; help you stay out of financial difficulty and perhaps even bankruptcy; allow you to sleep better. I offer this advice to my students every year. Nobody yet has accused me of encouraging un-American buying habits.

15) A safe investment.

I have found a place where you can make an investment. In fact, our family has made this investment for a number of years — about thirty-five years or more. We have found the safest place of all — the place that pays the highest rate of interest and the highest dividends. No investor has ever lost a penny. I would like to highly commend that place of investment to you. **We are investing heavily in the Kingdom of God.** The Bible tell us in the words of our Lord,

> Lay not up for yourselves treasures upon the earth where moth and rust doth corrupt and thieves break through and steal. But lay up for yourselves treasure in heaven where moth does not corrupt nor thieves break through and steal.

We are helping to support nine missionaries all over the world. Our dividends will be eternal souls in that day when we stand in eternity in the presence of our Lord. Those dividends will be "they that turn many to righteousness shall shine as the stars forever and ever." That is the soundest investment that could ever be made on this planet.

16) Pray for wisdom.

God will give us guidance. The Holy Spirit is our *paracletus*, our comforter, the one who has come to guide us into all truth. There is guidance and wisdom for the asking. He gives us the promise in Proverbs 3:5-6, "Trust in the Lord with all your heart, and lean not unto your own understanding. In all thy ways acknowledge Him, and He shall direct thy paths." Ask God for wisdom to know how to provide for your family in turbulent times. He tells us in James 1:5-6, "If any of you lack wisdom, let him ask of God, who giveth to all men liberally, and upbraideth not, and it shall be given him. But let him ask in faith, nothing wavering."

17) If hard times come, God will see you through!

If a money crash comes, and all indicators show that it will come; if depression comes, God will see you through. In 1929, our family lost everything we had. We lost our dairy. I was a lad of seven, and when I was nine and ten and eleven and twelve we went through the very heart of a terrible depression, the worst depression up to that time of the century. We lost our dairy farm. My father went out to work for a few dollars a day. We moved to a cotton farm in central California. I've gone to work with my father with the stars as a lad of ten, and I've worked through the day until the stars would come out at night. I worked my way through two colleges.

Not one day did God ever fail me. In fact, it was in those days of depression that our whole family was brought to the Lord. We didn't have adequate clothes with which to attend church, and one night in a little town in California, my father went into a shoe cobbler store, and while he was there the owner said, "You're new in our town. Have you found a church home?" My father said, "No, we don't have clothes that are good enough to wear to go to church." He replied, "We don't look at your clothes in our church. We love you for who you are."

My father went down the street and went into a grocery store. The owner said to him, "Your family is new in our area. Do you attend church anywhere?" My father gave him the same answer which was a truthful answer, "We haven't clothes that are really proper to attend church." The store owner replied, "We don't look at your clothes in our church. We will love you as you are." And he invited my father to church. It was the same church the shoe cobbler had invited him to attend.

The next Sunday our entire family was in that church. And it wasn't long until all of us came to know Jesus Christ as our Lord and Savior. It's not affluence that brings families to God. It's in times of great affluence that families drift from God and drift into worldliness and turn away from God. It's in times that are hard and times of financial depression that they turn to God. Isaiah said, "When the judgments of the Lord are in the earth the inhabitants thereof learn righteousness" (chapter 26:9). Almost every major, world-wide missionary society today was founded in the very heart of the Depression from 1929 to 1935 or 1936. God is not the God of inflation. Our God is not the God of depression. He is God! He is Sovereign! He owns "the cattle on a thousand hills." His name is *El Shaddai*, the God that is Enough, the All Sufficient One. He was enough for your yesterdays, He is enough for your todays, He will be enough for all your tomorrows, and He will be enough out yonder into all your eternities. "He is the same yesterday and today and forever."

There is a promise that has meant so much to me over the years. It is found in Philippians 4:19, "But my God shall supply all your need according to His riches in glory by Christ Jesus."

You Have Not One Atom to Fear!!

If you know the Lord Jesus Christ as your Savior and love and walk with Him, you need not be afraid. Nothing can touch you unless He permits. In Him alone is a place of safety, salvation, and security forever. The Lord gives us a wonderful promise in Hebrews 13:5-6,

> Let your conversation (your daily walk) be without covetness and be content with such things as you have for He hath said, "I will never leave you nor forsake you," so then we may boldly say, "The Lord is my helper, I will not fear what man shall do unto me."

And remember Proverbs 18:10, "The name of the Lord is a strong tower; the righteous runneth into it and is safe."

Satan's Masterpiece
"Babylon" — Back to the Future

Error is never set forth in its naked deformity lest it being thus exposed it should be detected; but is craftily decked out in attractive dress so as by its outward form to make it appear to the inexperienced, more truth than truth itself.
— Iraneaus, Bishop in Lyon, France
2nd Century A.D.

Try (test) the spirits whether they be of God.

— 1 John 4:1

Satan has devised a plan — a master blueprint — a plan of such monstrous subtlety and deception, that through it, he will deceive billions of earth's peoples, and even the very elect of God, if it were possible. That plan is to inaugurate a New World religion.

Is there such a religion in the world today? Incontrovertibly, yes. And it is moving over the planet like a giant nuclear (spiritual) cloud. Its satanic radiation and fallout is poisoning the minds of hundreds of millions of people. The nerve center of this evil octopus is in the United Nations plaza building in New York City. It was incorporated in 1922 by Alice Bailey, the author of *The Externalization of the*

91

Hierarchy. The information in her book was revealed to her, she claims, by a spirit guide called The Tibetan[1] (the Bible reveals that spirit guides are demons, 1 Timothy 4:1). It was incorporated under the title of *Lucifer Trust* and then changed a little later to *Lucis Trust.* Some of the titles of the New World religion are the following: *Planetary Initiative for Planetary Citizenry; The New Age of Aquarius; The Plan.* Some of its tenants are: Man is divine and is evolving into Godhood; by reincarnation you will live forever and not die; self-love is the greatest love of all; the worship and divinizing of Mother earth. Its major goals: to establish a one world government; a one world universal religion; to erase the name of Jesus Christ and all Christianity from the earth by the year 2000, and place a cosmic Christ on the throne of the world.

I have spent twelve years researching the religion of the New Age. It meets all the criteria to be the religion of the coming Antichrist. I am not alone in this. Hal Lindsey said on TBN telecast, "We now have a movement that is unparalleled in history called the New Age. This movement is preparing the way for the Antichrist rapidly." Constance Cumbey stated in her book *The Hidden Dangers of the Rainbow,* that **the "New" Age religion fulfills all the requirements of the Babylonian harlot church of the last days.**

How large is this religion? The New Age is sweeping America like wildfire. Polls reveal that sixty million are caught up in necromancy (talking with the spirits of the dead); forty million in the doctrine of reincarnation; fifty million in yoga and transcendental meditation, this is the religion of the Hindus; sixty million are caught in the global mind trap of astrology. I realize that there is some overlapping in these figures. But it is awesome to watch a great and good nation turning by the millions from the God of the Bible, from the divine light of Scripture and turning to the gods of the New Age.

The Bible reveals that the New Age religion began before time began. It began in eternity before the throne of the triune God.

Scene One:

"Thou art the anointed cherub that covereth."

How art thou fallen from heaven, O Lucifer, son of the morning! How art thou cut down to the ground, who didst weaken the nations! For thou hast said in thine heart, I will ascend into heaven, I will exalt my throne above the stars of God; I will sit also upon the mount of the congregation, in the sides of the north, I will ascend above the heights of the clouds, **I will be like the Most High.** Yet thou shalt be brought down to hell, to the sides of the pit (Isaiah 14:12-15).

In these passages the Bible reveals that Lucifer was the most beautiful archangel ever created — perfect in wisdom and beauty. Some Bible scholars believe that he led the angelic choirs of heaven and kept the entrance to the very throne of the triune God of glory. Then one day, iniquity was found in his heart. He said, "I will be like the most high. I will be as God."

Lucifer was the first great positive thinker of all time; the first to build his self image and build his self-esteem and love himself. The Bible tells us that he deceived one-third of the beautiful sinless angels of heaven by that awful lie, "Follow me and I will lead you to godhood." Lucifer, the Son of the Morning, led the first great rebellion at the very throne of God. He was banished forever. The "Son of the Morning" became the "Prince of Darkness," the Devil, Satan, the god of this world; and the angels, sinless beings, that had been given the power of free choice, became demons awaiting the judgment of the great day of God.

Scene Two:

A beautiful garden — the first man and woman have been created by God. They were given the power of choice as were the angels of heaven. Lucifer, now the arch foe of God, through the lips of a serpent channels a dual lie to our first parents. "Partake of the fruit of the tree of the knowledge of good and evil and ye shall be as gods, and ye shall not surely die" (by reincarnation you will live forever). They took the bait and through that lie all mankind joined in the great rebellion.

Scene Three

We leap across the span of human history to the last days. The Bible tells us what is going to take place just before Jesus Christ returns.

> Now we beseech you, brethren, by the coming of our Lord Jesus Christ, and by our gathering together unto him . . . Let no man deceive you by any means; for that day shall not come, except there come a great rebellion (this is the new revision), and that man of sin be revealed . . . . Even whose coming is after the working of Satan with all power and signs and lying wonders, and with all deceivableness of unrighteousness in them that perish, because they received not the love of the truth . . . God shall send them strong delusion, that they should believe **the lie** and be damned (2 Thessalonians 2:1-11).

The Great Lie

The lie that deceived one-third of the angels of heaven, the lie that deceived our first parents; Satan is using that lie, now at the end time, to deceive the entire world unless your name was written in the Book of Life from the foundation of the world. That awful lie that deceived the billions of angelic beings and brought mankind into the great rebellion against the triune God, that same lie, Lucifer will use to the hilt in the last days to deceive billions of earth's people.

The New Age religion is not new at all. It is as old as time and even goes back into eternity. It is the lie that man is divine, that he is a god, and through a series of reincarnations he will evolve to super-godhood, and will live forever. This is the genius of the New Age religion. It is the great lie. It has a thousand dazzling facets of deception. In the last twelve years I have spent about 3,000 hours of intense researching of the New Age. I have been almost overwhelmed by its labrynth of lies, deception, and subterfuge. It has staggered my imagination. It can only be what the Bible reveals "the mystery of iniquity," "the depth of Satan," "the doctrine of demons," "the great delusion of the last days."

At first I could not get a handle on it. Frankly, I literally went to my knees. I asked God the Holy Spirit to reveal it all to me so that I could warn His people. He is so faithful. He is the Spirit of truth, and He has come to guide us into all truth through His holy Word. And He did just that. He revealed to me the meaning of the New Age religion in one chapter of the Bible — in one verse — in one word —

Babylon
This is Truly Ancient Babylon, "Back to the Future"

> And there came one of the seven angels who had the seven bowls, and talked with me, saying unto me, "Come here; I will show unto thee the judgment of the great harlot that sitteth upon many waters; with whom the kings of the earth have committed fornication, and the inhabitants of the earth have been made drunk with the wine of her fornication." So he carried me away in the Spirit into the wilderness and I saw a woman sit upon a scarlet-colored beast, full of names of blasphemy, having seven heads and ten horns. And the woman was arrayed in purple and scarlet color, and bedecked with gold and precious stones and pearls, having a golden cup in her hand, full of abominations and filthiness of her fornication; and upon her forehead was a name written, **Mystery, Babylon the Great, the Mother of harlots and Abominations of the Earth** (Revelation 17:1-5).

Four thousand years ago, just after the flood, following the days of Noah, Lucis is described in Genesis 10:9 as a mighty hunter before the Lord (the Hebrew word is *against the Lord*). It was he who built the beautiful city of Babylon on the plain of Shinar on the banks of the Euphrates River. He became the world's first super dictator and led a great rebellion against the God of heaven. Nimrod's wife was one of the most beautiful women in the world but was licentious and sensual. Her name was Semiramis. In ancient Babylon the citizens rejected the Creator and embraced the lie of humanism — "The de-throning of God and the deifying of man." They turned to astrology and worshiped the sun and the moon and the stars and they began to worship the earth as their Mother Goddess, believing she was a living, breathing being, and her Satanic number in ancient Babylon was 666.

They worshiped the solar sun god, Lucifer. The city was laced with Satan worship, sensuality, black magic arts, and the occult. The state religion was the worship of their emperor Nimrod, "the god man", and the worship of the solar sun, Lucifer. Their religion spread like a cancer to the other nations of the world – Egypt, India, and even to Israel under Baal worship. It polluted the entire planet. They embraced the great lie of the serpent of Eden 2000 years before; that they were divine beings and through reincarnation they would never die. The Bible reveals that this Satanic religion will re-surface in the last days just before Jesus Christ returns, and that the religion of ancient Babylon will be the proto-type for the religion of all mankind in the end time.

The World Will Become One

Now if we could discover what Babylon was like 4000 years ago we will have in microcosm what the new world religion will be like just before the return of our Lord Jesus. Through the research of Brooks Alexander (his works are under the title, *Spiritual Counterfeits*) we know the Babylonian monarch was the focus of the occult, channeled through the activities of the priesthood. Nimrod was regarded as a divine being, a god-man. He synthesized a vast political and religious system into one. In Genesis 11 it is vividly described. The cry on the plain of Shinar at the Tower of Babel was **"we will be as one."**

Today, 4,000 years later, as we approach the seventh millennium, the political leaders of earth are calling for all nations to surrender their sovereignty and form the New

World Order — "one planet, one people." So, also, the great religious leaders are calling for all the religions of earth to surrender a measure of doctrine (to compromise) and form a universal One World Church.

One Planet — One People

Dr. Kurt Koch, professor, lectured at 100 universities in sixty-five countries on five continents. Subjects of expertise were New World Order, occultism, and parapsychology. He writes that his assessment of the coming New World Order under the United Nations will reduce everything to **one common denominator:**

> The system will be made up of a single currency, single centrally financed government, single tax system, single language, single political system, single world court of justice, single head (one individual leader) and single state religion.

> Each person will have a registered number, without which he will not be allowed to buy or sell; and there will be one universal world church. Anyone who refuses to take part in this universal system will have no right to exist.[2]

Babylon Comes to Chicago in 1993

In 1893, the world's representatives of the great religions met in Chicago, Illinois, to explore how all the religions of earth could come together in a universal world church. One hundred years later in 1993, on August 28th through September 6th, one hundred thirty of the most prestigious religions of earth met together again in the world parliament of religions. They met in Chicago, Illinois, to finalize plans for all religions to become one, to establish a One World church.

The Dalai Lama was there who believes that he is a man god. Joan Campbell, the feminist and director of the Marxistslanted National Council of Churches, was there. The Lucis Trust representatives of the New Age religion were there. Voodoo, high priests, and wicka groups, and witchcraft were all there. High free Masons attended. The Seventh Day Adventist church was represented. Serpent charmers and druids and Satan worshippers, liberal Baptists, Zoroastrians to Zen Buddhists were all represented. The World Council of churches and the powerful church of Rome were highly represented. They met to celebrate "unity in diversity."

Charles Colson of Prison Ministries, despite the pleas of evangelical pastors, came by personal invitation to receive the prestigious John Templeton award. He received his "thirty pieces of silver" (one million dollars). He was honored in the Rockefeller Chapel, presided over by Catholic Cardinal Joseph Bernardin, a supporter of the Eastern religions. Dr. Robert Muller, former Assistant Secretary General of the United Nations (for forty years director of thirty-two separate directorships), was there. He is one of the most powerful New Age leaders in the entire world.

Another man had previously received the John Templeton award. His name was Billy Graham. The American Humanist Association president Michael Werner was present and said, "This parliament of religions could pave the way for a New Age of humanism." Secular humanism is the de-throning of God and the deifying of man.

The declaration for the global ethic on September 5th, 1993, was signed, "**calling for the merger of all the religions of earth — the world religions to become one.**"[3] Directing it all from behind the scenes was the most evil genius on planet earth. His name was Lucifer, Satan the arch-deceiver of all time, the father of lies, the devil, the "god of this world." There was one who was not invited — my precious Savior Jesus Christ, the Lamb of Calvary, the Savior of the world was not welcome, nor were the hundreds of millions who love Him and have crowned Him their Lord.

What we saw in Chicago was nothing less than the Satanically inspired global church of Satan right out of Babylon, Egypt and Rome. This gala extravaganza was mainly "bank-rolled" by the international banker David Rockefeller, one of the board members of the Lucis Trust, which is the nerve center of the New Age religion, centered in the United Nations. This event will be the kick-off of a seven year New Age plan first formulated by the Club of Rome, a key planning group under the control of the Illuminati Hierarchy. The plan calls for the initiation of all humanity by the year 2000. Hail mystery Babylon!

The Mystery "Initiation"

What is this initiation of all humanity? David Spangler is the director of Planetary Initiative for Planetary Citizenry in the United Nations. He said that the Luciferian initiation is the heart and core of the New Age religion. Malachi Martin, the Roman priest, who wrote the very famous book *The Keys of this Blood* quotes David Spangler,

> At some point each of us faces the presence of Lucifer. Lucifer comes to give us the gift of wholeness — that is the Luciferian initiation. It is one that many people now and in the days to come will be facing. It is an initiation into the New Age.[4]

Lucifer is Satan, the master deceiver, the prince of the power of the air. **The Luciferian initiation is the pledge to worship Lucifer (Satan).**

Constance Cumbey who wrote the splendid book *The Hidden Dangers of the Rainbow* reveals that the New Age leader David Spangler, who is right on top of the Planetary Citizenry which is the secretariat for a planetary initiative, says that in order to enter the New Age we must take a Luciferic initiation. He says, "We are heading into a vast planetary mass initiation of people. Benjamin Creme has declared that the revitalized Christian churches as well as the Masonic lodges will be used for purposes of giving these mass planetary initiations."[5]

"They intend to give us our mark," Mrs. Cumbey writes, "or a number."

The Mark which is intended to be given is revealed by God in Revelation 13:16-18. It will truly be a New Age of Satanism. It is called the Mark of the Beast or 666. Dr. David P. Ramage, president of McCormick Seminary in Chicago, revealed that the World Parliament of Religions formed an ethics committee on September 5, 1993, to implement the plan for all religions of earth to unite as quickly as possible into a world body. Mystery Babylon has returned! The great whore is about to take center stage as we approach the close of the grace age. The Satanic religion of ancient Babylon has risen its beastly head in the form of the religion of the New Age. All the great religions are merging. The Apostate Christian World Council of Churches is abandoning its faith in Jesus Christ. The global leaders, blinded by the prince of darkness, are rushing to establish a Satanic counterfeit church described in Revelation 17 as Babylon, the great whore. **We are watching Babylon "back to the future."**

Robert Muller, former Assistant Secretary General of the United Nations in his last famous book *The New Genesis* is calling for a cosmic Christ to take the throne of the world by the year 2000. He describes this new world order "like a glorious aphrodite emerging from the sea."[6] Aphrodite is the ancient Greek version of the Babylonian mother goddess who polluted the whole world with Satanism.

The Beast and the Woman

The Bible pictures her as "the great whore who sits on many waters" (Revelation 17:1). This is what John the Apostle saw nearly twenty centuries ago unfolding like a giant kaleidoscope. He saw a beast carrying a woman,

> So he carried me away in the Spirit into the wilderness and I saw a woman sit upon a scarlet-colored beast, full of names of blasphemy, having seven heads and ten horns (Revelation 17:3).

A beast with seven heads and ten horns. In the Bible God often reveals His truths in symbolism.

The picture is clear. When you compare this verse with Daniel 7:23-24 and Revelation 13:1, we discover the Beast is the leader of the last days super power, a revived Roman empire, a ten nation empire of the old Roman world. The Beast is carrying a woman. Her name? "The Great Whore" of Babylon. She is the counterfeit, the last days Satanic world church, a counterfeit of the pure, chaste Bride of the Lamb, the church of Jesus Christ. The vast political power of the New World Order has become one. With the ecclesiastical power of the world, church and state will have become one as in ancient Babylon. Revelation 17:9, "The seven heads are seven mountains, on which the woman sitteth;" and verse 18 "And the woman whom thou sawest is that great city, which reigneth over the kings of the earth." The great whore, the false Satanic church of the end time is depicted as a city sitting on seven mountains and "reigning over the kings of the earth."

One hundred years ago, Alexander Hislop wrote the book *The Two Babylons*. It is the most documented book I have ever read. After two hundred eighty-seven pages, this is his final conclusion:

> Xerxes and many of the medo-Persian kings banished its priests from Babylon and labored to root it out of their empire. But it found a secure retreat in Pergamos, and Satan's seat (Revelation 2) was erected there. It took a higher flight and seated itself on the throne of Imperial Rome. **The Babylonian's goddess, seated in glory on the seven hills of Rome.**[7]

Malachi Martin in his book *The Keys of this Blood*, which was endorsed by the Vatican, states,

> At the round table of international politics, no ruler could command, no government could function without the nod of the Roman pope.[8]

History is clear. Only one ecclesiastical power has ruled over the kings of the earth for almost fifteen centuries. That power is Rome.[9]

Reverend Hislop reveals that the Roman church incorporated the very core of the mysteries of the Babylonian doctrine and ritual of the worship and veneration of their queen of heaven, Mary, whom they place even above Jesus Christ. He continues,

> Every statement in Scripture shows that it was truly described as Satan's masterpiece — the perfection of his policy for ensnaring the world. He warns of the queen of heaven in the worship and veneration of Mary and her exaltation above Jesus Christ.[10]

The Bible says:

> For there is one God, and one mediator between God
> and men, the man, Christ Jesus (1 Timothy 2:5).

Cardinal Alphonsus de Liguori, in his book *The Glories of
Mary* states, "He falls and is lost who has no recourse to
Mary. We shall be heard more quickly if we have recourse to
Mary and call on her holy name than we should if we called
on the name of Jesus our Savior." He says,

> Many things are asked from God and are not granted:
> they are asked of Mary and they are obtained . . . she is
> even the queen of hell.[11]

Then the Cardinal makes this amazing statement:

> All power is given to thee in heaven and on earth; at
> the command of Mary all obey her; even God Himself.
> God has placed the whole church under the command of
> Mary.[12]

Our Lord Jesus Christ said, "All power is given unto Me
in heaven and in earth" (Matthew 28:18).

Reverend Hislop continues, **"It is against Babylon that
sits on seven hills that the saints are warned."**

When Christianity first became the state religion under
Emperor Constantine he was granted the title of Pontifex
Maximus. Dr. John Walvoord, president of Dallas
Theological Seminary, writes in his commentary *The Bible
Knowledge,*[13]

> The Babylonian cultists moved to Pergamos where
> one of the seven churches of Asia Minor was located
> (Revelation 2:12-17).

> Crowns in the shape of fish heads were worn by the
> chief priests of the Babylonian cult to honor the fish god.
> The crown bore the words Keeper of the Bridge symbolic
> of the bridge between man and Satan. This handle was
> adopted by the Roman emperors who used the Latin title
> "Pontifex Maximus." The early Pontiff, when Christianity
> became the state religion, was given the title of Pontifex
> Maximus. Pontifex Maximus meant the bridge between
> man and Satan. Pontiff means the "keeper of the bridge."

The same title was later given to the bishop of Rome and
he was called The Pope and is today called The Pontiff.[14]

Pastor Barry Smith, in his two books *The First Warning*
and *the Second Warning* documents that the official title of the
Roman Pontiff is **Vicarius Felii Dei** — the Vicar of the son of
God. This is the official name of the Roman Pontiff given by
the Roman Catholic church — the Vicar of the son of God,
the representative of Jesus Christ on earth. The Roman
numerals of those three words spell out 666. The Bible tells
me that it is the Holy Ghost who is come to represent Jesus
Christ on earth and glorify Him as the Son of God.[15]

The Great Merger

Mr. Gary Kah in his book *Enroute to Global Occupation*
tells us that he discovered the plan for the merger of the
New Age religion, the order of Free Masonry, and the one
billion members of the Roman church. Also the World
Council of Churches representing the mainline protestant
denominations are privately pushing for unification with
Rome. After the Pope's visit to Los Angeles a few years ago,
the Los Angeles Times reported that Robert Schuller of the
Crystal Cathedral spoke to the Arch Bishop of the Los
Angeles Diocese saying that we protestants should go back
to the mother church and say, "What must we do to come
home?" The stampede is on!

The Oregonian, the largest newspaper in the State of
Oregon, on September the 22nd, 1992, quoted Billy Graham
at a news conference in Portland as calling for "a One
Merged church."[16]

Robert Muller, former Assistant Secretary General of the
United Nations, now president of the Peace University in
Costa Rica, called for the Roman Pontiff to come and address
the United Nations and present himself as the head of the
world church.

Texe Marrs in his book *The Millennium* reveals the Order
of the Illuminati has established six global goals and their
sixth goal is:

The Order desires the Vatican to be the fountain head
and headquarters of the New World religion, and intends

that the Pontiff of the Roman church become the supreme
Pontiff of the whole world. He is to be the king priest to
marshall the spiritual resources of the planet and all
religions to become one, and that God has given divine
authority and absolute rights and responsibilities to the
world leader.[17]

There it is. And all who refuse to join will be held to
ridicule and called non-conformists and right-winged
extremists. Who will be the head of this universal world
church called Babylon?

Again we quote from Malachi Martin's book *The Keys of
this Blood,*

> In essence Pope John Paul seems to perceive what the
> New World order should be. The Pontiff is not only a
> calculated blueprint for the New World Order but it is
> determined that he shall lead it. Pope John is determined
> to endure his Pontificate with an international profile and
> among leaders and nations indicating a position for
> himself as a special leader among leaders because in the
> competition **he plans to emerge the victor**.

> John Paul sees himself not as one leader among many
> but as one by virtue of his exalted position should be the
> **supreme authority**.[18]

"Church and State Become One"

The church and state will have become one. The Satanic
trinity of Babylon will surface again (Revelation 13:4). This is
Satan's masterpiece. The Satanic trinity of the end times.
The dragon Lucifer, Satan. The Beast, the head of the New
World Order, the Antichrist. The false prophet who by virtue
of "his exalted office", causing all the world to worship the
first beast – the Antichrist as God.

> And he exerciseth all the power of the first beast
> before him, and causeth the earth and them who dwell on
> it to worship the first beast, whose deadly wound was
> healed (Revelation 13:12).

The Satanic trinity of ancient Babylon will have re-emerged and the world-wide worship of Lucifer and the world dictator will be mandated.

And he hath power to give life unto the image of the Beast, that the image of the Beast should both speak, and cause that as many as would not worship the image of the Beast should be killed (Revelation 13:15).

John Cotter in his book *A Study in Syncrotism, the Background and Apparatus of the Emerging One World Church* wrote of "the universal brotherhood which is the spiritual arm of the United Nations – a One World Government." This plan began in the United Nations almost forty-five years ago under the term **"syncretism – the merger of conflicting religions and philosophic ideologies into one."**

This plan has emerged in the Parliament of Religions called *Unity in Diversity*. That plan is about to crest — all the great religious bodies merging and fusing to form the last day universal world church. The world Parliament of Religions laid down the final plank, "a world ethic to unite all faiths into a One World Body." Billions will be signing up. The twentieth century Tower of Babel is almost complete.

If Lucifer can pull it off (the Bible says he will), then there will be unleashed in the world the greatest force that mankind has ever known – it will propel a man (the Beast, the leader of the revived Roman empire) to the throne of the world. The gavel of the "world federation earth," the great world tribunal, the New World Order will be in the hands of the most powerful dictator ever known in human history. That man will be the Beast, the man of sin, the son of perdition, the world's great Antichrist.

"The Goddess is Back"

In Babylon they worship the solar sun Lucifer. They worship the goddess Mother Earth, and when Nimrod was slain with the sword, Semiramis, his beautiful but lustful wife, and announce to the citizens of Babylon that she had become pregnant by the solar sun god Lucifer (Satan pulled off a counterfeit, fake virgin birth), and the son she bore she claimed was a reincarnation of Nimrod the world dictator. She named her son Tamuz. The citizens of Babylon worshiped the solar sun god Lucifer, the goddess earth — whose Satanic number was 666, and the son, supposedly Nimrod reincarnated. Satan produced a counterfeit trinity, a mockery of the triune God of heaven, the blessed Father, Son, and Holy Spirit.

Earth was their goddess. They worshiped the earth as a living, breathing being. In the ancient city of Babylon they had an *earth agenda*. It was actually witchcraft. They worshiped the son, the moon, and the stars and their goddess mother earth. The Bible describes this in Romans 1:25,

> Who changed the truth of God into a lie, and worshiped and served the creature more than the Creator, who is blessed forever.

I recently tuned in to a telecast. It portrayed beautiful Yosemite in California. A lovely feminine voice said, "We should worship the divine Mother Earth."

Ted Turner, the powerful voice of CNN, "the King of News," has unveiled his ten new commandments. He tells us that the ten commandments of the Bible are now obsolete. He has written ten new commandments. We now have the Ted Turner Commandments. He says, "The first commandment is we should love Mother Earth." The Christian mandate that our Lord gave to His people was, "Thou shalt love the Lord thy God with all thy heart and with all thy soul and all thy mind and all thy strength and thy neighbor as thyself."

Matthew Fox, an ex-Roman Catholic priest, wrote the book *The Coming of the Cosmic Christ*. This man has been deceived by the Gaia hypothesis. I quote, "Mother Earth has been nailed to the cross — we have crucified Mother Earth."[19] The Bible tells us that we crucified Jesus Christ the Lord of Glory, the creator of the heavens and the earth.

It is incredible. Modern 20th century man, the most enlightened generation which ever lived — with all our advanced technology, going back to witchcraft — the worship of the sun and the stars and Mother Earth. Even the popular astronomer Carl Sagan who reveres the cosmos said, "Does it not make sense to revere the sun and stars?"[20]

"The goddess is back!" Dr. Dennis Cuddy, Ph.D., in his book *The Dawning of the New Age, New World Order* quotes Mary Daley, who teaches feminist ethics at Boston College Theology Department,

> I took the concept of the second coming of Christ and said the real concept would be the second coming of women with the celebration of the goddess.[21]

Barbara Kelly of Eugene, Oregon, founder of *Save our Eco Systems*, wrote, "We all have one mother, Gaia, preserving her is the highest good. This is my religion." — The Gaia hypothesis.

Ted Turner, via the television program *Captain Planet and the Planeteers*, portrays Gaia, the earth goddess, who gives super powers. The goddess is back. 4000 years later modern twentieth century homo sapiens have come full cycle. Their goddess Mother Earth had the triple six as her symbol in ancient Babylon. In the 1990s, the Wicka groups that are springing up by the thousands throughout America sit in a circle and in groups of three sixes, and they worship their mother goddess.

Readers Digest described Ted Turner's broadcasting system New Age cartoon series *Captain Planet and the Planeteers* as "the slickest, political propaganda piece ever aimed at America's young people, promoting a leftist agenda."[22]

"Earth Agenda — Save Mother Earth"

The Los Angeles Times announced the super-mega extravaganza. The date was to be April the 22nd, 1990, "Earth Day." President Bush issued a proclamation called Earth Day.[23] Hollywood stars supported it. Norman Lear of the people for the American Way supported it. This arch foe of Christianity backed it and promoted it. Now, we are all for clean air and pure water and wildlife and preserving our forests. But there was a hidden agenda.

Earth Day actually began in 1970. New Agers have a secret networking language of symbolism. The ploy on the first Earth Day? "Meditate for world peace." The symbol was the circle with the broken cross.

Through that symbol they launched Earth Day in New Age language. The broken cross with the bars pointing downward was a mockery of our crucified Lord Jesus and total rejection of Christianity. This is the meaning of their peace symbol and thousands of Christians were "taken in." The preparation for Earth Day was carefully crafted and there was a conditioning of earth's millions as it was fine tuned for April 22nd, 1990.

1986 — "World Instant Cooperation." One billion people were linked together in a giant mind link meditating for world peace. The master mind behind it all was John Randolph Price of the Quartus Foundation in Texas. He reveals in his book *Planetary Commission,* "When millions of us little gods meditate for world peace we will create a critical mass; a new world religion will flood the souls of all mankind, and we will bring forth a new world Christ."[24]

Then came harmonic convergence in 1987, organized and orchestrated by Jose Aquellas, another powerful New Age devotee. This mind link boasted of two billion people meditating for world peace. Behind the scenes he called for 144,000 New Agers to become the nuptial bride of Lucifer — to bring Lucifer back so Gaia, Mother Earth, could be healed.

Then the United Nations proclaimed Earth Day April 22nd, 1990, and 2.5 billion people were linked together by telecommunications satellite throughout the planet. **The United Nations endorsed the great invocation as the official prayer of Earth Day.**

"The Great Invocation" — Satan's Prayer

Now, the New Agers not only used the secret language of symbolism but they have buzz words; a double-speak language, a spin-out language, "the feasible lie." This is the Great Invocation. The translation is from *The Mystery Mark* by Texe Marrs.[25]

From the point of Light within the Mind of God
Let light stream forth into the minds of men.
Let Light descend on earth.

(Translation: They mean Lucifer, their false god to descend to earth.)

From the point of Love within the Heart of God
Let love stream forth into the hearts of men.
May Christ return to Earth.

(Translation: May Lucifer come and their false New Age Christ appear.)

From the center where the Will of God is known
Let purpose guide the little wills of men —
The purpose which the Masters know and serve.

(Translation: From Shamballa (hell), where Satan and his demons reside, let Satan's plan to rule the universe and have men worship him as god prevail.)

From the center which we call the race of men
Let the Plan of Love and Light work out
And may it seal the door where evil dwells.

(Translation: May Satan's plan succeed in extinguishing all traces of the God of heaven and the elimination of all who love His Word.)

Let Light and Love and Power restore the Plan on Earth.

Hidden Danger of the Triangle

Earth Day 1990 was Satan's Day. Their symbol flashed across the television screens of the world with 2.5 billion people watching. The symbol? **The triangle** –– the Babylonian symbol of the Satanic trinity of ancient Babylon, a mockery of the Holy Triune God. The symbol of the triangle is the symbol of the Lucis Trust, the nerve center of the New Age Religion in the United Nations. It is actually the New Age symbol of their god Lucifer.

Alice Bailey wrote about the point of the triangle that represents Shamballa, the spirit kingdom of Lord Matreya, the false New Age coming world Christ.[26]

Benjamin Creme, director of the New Age religion of North America, links the triangle with the coming world ruler, whom he calls "the Christ." Remember, it's a double-speak language, and to him the Christ is the one whom the Bible calls the Antichrist.

Barbara Walker, in the *New Age Encyclopedia*, says, "The triangle is the universal symbol of the mother goddess."

The Tibetan spirit guide, which is a demon, reveals that the triangle through the prayer, the Great Invocation, represents the combined energies of the solar father Lucifer, the Christ, Antichrist, and the hierarchy kingdom of Lucifer. This was the secret symbolism of Earth Day, and it was a call, through the Great Invocation, for the coming kingdom of Lucifer; for the Antichrist to come and set up his reign on earth.

We've been duped! The master con-artist Lucifer is deceiving the billions of people under the ploy of peace. Meditate for world peace. 2600 years ago Daniel wrote by divine inspiration, "By peace He shall destroy many." This prophecy is being re-enacted on the television screens of the world before our eyes.

Is it coincidence that the symbol of the New World Order, the coming One World Government, is the triangle with the all-seeing eye of Lucifer at the top? Is it coincidence the symbol of the Lucis Trust in the United Nations is the triangle? The symbol of the New Mint in Fort Worth, Texas, is the supreme symbol of Satan — the triangle within the circle. Is it coincidence the symbol of the new educational agenda "America 2000" is the triangle, and also the hexagram, which is the six points, the ultimate symbol of Lucifer himself?

Then there followed the greatest global conference of them all. The Rio Summit in June,1992, was touted as the greatest conference in the history of mankind. The title? **UNCED — The United Nations Conference Environmental Development.** One hundred seventy-seven nations of the world were represented. Al Gore, "Mr. Environmentalist," led the American delegation. The Dalai Lama was there, the man who claims to be god. The leaders of the world religions attended and had a separate conference. Behind it all was the full power of the New Age religion.

New Age Secret "Mecca"

Let's take a good, hard look at the chairman of the Rio Summit — UNCED 1992. His name is Maurice Strong — the Canadian multi-millionaire, whom the New York Times called the Custodian of the Planet. He founded one of the great New Age centers of the world, in Southern Colorado, in the San Luis Valley called the Baca, just under the San de Christo Mountains. The meaning in Spanish is *the mountains of the blood of Jesus Christ.* It is a 160,000 acre paradise. The Ashrams of India were represented, who teach that man is evolving into super godhood. They conduct fire ceremonies and place the ashes in their foreheads and worship their Hindu god Agni (who is the god Lucifer). The triple six is the predominant number of the Baca.

Shirley MacLaine has built an occultic channeling center at the Baca. The Temple of Babylon has already been built. It is a replica of the ancient Temple of Babylon.

George Hunt has given me the manuscript of his eye-witness account as well as pictures of the fire ceremonies that have taken place at the Baca and the Temple of Babylon. The elite of the planet visit this New Age retreat.

Maurice Strong is the friend of some of the global leaders of earth — David Rockefeller of the Council of Foreign Relations; Baron Edmund De Rothschild of London, who sets the gold standard of the world. Mr. Strong and his wife Hanna are members of the Baha'i faith, which is calling for all religions of earth to form the One World church.

The Roman Pontiff has his personal representative there at the Baca and a carmalite Roman priest, also, who represents one billion members of the Roman church. Mr. Hunt asked the carmalite priest, "Why are they incantating at the Babylonian temple?" His reply, "When heaven and earth are wed they will bring forth a son."[27]

This is one of the most awesome things I have ever encountered in my entire life time. "Bring forth a son." Could it possibly be the son that will be brought forth will be the counterfeit Christ, the **son of perdition, Lucifer incarnate in a man, the Antichrist?**

In the New Age book *Two Disciples, the Rainbow Bridge,* "These authors reveal that planet earth as a network of light composes an interlocking triangle energy force fields. They link up with these universal force fields. You will be one with God when enough people of earth link up to this network. They claim the New Age Christ and all his hierarchy of spirits will appear to establish their New Age kingdom and the sons of men will be one."[28]

Do you now understand what these mega extravaganza world meditation days are all about?

The Day of the Declaration of Antichrist
A Counterfeit Day of Pentecost

New Age leader Barbara Marx Hubbard, an executive director of the world's Future Society, former advisor to President Bush and Reagan, and candidate for the vice-presidency of the United States in 1984 believes

> . . . that the World Healing Day would trigger a planetary Pentecost . . . a mass transfiguration and empowerment of billions at once . . . a second coming through lifting our consciousness, transforming ourselves as Christ transformed Himself . . . such events are now being planned.[29]

Benjamin Creme, North American director of the New Age movement believes that when the world is ready for the appearance of the Christ, there will be a day of declaration. On that day, he says,

> The new world Christ will be invited to address all the world through the world-wide television and radio hook-ups. At that time he will overshadow all humanity . . . he will communicate with us telepathically on our T.V. screens. We will see this man and we will silently hear his words drop into our minds in our own language. We could then turn off the sound on our own television sets and still hear him. Everybody, everywhere will hear no matter what they are doing. (This will be a counterfeit Pentecost.) In this way, by overshadowing, he will reveal his true nature, inspiring within all men and women the certainty that this man is indeed the Christ . . . . And simultaneously throughout the world hundreds and thousands of healing, cures (apparently miraculous cures)

will reinforce if necessary, that this is the Christ they are watching.[30]

The Bible reveals this very thing will take place.

> And the Beast (the Antichrist) shall ascend out of the bottomless pit . . . and all they that dwell on the earth shall wonder . . . **when they behold the Beast** (Revelation 17:8).

> And then shall that wicked one be revealed . . . whose coming is after the working of Satan, with **all power and signs and lying wonders**, with all deceivableness of unrighteousness (2 Thessalonians 2:9-11).

Beverly Galyean, psychologist of confluent education (this literally swept the schools of Southern California) taught that the chief goal of education was to "re-own our godhood." She instructed the little children to look into the sun, and as you do, the face of a wise person will appear. "Listen to this person speaking, these wise persons and mystical spirit guides." She says, "We don't call them spirit guides in the public schools. We call them imagery guides."

These are mystical spirit guides which are literal demons — and through these occultic methods, millions of school children of America are subtly being conditioned for the Day of the Declaration of the coming world leader. When he makes his declaration millions of the spirit guides will identify him to the children and the youth as **Mr. Good Guy.**

These plans for the human race could only have been strategized by a genius far beyond the ingenuity of man, synchronizing and orchestrating it from behind the scenes.

Willis Harmon of the Stanford Research Institute (humanistic psychologist, professor of psychology at Stanford University), president of Noetic Sciences and advisor to presidents,

> There seems no reason to doubt that my creative mind might have in mind a plan; this idea of a plan coming from beyond consciousness seems plausible.[31]

"A plan coming from beyond consciousness." Yes, the Bible reveals there is just such a plan and that the mastermind beyond it is none other than Lucifer himself, the prince of the power of the air and through this plan he will deceive the whole world.

> And the great dragon was cast out, that old serpent called the devil and Satan, which deceiveth the whole world (Revelation 12:9).

It is fascinating to me, throughout my research, to discover that the two New Age books, *The Externalization of the Hierarchy* by Alice Bailey, and *The New Genesis* by Robert Muller, both reveal they received their information from the same spirit guide who calls himself Djwhal Khul. God's Word identifies spirit guides as demons.

> Now the Spirit speaketh expressly, that in the latter times some shall depart from the faith, giving heed to seducing spirits (Greek word is planos — seducing or deceiving spirits — demons) and doctrines of devils (1 Timothy 4:1).

A World Mind

But the plan of the New Age has even a deeper dimension for the sons of men to become one. The plan is:

> The planet earth and man (all animal and plant life) will make up a world body, collectively known as a world of mind. The body will constitute a world government which will act for the good of all humanity. The world mind will exercise total control over every aspect of life on earth.[32]

God's Word preempted and revealed this demonic plan nearly 2000 years ago.

> And the ten horns which thou sawest are ten kings, who have received no kingdom as yet, but receive power as kings one hour with the Beast. **These have one mind,** and shall give their power and strength unto the Beast (Revelation 17:12-13).

At a symposium in 1984, Robert Muller said,

> We are beginning to link together to form **One World,** minds and souls. Let go of our own beliefs (crap stuff).

> We stand now at the threshold of the first spiritualization of humanity — this is probably what the second coming is all about. It has nothing to do with an individual coming, it's with the Christ in all of us. The Christ did not come to say there was only one Son of God.[33]

(Muller called our beliefs "crap stuff." This man is blaspheming our great God and Savior Jesus Christ.)

Some 14,000 Catholic educators attended the National Catholic Education Association meeting in St. Louis, Missouri. The theme was "The Gateway to Global Understanding." Robert Muller was the key note speaker. He calls himself the chief of cosmic optimism. He told Sister Joan, "We know so much about the universe that we are probably of divine nature."[34]

That is cosmic divine beings (the lie of Genesis), and God is the cosmos (Romans 1:25). In his address to the convention, "We are cosmic, divine beings, an integral part of the universe."[35] In the book *The New Genesis* he writes,

> And the Lord looked down on earth and said (his God is not the God of the Bible), "At last you are on the right path . . . you have brought heaven down to earth . . . I will now leave you . . . I turn my sight to other troubled celestial bodies . . . I now pronounce you 'Planet God' . . ."[36]

Robert Muller, this brilliant former Assistant Secretary General of the United Nations, has been deceived by the lie of the serpent of Eden, and unless he draws back he will lose his immortal soul. He has been duped by the master liar of the universe. The New Age religion teaches that man is evolving into a super race, solar man — super beings.

Thomas Erenzeller, president of the World Federalist Association, said, "The dawn of the solar age will herald the coming of a new solar race which will last for centuries even millennia."[37]

In Caryl Matrisciana *The Gods of the New Age*, Dr. Johanes Aagaard, a world expert on Hinduism wrote, "The New Age really means the Aquarian Age, the enlightened man, **the age of super man.**"

The New Age goal is to develop a world mind or a giant super world brain comprised of a new species and a new race, the race of "solar man", a race of super beings and divine gods. That's what the New Agers are saying. All men and women linked together in a super world brain. In the book *Gods of Aquarius*:

> The only viable solution is to link the brains of all men into one giant super brain. It has been the entire species that have been developing and it must be linked into one super being. A synthesis of human minds in a world brain.

It almost staggers one's mind to realize the goal of the Illuminati is that all men's minds must be linked together into one giant super brain which will bring billions of human cells and link them to a cosmic consciousness (translation: a One World religion). Anthony Sutton in his book *Skull and Bones, America's Secret Establishment* discovered this horrendous plan. "The whole of the human race is going to evolve an effective soul of its own — an emergence of a universal soul. There will be a great unification of the entire human race ushering into existence a new era, a new age, a new dawn of unique world power.[38]

This is the ultimate syncretism fusing all religious and political life on earth into a world mind. This is what John saw almost twenty centuries ago as he penned the book of the Revelation. **"These have one mind and shall give their power and strength unto the Beast"** (Revelation 17:13).

At the command center will be none other than a **super being**, the man the Bible calls the Antichrist, endued with all the energies of Lucifer who is the driving, accelerating, manipulating force behind it all — his ultimate goal: the world-wide worship of all mankind (Revelation 13:8).

Robert Muller wrote about seeing a picture of Jesus Christ standing outside the United Nations and knocking for admission. Then he says,

> I often visualize in my mind another even more accurate painting; that of the United Nations which would become the body of Christ. — The United Nations, the Body of Christ.[39]

In those words by Robert Muller there is reflected the most **horrendous counterfeit of counterfeits**: this brilliant man, now president of the Peace University in Costa Rica, has believed the great lie. He has bought the counterfeit.

The surest, quickest way to discern a counterfeit is to lay it down beside the genuine. Let's check out this counterfeit against the truth of the Word of God and put it under the ultra violet light of the Word of God.

> Beloved, believe not every spirit but try (test) the spirits and see if they be of God (1 John 4:4).

A world brain made up of 5.5 billion souls (human cells with Lucifer as the head of the body) –– this is the **horrendous mystery of iniquity**, the stark **counterfeit of all counterfeits.**

God's Plan of Salvation
The Genuine Plan

> Great is the mystery of godliness, God was manifest in the flesh (1 Timothy 3:16).

> But now in Christ Jesus, you who were sometimes afar off and made nigh through the blood of Christ. For He is our peace who has made **both one** and has broken down the middle wall of partition between us, so making peace. . . to make in Himself of twain **one new man** . . . for we are members of His body, of His flesh and of His bones . . . this is a great mystery, but I speak of **Christ and His church** (Ephesians 2:14-16; 5:30, 32).

> The Church which is His Body . . . (Ephesians 1:22-23).

The sons and daughters of Adam's fallen race, through faith in the blood of Calvary's lamb, ransomed, redeemed, born into the kingdom of God by the new birth (John 3:5-7), made members of His body, His church, His bride, new creations in Christ Jesus (2 Corinthians 5:17), delivered from the power of darkness, translated into the kingdom of God's own dear Son (Colossians 1:13-14), a chosen generation (a new race), a royal priesthood (1 Peter 2:9).

> Unto Him who loved us and washed us from our sins in His own blood and has made us kings and priests (a

kingdom of priests) unto God and His Father, to whom be glory and dominion forever and ever. Amen (Revelation 1:5).

And to live and reign with Him on His millennial throne (Revelation 20:6).

This is the plan of the triune God of heaven from the foundation of the world.

The Great Counterfeit

But Satan, Lucifer, has devised a counterfeit plan — a plan of such subtlety and immensity, that through it, he will deceive the whole world.

Satan holds up the flashing, glittering, counterfeit: "You are divine beings!" (The great lie of the serpent of Eden — "You shall be as gods" — and by reincarnation you will never die. The awful genius of this lie is reflected in the words of Benjamin Creme, director of the New Age movement of North America, "When the New Age comes, we will live as gods and not die." Lucifer is saying to this "enlightened", hi-tech scientific generation, "I, Lucifer, Son of the Morning, will lead you to the golden age." "Man will become a new race of divinized solar beings, a race of super men; all mankind will be one; the United Nations will become the body of Christ" — the cosmic Christ will take the millennial throne of the world.

In reality **man will become a race of demonized beings,** having taken the Mark of the Beast they will be sealed forever to the kingdom of Satan . . . deceived and deluded by the lie, worshipping a cosmic Christ who will be none other than the man whom the Bible calls the Beast, the man of sin, the Antichrist himself. And through that man (the last great dictator of history) Lucifer will demand the worship of the entire world. All the billions of earth's people will worship him as god unless you know Jesus Christ as your Savior.

And all they that dwell upon the earth shall worship him, whose names are not written in the book of life of the

Lamb slain from the foundation of the world
(Revelation 13:8).

The Greatest Lie Ever Told

The citizens of the city of Babylon embraced the great lie
(that they were divine beings and through reincarnation they
would never die).

Come down, and sit in the dust, O virgin daughter of
Babylon.

Therefore, hear now this, thou that art given to
pleasures, that dwellest carelessly, that sayest in thine
heart, I am, and none else beside me.

For thou hast trusted in thy wickedness; thou hast
said, None seeth me. Thy wisdom and thy knowledge, it
hath perverted thee; and thou hast said in thine heart, I
am, and none else beside me (Isaiah 47:1, 8, 10).

The name *I am* was reserved by the true transcendent
God of heaven, described in Exodus 3:14 — **"I am that I
am."** That is the name Jehovah God reserved for Himself.
The Hindus engraved the words Om or Aum on a golden
triangle which stood for the creation of the worlds. This is
the ancient lie of the serpent that is taking America by storm.

Shirley MacLaine is "Out on a Limb"

In the four hour prime-time telecast, Shirley Maclaine
spoke about UFOs that came to earth in the day of Atlantis
(this is the New Age code word for the Day of Noah
described in Genesis 6). She also told of sighting UFOs on
her trip to the High Peruvian Mountains in South America.
Her mentor Ken Ryerson told her of extraterrestrials coming
to the earth from the Pleiades.

Jaques Vallee, the world's most renowned astro physist
said, "UFOs are real but probably not physical: they are part

of some evil scheme for the victimization of humans and one of their major purposes is to manipulate human consciousness and to program mankind for some ultimate deception."[40]

> I believe there is a machinery of mass manipulation behind the UFO phenomenon . . . they are helping create a new belief system . . . they are designed to help change belief systems, and that the technology we observe is only the incidental support for a world-wide enterprise of **subliminal seduction**.[41]

Subliminal seduction. The Bible reveals in 1 Timothy 4:1 that " . . . men shall give heed to seducing spirits." The Greek word is *planos: seducing, deceiving demons.*

A former intelligence officer has come to know Jesus Christ (I am not at liberty to reveal all that he has told me) but he believes that UFO's (in the light of Genesis 6) are alien beings, extra-terrestrials, and that they are real. He believes they are demonic beings who have come to deceive mankind and lead them into the great delusion of the last days (2 Thessalonians 2:9-11).

I watched that awful lie play across the television screens of America for four hours, prime time on ABC television network. Shirley MacLaine lifted up her arms at Malibu and said, **"I am God."** The New Agers are chanting all over the world *Om*, which means *I am God*.

John Randolph Price, the mastermind behind World Instant Cooperation in 1986, said in his book *Planetary Commission*, "I am the Christ, the Son of the living God."[42]

Norman Vincent Peale, on a national telecast, said, "Affirm with me (as he told millions) I am a child of God."

I hear the hiss of the serpent in the great halls of academia. M. Scott Peck of Harvard University wrote,

> We may define the goal of spiritual growth to be the attainment of godhood. It is the individual to become totally and wholly god.[43]

This is the lie embraced by the six million members of the Mormon Church — "we can become gods some day." It is the lie taught by Carl Jung, the father of modern psychology. He says, "The arch type of self is the same thing as god, who I really am in my deepest, truest self is god."

Eric Fromm, one of America's most popular psychologists, wrote the book *Ye Shall Be as Gods* (the lie of the serpent of Eden). This lie has been embraced by the order of Free Masonry. In the closing ritual ceremony for the royal art degree, the candidate is asked, "Brother Inspector, what are you?" He replies, "I am that I am."[44]
In *The Lost Keys of Free Masonry*, page 92, I read,

> Man is a god in the making, and he is being molded on the potter's wheel. When the light shines out to lift and preserve all things he receives the triple crown of godhood.[45]

This is the lie that deceived one-third of the angels of heaven. This same old lie deceived our first parents in Eden — "Ye shall be as gods, and ye shall not surely die." This is the lie that arch deceiver, the father of lies will use to deceive billions of earth's people in the last days. It is described in 2 Thessalonians 2:9-11.

> Even him whose coming is after the working of Satan with all power and signs and lying wonders, and with all deceivableness of unrighteousness in them that perish, because they received not the love of the truth, that they might be saved. And for this cause God shall send them strong delusion, that they should **believe the lie**.

What Does John Denver and Norman Lear have in Common?

The lie is found in the words of Bernadette Roberts, "One glimpse of godhood and no one would ever want God back (the God of the Bible)."[46]
This is the lie that is at the root of all false religions, from Hinduism, Zen Buddhism Rosicrucians, to the cult of EST and Dyanetics (Scientology), "Kneel to your own self and worship your own being: God dwells with you as you."[47]
This is the lie of the new cult of Est that is sweeping into the highest echelons of the executives and the multi-lateral corporations of America. EST teaches, "You are the perfect you. You are god. Take charge of your life as god." It has

spawned John Denver the folk singer, who says he will be a god some day, and Norman Lear, the arch foe of Christianity. The lie flashes across television screens of America — Dyanetics can change your life. Dyanetics is scientology that teaches we are Thetans and we can evolve into gods. I watched this lie even in some televangelists.

Kenneth Copeland: "You don't have a god within: you are one."[48]

The Bible tells us that man is a fallen being, and only through the blood of Jesus Christ can he be reconciled to God. Hebrews 9:27 gives the lie to reincarnation, "For it is appointed unto men once to die, and after that the judgment."

Earl Paulk said, "Until we comprehend that we are little gods, we cannot manifest the kingdom of God."[49]

Free Masonry: "The only personal God Free Masonry accepts is humanity in toto. Humanity is therefore the only personal God that there is."[50]

The Bible tells us that we are the sons and daughters of God only through faith in Jesus Christ. God, the eternal creator, answered them in ancient Babylon as they were **chanting the "Om," I am and there is none else.** The eternal Creator God, creator of heaven and earth, answered them in Isaiah 42:8, **"I am the Lord God; that is my name, and my glory will I not give to another."** He said to Moses in Exodus, "I am that I am, (the eternal self-existent, transcendent God)." **This is the name our Lord Jesus Christ used to attest His deity, "Before Abraham was, I am;** who existed from eternity to eternity."

"*I am* Alpha and Omega, the beginning and the ending" (Revelation 1:8), "The first and the last, the Almighty." "*I am* He that liveth and was dead, and behold *I am* alive forevermore."

God's Holy Word reveals that some day the evil lie that began in the heart of Lucifer, before the very throne of God — the lie that deceived the billions of sinless angels, the lie that brought all mankind into the great rebellion — **that lie will be expunged forever from the universe.**

And there shall in no wise enter in anything that defileth neither whatsoever worketh an abomination or maketh a lie but they which are written in the Lamb's book of life (Revelation 21:27).

And He who is "the way, the truth and the life" — Jesus Christ our Lord, shall reign in the midst of the throne forever and forever. All the signs of this hour point to one great reality: man's long night of despair is almost over. **The globe is sprinting to the finish line of history**, when our Lord Jesus Christ will return in power and great glory, great Babylon will be destroyed in one hour.

> And the kings of the earth . . . shall bewail her (Babylon), and lament for her . . . saying, Alas, alas, that great city, Babylon, that mighty city! **For in one hour is thy judgment come** (Revelation 18:9-10).

The kingdom of the Antichrist will crumble and King Jesus will set up His everlasting kingdom. And the words of the song shall become a reality:

> For the darkness shall turn to the dawning,
> And the dawning to noon day bright,
> And Christ's great kingdom shall come to earth
> The kingdom of love and light.

Is There a Way out of the New Age?

Randall Baer was a young man who had a meteoric rise in the New Age Hierarchy of America, to be at the top on the New Age speaking tour. Thousands of New Agers flocked to hear him. His books reached the best seller list and he soon became an international expert in crystal power. A New Age magazine called him, "Light years ahead of all other entries."

He was into astral travel, scintillating psychodellic experiences, etc. Let him tell the story:

> One night I was in the "Ascension Chamber." My spirit was roaming the farthest reaches of heavenly light that I had ever perceived. That night I had an experience that would change my life forever.

Waves of bliss radiated through my spirit. Suddenly another force stepped in . . . what I saw was the face of devouring darkness. Behind the glitter and facade of beauty lay a massively powerful, wildly churning face of absolute hatred and unspeakable abominations. The face of demons filled with the power of Satan. This devouring force was now closing in on me.

He **tells of unspeakable anguish of soul**. Then one day he says,

My wife Vicki suggested that I pray the prayer as the Christians do. This possibility had not yet crossed my mind. So, with sincerity born of deep need, I prayed an S.O.S. prayer something like this: "Jesus, I really need your help." I continued to pray for several weeks and then one night I was watching the *700 Club*. Pat Robertson called on the unsaved viewers to pray with him. A deep conviction came over me. I got up from the bed and knelt on the floor with my hands on the T.V. set.

As the prayer progressed, I felt the hand of Jesus reach deep into my innermost being with an Almighty power that was both piercing to the core and yet completely gentle.

By the end of the prayer I was so filled to overflowing with the power of His presence . . . a powerful but gentle quaking in the spirit happened in every fiber of my being. Weeping uncontrollably I dropped to the floor . . . I felt the conviction of the Holy Spirit pierce my heart — continuous prayer poured from my lips in repentance and praise of His majesty and saving grace. I had never prayed like this before . . . It was like an effortless stream of sweet water pouring through me in rejoicing and honoring Christ Jesus as my Lord and personal Savior.

The Lord had cut through the horrific Satanic bondage and set me free as He received me into His Body, and washed my scarlet sins as white as snow. I was captive but now I was free. With an absolute certainty I knew this was what I had been looking for all of my life and had never found until now.

This made even the most powerful mystical New Age experience completely pale in comparison to our heavenly Father's infinitely greater power and glory. Satan's glowing counterfeit fineries are as cheap filthy rags compared to the truth.

A prodigal son had returned home, destitute and unworthy, but was met with loving arms and a wonderful feast. It was hard to fathom the greater love of Jesus that could forgive so much sin. Continually that passage in John 14:6 kept coming to my mind, "I am the way, the truth, and the life, no man cometh to the Father but by Me."

I could not bear the thought of the multitudes of well intentioned New Agers who I knew were walking the path of destruction. Who would warn them? In fifteen years as a New Ager I had come across only one person witnessing to me of Jesus Christ.

Just before he began a speaking tour of television appearances Randall Baer's car was found in a mountain area of Colorado. The car was 330 feet down over a cliff and there were no skid marks at the top. Randall Baer gave his life that you might have this testimony.

Before his death he wrote these words,

Satan is the author of the New Age. The saddest part of all is that millions of New Agers today haven't a clue to the fact that they are caught up in a masterful powerful delusion that leads only to the Lake of Fire. Today my heart breaks when I think of all the people, young and old, who are flocking toward the false light of the New Age like moths to a flame.[51]

The New Age "Final Solution"

In the great city of Babylon, on the Euphrates River, all who believed and served the true God in heaven, the creator of heaven and earth, were marked for elimination. In the new Babylon that is springing to life before our eyes, the

religion of the New Age is running right on schedule. Alice
Bailey wrote,

> A violent streptococcus germ, an infection, makes its
> presence felt in infected areas in the body of humanity. A
> surgical operation must be necessary . . . to get rid of the
> fever. It is no disaster, but it has to go.[52]

She is talking about all who believe in the Lord God of
heaven.

Dr. Rebecca Brown Yoder, M.D., told me that she heard
Benjamin Creme speak in San Francisco, California:

> There are two major enemies of mankind --
> fundamental Christians and Jews. These must be
> removed if civilization is to survive. All who refuse the
> Luciferian initiation will be given the sword of cleavage.

**There is only one thing standing in the way of the New
Age religion, and that is the church of Jesus Christ.**

This is War

Hal Lindsey said on *TBN*, "The church of Jesus Christ is
about to come under attack, as at no time in history since the
first century.

Jose Aquellas, who designed Harmonic Convergence
Day in 1987 (but behind the scenes he called for the removal
of all Christians from the planet in order for Lucifer to return
and so Gaia [the earth] could be healed), stated, **"This is war
— the moral equivalent of war."**

That war has already begun. The New Age religion of
the Antichrist has declared war on the saints.

In America now they are blaspheming the name of our
God. The National Endowment for the Arts gave a man first
prize for his portrayal of the pure Son of God, my Savior, in a
bottle of urine. Christians protested to the Congress, and the
answer of the American Congress was to give the N.E.A. a
raise of three million dollars.

Recently a national cartoon depicted fundamental
Christians as rats pulling the G.O.P. on a cart into a
gospel mission in a downtown building, and over the

mission were the words *Jesus Saves*. The rats were depicted as fundamental, Bible-believing Christians. (The Nazis did this exact thing against the Jews in the 1930's just before they began a mass campaign of persecution.) If they had done that to Jews or blacks there would have been race riots across America. But they do it to Christians because they know that they can get by with it.

A national poll was recently taken, and the question was asked, "Of the three groups in America — Neo-Nazis, white supremists, and fundamental, Bible-believing Christians — which is the most dangerous?" The majority answered, "Fundamental, Bible-believing Christians." In high circles of power the Cult Awareness Network, now directed by former U.S. Congressman Ryan's daughter, is bringing about a mindset that, "Unless you are a member of the old-line churches (the World Council of Churches), you are almost regarded as a cultist."

In some circles a cult is being defined as those fundamental Christians who believe the Bible, home-school their children, who believe in their Constitutional rights to own and bear arms, and are not "politically correct" in the New World Order.

In the summer of 1993, the homosexuals marched, almost one million strong, in Washington, D.C. The television cameras (conveniently) didn't show some of them chanting: "Christians to the lions."

A few months ago, a Christian was arrested in St. Helens, Oregon. His crime? He had invited one of his employees to come to the Bible church where he attended and told him that he was praying that he would become a Christian. He was fined $3,000.00 He asked the judge, "What crime have I committed? What law did I break?" The judge replied, "We make the law in this court."

Listen to Dr. M. Scott Peck of Harvard University. (Friends, this man is reaching millions in his call for a New World Order.) He writes in his book *Marching to a Different Drum Beat*,

> There are negative forces — the Christian church and nationalism (he means the sovereignty of this great nation) — these threaten to destroy the world. They are standing in the way of the giant leap forward in the

evolution of man's global consciousness (a world community of nations).[53]

This plan of the New Age religion has been articulated well by Barbara Marx Hubbard, executive director of the World Federalists Society. In her book *The Apple of Eden's Eye* she states,

> People who do not accept the New Age teaching (including Bible believing Christians) are an evolutionary drag on humanity and must capitulate or be killed.[54]

Alice Bailey, the high priestess of the New Age, wrote, "All the people of the Book must go . . . this includes all those who believe in the Lord God."

In The Satanic Bible *The Keys of Enoch*, they make it clear that the removal of Christians will be a holy act.

> The death and passing from the scene of the unbelievers (Christians) in the New Age will open the earth up for a higher spiritual frequency. This will allow a new communion to occur as the higher angelic beings (demons) join and merge with the holier race of humans who have become gods.[55]

Our Lord warned us:

> . . . Yea, the time cometh that whosoever killeth you, will think that he does God service (John 16:2).

The emerging view of the world's leading thinkers — "The two greatest stumbling blocks to world peace and the New World Order are national sovereignty and Christianity."

Mortimer Adler said it, "All religions are willing to compromise, but one – Christianity. This will lead to World War III!"

The battle ahead will be over doctrine. Paul wrote to Timothy about the last days.

> For the time will come when they shall not endure sound doctrine, but after their own lusts shall they heap to themselves teachers having itching ears (telling them what they want to hear). And they shall turn away their ears from the truth and be turned unto fables (2 Timothy 4:3-4).

"Unwilling to Compromise"

What doctrine shall we who love and serve the risen Lord of glory, compromise?

- The deity of our Lord Jesus Christ?
- His divine blood that was shed on Calvary's cross to redeem us to God?
- His bodily resurrection from the dead and ascension to the right hand of the Father?
- His return in power and great glory to reign as King of Kings and Lord of Lords?

No! **Our faith is non-negotiable.** The coming battle will be over the Word of God and the testimony of Jesus Christ. The **battle lines are being formed right there.**

As in the first century under the Imperial Emperor of Rome, John the Apostle wrote in the book of the Revelation,

> I, John, who also am your brother and companion in tribulation . . . was in the Isle which is called Patmos **for the Word of God and the testimony of Jesus Christ** (Revelation 1:9).

So it will be in the last days under the last great world dictator the Antichrist (the leader of the revived Roman empire).

The Word of God and the Testimony of Jesus

> And the dragon (Satan) went forth to make war (with those) which **keep the commandments of God and have the testimony of Jesus Christ** (Revelation 12:17).

In the Days of the Reformation, the battle was over the Word of God. The cry of the reformers, "Solo Scriptura," "only the Scriptures."

Martin Luther stood before the great Roman church to defend his stand on the doctrine of the Scripture, "The just shall live by faith." With these words he won the battle against all the power of Rome:

> Here I stand, I can do naught else, my conscience is chained to the Word of God.

The Final Victory

The church of Jesus Christ has powerful enemies: It is facing its greatest danger, but it is facing its greatest challenge and its greatest opportunity.

But the church will never be defeated. It will emerge a glorious church, without spot or wrinkle, washed in the blood of the Lamb. Our Commander in Chief said,

> Upon this rock (the testimony that Jesus Christ is the Son of the Living God) will I build My church and the gates of hell shall not prevail against it (Matthew 16:18).

Our victory was pre-written by our God in Revelation 12:11:

> And they overcame him (Satan) by the blood of the Lamb, and the **word of their testimony** and they loved not their lives unto death.

> Who shall separate us from the love of God? Shall tribulation, or distress, or persecution, or famine, or nakedness, or peril, or sword? . . . **Nay, in all these things we are more than conquerors through Him that loved us.** For I am persuaded that neither death, nor life, nor angels, nor principalities, nor powers, nor things present, nor things to come . . . shall be able to separate us from the love of God, which is in Christ Jesus, our Lord (Romans 8:35-39).

SEVEN

America 2000
Strategy (or Tragedy) for Education

Regarding his statements on improving American schools, George Bush stated: "There will be no renaissance without revolution." — George Bush
Los Angeles Times, April 18, 1991

If schools teach dependence on ones self, they are more revolutionary than any conspiracy to overthrow the government!
— M.J. Blackham, *Humanist Magazine*
September-October 1981

This chapter will crystallize around the theme *The New Educational Program for America* which will affect every child in this nation in 110,000 school districts. *America 2000* was implemented by former President Bush and his Secretary of Education Lamar Alexander. It is now being accelerated in a far more intensified manner by President Clinton, as the reader will discover later in this chapter.

It is the most innovative plan ever devised for the schools of this nation. On the surface it looks good. They say it will be the centerpiece of our national education strategy. It is a

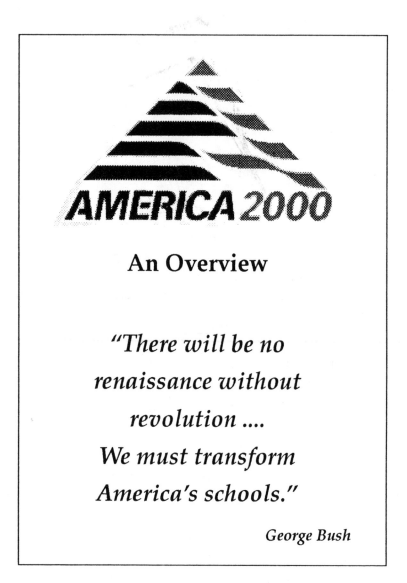

An Overview

"There will be no renaissance without revolution .... We must transform America's schools."

George Bush

The official logo of America 2000 *– the new strategy for education for all American schools.*

strategy, they say, to reinvent American education, to design new American schools for the year 2000 and beyond.

But as you study it, friends, there is a hidden agenda that is frightening. In her book *A Critique of America 2000, Citizens for Excellence*, by Kathi Simonds, we have this quotation, (when this information is studied with other research, as *Education and the New World Order* by B.K. Eakman, one can see clearly a subversive agenda of the education bureaucracy),

> If the behaviorists behind these goals are allowed to have their way we will lose our freedoms we hold so dear, our children will be indoctrinated into a globalist, One World Order, where Christianity is simply unacceptable.[1]

The Hidden Agenda

The subtle, hidden agenda is to condition your children and grandchildren to be what they call P.C., politically correct. That is their actual wording. Their goal is to condition our children to be politically correct for the New World Order, the secret code word for a One World Government; brainwashed into an occultic religion of the New Age. It is my purpose to expose this evil plan that portends grave danger to every school child in the United States, from preschool through the twelfth grade level. I will give you some carefully researched information. I draw heavily upon superbly documented books. One is called *The Dawning of the New Age, the New World Order*, by Dr. Dennis Cuddy, Ph.D. from North Carolina University and *Educating for the New World Order*, by B.K. Eakman.

Let's look at this man Lamar Alexander, former governor of Tennessee, whom President Bush nominated and who was confirmed by the Senate to be the Secretary of Education in the President's Cabinet. He says, "The volume (he's talking about a certain book) has changed my thinking during the past ten years." He also goes on to say that he has tried to read this book once or twice every year since the 1970s.[2] The book is called *A God Within*, and when we understand about the book we will understand about this man's philosophy.

The author of this book is René DuBos. I want to quote him. He says, "Apparently certain drugs can help develop an inspired state."[3]

What is this God Within?

A God Within is not the God of the Holy Bible, but a pantheistic god where plants are brothers and sisters. He speaks about reincarnation,

> You shall have the power to degenerate into lower forms of life. You shall have the power to be reborn into higher forms which are divine.[4]

That is pure reincarnation. This book is simply about a lie. A lie that man is divine and that by reincarnation he will never die. A lie that was perpetrated by the father of lies and channeled through the lips of a serpent in the Garden nearly 6000 years ago. The lie that deceived our first parents and drew the billions of earth into the great rebellion of Lucifer. The dual lie of Eden in Genesis 3, "You shall be as gods, and you will not surely die."

This is the lie that is found in Karl Jung's books, who, with Sigmund Freud laid the foundation for all modern psychology and psychiatry. "Who am I? I am really God," Karl Jung said. "You are God." This is the lie that is the very genius of the New Age religion that is deceiving hundreds of millions of people. This is the core teaching of Galyean's psychology that is sweeping the public schools in Southern California like wild fire. The heart of that is for the children to "reown their godhood." This book, *A God Within*, and its awful lie, has captivated Lamar Alexander.

Marilyn Ferguson is the most powerful spokeswoman for the New Age religion in America and has written a book entitled *The Aquarian Conspiracy*. Her logo contains the numbers 666. She says of Lamar Alexander, who has tried to read the book *A God Within* at least once or twice a year since the 70's, "He is one of many authors whose thinking was influential in the writing of *The Aquarian Conspiracy*."[5] She endorses his philosophy concerning the New Age completely. Moreover, in her own book she reveals,

There are legions of conspirators. Their lives have become revolutions. They are in every town and village and institution in America. These are more involved in education than any other category of work. Education is humanistic. Its humanistic methods are linking in national networks across the nation.[6]

Friends, secular humanism is atheism. It's the dethroning of God and the deifying of man.

Mastery Learning

Mr. Alexander who was confirmed on March 14th, 1991, by the United States government as Secretary of Education, is the man that now sends his son to private school. He made a speech in Wichita, Kansas, on November 1, 1989, in which he says, "I envision America going through its own perestroika." His wife has been associated with Planned Parenthood. He said, "The brand new American school will serve children from the ages of three months to eighteen years, which will be open from 6:00 A.M. to 6:00 P.M."[7]

Watch out! Let me describe that hidden agenda. In other words, they'll have more time away from the home, away from parental influence for twelve hours. They will be brought under the control of the State. That is the goal already in full swing under the code phrases Operant Conditioning Mastery Learning. The child, they say, is a global citizen. Condition their minds from National sovereignty and away from America's founding fathers, away from family values towards state control. Draw the child away from belief in God and condition him or her toward a new global consciousness — the code words for a One World Government and a New World religion.

What are Some of "America 2000" Major Tenents?

Let's take an even closer look. Here are some of the major points of America 2000. In their syllabus: 1) National assessment tests will be administered in the fourth, the eighth, and the twelfth grades. Testing for what? One-half the testing will be on cognitive learning, which will be math, science, history, geography, and so on. The other half will be on effective learning or psychological behavior modification. Do you think that the testing will be all on academic achievement? No. Your child's answers must be politically correct. If the child's answers are not politically correct they will be targeted to be re-processed.

America 2000, Strategy for Education requires a system of federal computers — listen to this — to track assessment tests results. Then both the child and parents' attitude will be targeted for re-training unless the child and the parents are politically correct. But there is more. This is incredible. The plan calls for grouping all schools in a community under public schools, private, public, or home schools. One thing is clear. **This will bring all Christian schools under state control.**

They Marched for Freedom

America 2000 requires all teachers and administrators to be trained in the new methods. There is a heavy emphasis on training parents on how to properly train their own children and conform to the new governmental state and federal standards, in other words, state-controlled schools. Let's digress just for a moment. Dr. Dennis Cuddy, in his masterful book *Dawning of the New Age and the New World Order* tells us on page 353 of a woman who ran for office of Superintendent of Education in Arizona. Her name was Ann Herzler and when she was in France in 1984, she saw a million people marching in the streets of Paris because the national government was about to take over the schools in France. She saw the people force the resignation of the entire executive branch of the government except the President. She then quotes a woman who had her Ph.D. from Columbia University who said,

> Americans are fools. Don't you know there is a world-wide movement to bring all schools under state-control. No government should control education because education must remain in the hands of the people to remain free. Parents have to say how they want their

children to be educated. We did not march in Paris for
religious purposes. We marched for freedom. You
Americans had better wake up or you are going to lose
your freedoms.[8]

State Control of American Schools

All areas of America 2000 plan to create a greater
dependency on control by the Federal government. It is now
clear to this writer that America 2000 is a plan to bring all
American schools under the control of the state. When that
happens our freedoms will be gone forever. Remember the
former president of the United States, George Bush, is a
member deeply involved in the order of Skull and Bones,
America's secret establishment. It is America's most
powerful, esoteric secret society, set up and controlled by the
Illuminati, called the Order, to create a new synthesis, a
world order where the state is all-powerful, is absolute, and
the individual can only find freedom in blind obedience to
the state. That's exactly what Skull and Bones is all about.
The plan is unfolding with precision to capture the minds of
the children and youth of this nation.

Adolf Hitler said, before World War II, **"Give me one
generation of youth and I will take the world."** He almost
pulled it off. How did the Nazis do it? They did it in the
classroom. Hitler said, "Your child belongs to us already.
This is the new reich. We will give its youth to no one, but
will itself take youth and give to youth its own education and
its own upbringing."

In Mario Trapp's book the *Story of the Trapp Family Singers*
she says,

> We were told by the Nazis at the school assembly that
> our parents are nice, old fashioned people, who don't
> understand the new party. We should leave them alone
> and not bother. We are the hope of the nation, the nation
> of the world. We should never mention at home what we
> learn at school now.[9]

This same program is in full swing and has been in full swing for a number of years in the schools of America. The new teachers, the change agents for behavior modification say, "Do not tell your parents what you are learning in the school."

Behavior Modification (or Behavior Destruction)

Under the euphemism Behavior Modification our children are being taught guided imagery, visualization, which is contact with occultic powers; and altered states of consciousness, in which you open your mind to demonic forces or occultic beings. This is nothing but the Hindu religion. We can't have the Bible; we can't have prayer, but we can have an inundation of the Hindu religion into our schools. They are teaching sex education with unmentionable practices. This sort of thing is going on right now in our state of Oregon.

"Project 10"

Their Project Ten was started in 1984 by an admitted lesbian, Virginia Uribe, as a way for the Gay Rights Movement to gain access to children in the Los Angeles public school system. Ostensibly, Project Ten is supposed to provide counseling to young people who are suffering emotional problems because of their homosexual lifestyle. In reality, however, Project Ten does not assist children in recovering from homosexuality, it encourages them to embrace and further explore homosexual behavior, often with the assistance of outside groups. This is now being introduced in the schools in Oregon.

Homosexuals invited into the Classroom

Project Ten is not limited to children that have already developed a homosexual behavior pattern, however. Under Project Ten, practicing homosexuals are invited into the classroom, now hear this, without parental knowledge or consent. That's what the schools are doing, while saying, "Do not tell your parents." Homosexuals are being invited in to counsel the students about homosexuality. Students are told that one out of ten of them is a homosexual tendency. This is a disproved myth. They are telling them that if they repress their homosexual desires they may develop serious emotional problems, and perhaps even commit suicide. Friends, that has totally been discredited; that is a lie. Outraged parent groups in Los Angeles charge that Project Ten recruits emotionally confused and naively open-minded children into homosexuality.

On April the 23rd and 24th, 1992, a coalition of homosexual groups and government agencies met in Beaverton, Oregon, to introduce Project Ten to Oregon educators. Project Ten founder Uribe advised local activists not to wait for permission from the school boards to implement Project Ten. Instead, she told them to take it upon themselves to start Project Ten in their schools because, she said, it's easier to say "I'm sorry" than to say "May I please." Uribe also encouraged teachers and counselors not to limit their efforts to high school and junior high, but to start Project Ten in elementary schools. Indeed, parents from several school districts have already called to complain that their children's teachers have already started teaching Project Ten in the middle school classes.[10]

Find Out What Your Child is Being Taught

I received a letter from a close friend of mine in Spokane. It is a bulletin put out to warn every believer in that area and in the state, we should say, America. It's entitled, "Find Out What Our Schools Teach." I'm going to quote Sandy Ogle:

> I have been following the Jeffrey Dahlmer Case. Do you wonder what would possess a man to want to have sexual relations with a dead body? In May, 1989, we had a meeting at Mead Jr. High School (now, Mead is just at the northern fringe of Spokane), which was attended by the Mead Sex Education Board and about 300 parents. There was a disagreement over what was being taught for the AIDS sex education program. We found out at that

meeting that Mead High School did in fact teach the students about having sex with a corpse, as well as the practices of bestiality and homosexuality.[11]

One can hardly believe what followed but it is absolutely documented. They also discussed a homosexual student who had brought his adult lover to class to share with the students their relationship in a question/answer time . To top it off the statement was made that marriage is of no value, and we can't teach it![12]

The NEA Track Record

Are these the types of classes needed to further a student's life skills? Is this what behavior modification is all about? Apparently so. It creates more Jeffrey Dahlmers. It is no wonder that our SAT scores are going down while violence of all types, rape, drugs, alcohol, knives and guns in schools, are running rampant. Do you know what is being taught in the curriculum in your school district? If you don't, you had better check it out. I think that the "professionals" owe it to us parents and tax-payers to give our children the type of education that will help them grow into responsible adults.

Witchcraft Replaces Christianity

The kids in a private school in the Pacific Northwest, were not allowed to celebrate a traditional Christmas last year. School authorities had decided that would be wrong. Religion is not permissible in the classroom. Church and state must be kept separate, right?

Since *Christmas* is a Christian holiday, school officials decided that the very word *Christmas* must be forbidden to be spoken. And in place of the annual Christmas event, the school kids would be required to participate in a Winter Solstice program. On December 18, the Winter Solstice was celebrated in the school's auditorium. The theme, "To Celebrate the Return of Light."

CELEBRATE THE RETURN OF THE LIGHT

*Bulletin cover from a private school
in a large city in Oregon – in lieu of Christmas –
a celebration of the Winter Solstice.*

The cover of the official printed program handed out to the students and their parents was very revealing. It depicted the Babylonian Sun God (Lucifer, god of Light) and the moon goddess. Inside the printed program is found this description of the Winter Solstice program:

> Each child will partake of the sun and moon cake before entering the auditorium, where they will seat themselves according to their astrological signs . . . chanting will begin on entering the auditorium. The Sun God and Moon Goddess will enter with each attendant.[13]

A Witchcraft and Satan Ceremony

This is nothing but a celebration that is historically a witchcraft satanic holiday. The cakes to be eaten are the same ones devoured by the heathen worshippers of the Sun God Baal and the Goddess Astoreth (the Moon Goddess) in the ritual denounced as an abomination by God in the Bible.

The Taking of the Mark

In one segment of the solstice program, kids came in with **bar codes stamped on their foreheads**. Children who did not have the bar codes were rejected. Only those with the bar codes were deemed "to be worthy and good." To understand this, please read Revelation 13:16-18. To receive the Mark was to give allegiance to the Antichrist. Remember this event replaced the Christmas program.

Separation of Church & State??

Separation of Church and State? Christmas was a religious event and therefore unlawful, so instead, the kids were treated to one of the most pagan witchcraft, occultic satanic New Age Religious rituals imaginable. Apparently it is **only the Christian** religion that is banned from our schools, **not the pagan religion of the devil**.

Lamar Alexander, by his favorite book *A God Within* says, "We are all gods." That seems to be his molding philosophy. The concept that man is god is so false. One writer pointed out that this is pantheism. This is pure Hinduism. Everything is permissible. If everything is god, which pantheism is, we're god, we're all things in god; god is a part of us. If everything is god, then there is no way of making any distinction between good and evil. This is the religion of the Hindus, and it is flooding the schools of America. This is the religion that left India the most morally, spiritually, bankrupt nation on earth. And now it is rolling across America like a flood tide, inundating our schools.

One New Age educator said not long ago,

> When the crazies (and the crazies according to her are Bible-fearing, Bible-loving parents) find out what we're doing, it will be too late because we will have already captured their kids!

The "Change Agent"

The priority of the National Education Association, the N.E.A., is change agents. Teacher education is built around the philosophy that they are **change agents**. According to the congressional record in 1974, the United States Office of Education gave a grant of 5.9 million dollars for 500 change agents to be trained at twenty-one universities. They knew if advocating change was blatant, there would be an outcry from the parents. There, the National Training Laboratories Institute for Applied Behavioral Science newsletter put out the guidelines:

> Couch the language of change in the language of the status quo. These are always broad enough to encompass innovation.

That means a planned deception under double-speak language.

Educating for the New World Order/ One World Government

Now, at about the same time, concerning the adolescent literature movement, which included home, sexuality, rebellion, and so forth, Sheila Schwartz, in the January and February, 1976, issue of the *Humanist Magazine* expressed her thankfulness like this,

> The crazies (that's the fundamental believers in God and the Bible and morals) don't do all that much reading. **If they did they'd find they had already been defeated.**[14]

In September, 1976, Harold Shane, Phi Beta Kappian said, "We will educate our young for planetary service and eventually for some form of world citizen." They're talking about the New World Order for the One World Government.

James Covell, author of *Showgun*, published children's stories depicting how in the short period of time "your school children's thinking," he said, "could be so manipulated by **change agents** that they would consider cutting into pieces the American flag. They'd consider doing that a wonderful thing."

Parents as Teachers — Watch Out!

America 2000 will establish a parent association of teachers; Parents as Teachers is the technical name for it — P.A.T. It will be a program in every school in America. It sounds great — parents as teachers. But what do they mean? The training of parents is to offset the real parental involvement of Christian parents and their influence in the schools across this country. The plan is to teach parents to go along with all school programs and to alter their political opinions to conform. My understanding of this strategy for education is if the child is found by testing not to be **Politically Correct**, the school authorities can reprogram him or her. If this fails they can come into your home and train the parents to be Politically Correct. In other words, condition them. If this does not work with the parents, they can then take the child out of the home and place him in a state controlled institution.

Betina Dobbs, former consultant of the United States Department of Health and president of Guardians of Education for the state of Maine says of the program, "It will result in the state control of the children and reduce parents to the status of breeders and supervised custodians."[15]

Now let's go back to this new innovative program under Lamar Alexander's *America 2000*.

> A parent educator binds herself or himself to a family through home visits or school visits. This is to help the parent feel more comfortable about leaving their child at the sitter.

A Computer Number From Birth to Death

Now, remember Lamar Alexander's plan, to take your child from the age of three months to eighteen years from 6:00 A.M. to 6:00 P.M. Both parent and child are evaluated under the guise of educational screening. The child is given a personal computer code number by which he can be tracked the rest of his life! Wow! The state can have him or her under total surveillance for the rest of his or her life. Are they planning for us a police state? Well, what do you say? There are twelve computer code definitions which label your child "at risk" since their expectation is that your child will be found mentally ill. There is no code for "normal" set up. Now, let me repeat that again. Since their expectation is that your child will be found mentally ill, there is no code set up for normal. What do you think they claim is a mentally ill child?[16]

Well, Dr. Pierce of Harvard University, a Ph. D., a very brilliant, but not a very wise man wrote,

> Every child in America entering school at the age of five is mentally ill, because he comes to school with certain allegiances toward our founding fathers, toward our elected officials, toward his parents, toward a belief in a supernatural Being, toward the sovereignty of this nation as a separate entity. It's up to you teachers to make

all of these sick children well by creating the international children of the future.[17]

My friends, that comes from a sick mind.
Mrs. Dobbs whom I quoted before, is quoted further,

> The next step is to change the parent/child relationship replacing it with a change agent, or a certified parent educator who will supply free medical care, free nutritional counseling, free food, free mental health services, increased overtime with parents finding schools that will provide free daycare, free overnight care, free camps, and additional free education.

These imposed services will be paid for with guess whose money? That is right. With your tax dollars and mine and the loss of our freedoms, not to mention the real loss of our children . . .

I have the manuscript before me of *America 2000*. Let's check out *Restructuring American Society*. Under that title, let me read,

> Congress now has fourteen house and senate bills under consideration to implement these programs. Two of these have already become law.

Home Schooling "Targeted"

America 2000 is a nine year national plan to include all 110,000 public and private schools. That includes home-schooling. Did you hear that? This includes all home schooling in America, every American community, every American home, and will change everyone's lifestyle and attitudes.

One of the main **goals of the globalists' movement is to condition the child in the school away from nationalism and patriotism.** They are actually saying that the representative democracy in the United States now is unhealthy and destructive. In a publication called *Education for International Understanding in American Schools* it is stated,

Enduring peace cannot be achieved until the nation states surrender to a world organization.

New World Order Agenda

That is the New World Order that former President Bush has been encouraging 145 times since September of 1990 — a New World Order, the secret code for a One World Government. Remember, in the plan *America 2000*, your child's answers will have an assessment test. They must be Politically Correct or he or she will be targeted for re-training. I'm convinced that P.C. is the code word for conditioning for a One World Government –– America yielding sovereignty to a world central authority, the United Nations. And when we do, our constitution will be gone; our Bill of Rights will be gone! Americans will be serfs in a futile system, controlled by the elite; a globalist mind-set for the New World Order or a One World Government. This is being pushed upon our children under the code words in *America 2000*, Politically Correct. Politically Correct is their double-tongue language to brainwash the school children of this nation toward the One World Government.

The National Education Association Journal, proclaimed:

> In the struggle to establish an adequate world government the teacher can do much to prepare the hearts and minds of the children for global understanding. At the top of all the agencies which will assure the coming of world government must stand the school . . . the teacher.[18]

For forty-six years the N.E.A. has been on a course to subvert the constitution of the United States of America.

President Clinton's Agenda for American Education

What will President Clinton's agenda be for his program of education? The *Midnight Messenger* describes his Governor's school for the elite "gifted" — the cream of high school students which he implemented in Arkansas when he was governor. The program was six weeks of intensive, secluded training. Here are eye-witness, verbatim testimonies of some of the students who took the course.

"They are getting away from more objective, substantive learning into this subjective area of feelings" (Mark Lowery).

"You would think that there would be some academic challenges . . . getting ready for college . . . The main textbook that I remember from there is a book called *Zen and the Art of Motorcycle Maintenance*" (Steve Roberts).

Promotion of an All-Inclusive Pantheistic Spirituality: "It was like that Baha'i idea. How you have Islam, Baha'i, Muslim, Christianity . . . they are all different kinds of trees, but underneath, its root system grows together (and) is the same god" (Steve Allen).

Instill the Target Beliefs — A "New" Social and Political Agenda: "I think that the whole intent of the Governor's School is to pick the four, five, or six students that could be political leaders and then mold their minds into this more liberal and humanistic thinking. The greatest influence of the Governor's School is to promote the thought that to be considered intellectual by your peers, you have to be a liberal thinker. (This is) not teaching but indoctrination" (Mark Lowery).

"Prominent themes promoted by this school include radical homosexuality, socialism, pacifism and a consistent hostility towards Western civilization, especially (America's) Biblical foundations" (Jeoffrey Botkin).

Immersed in a Fantasy World Where All Seems Perfect: The transition back to reality — to home, family and normal life -- wasn't easy. For some it was devastating.

"When I came back home, I sort of wrote a suicide note to myself," confessed LeAndrew Crawford. "Not actually wanting to kill myself, but wanting to kill the reality of what society had been teaching me for so long . . . I was totally down, because my family just didn't feel like my family . . . I didn't want to be back."

Brandon Hawk did commit suicide within a year after attending Governor's School. Hearing about his death, concerned parents contacted Brandon's parents. "They see the same thing in their kids as we saw in Brandon," his father explained. "They just walk off and leave the family."

Unusual Learning Experience: In a documentary promoting his school, Bill Clinton shared his enthusiasm for his educational model: "It would be impossible for me to describe to you just how exciting and unusual this educational experience is."

"It was Bill Clinton's idea," said Bill Oonk, "his educational masterpiece."

"Students. Totally ignore your parents. Listen to them, but then forget them. Because you need to start using your own stuff" (Guest speaker, Ellen Gilchrist, author of *The Annunciation* and *In the Land of Dreamy Dreams*, quoted by a student).

"The instructors tear down our authority figures. They convince the student that, **'You're the elite'** and the reason why you are not going to be understood when you go home — not by your parents, your friends, your pastor or anybody — is that you have been treated to think that you can't handle your own life.' Intellectual and cultural elitism gives them the right to say, 'We know better than you!' " (Mark Lowery, former director of Governor's School publicity).

"But," said former student LeAndrew Crawford, "we learned about gay life, and the things our parent's said, 'This is wrong. You shouldn't see this!' "[19]

Flash Point, Texe Marrs – June 1993

Nightmare in Little Rock

"The Governor's School is one of my proudest achievements," boasted Bill Clinton as he welcomed the new students, the gifted teenage boys and girls. The cream of Arkansas' high schoolers had been recruited from across the state. They were made to feel special, elitist, superior to the common rabble outside the Governor's School. They were told they were the 'chosen ones' who would revolutionize the world and overturn despised traditional values.

Why, then, did one student commit suicide shortly after graduation? Why did so many others experience severe depression? And why did parents complain that their children were 'changed' beyond recognition, used as experimental guinea pigs, and their minds destroyed?

Trained to Reject Christianity

Brought to Little Rock by Bill and Hillary Clinton, the students of the Governor's School were instructed *not* to call home. Then, isolated for weeks on end, they were subjected to the most intense, Nazi-like indoctrination and mind control program imaginable. Daily, their minds were bombarded with pro-lesbian and homosexual propaganda. Through films and videos, their thinking was infused with images of rioting, bloodshed, murder, anarchy and rebellion. Instructors winked at sexual promiscuity and profanity among the students. They were taught by radical feminists, abortionists and goddess worshippers, guided in New Age 'therapy' exercises, and **trained to reject the 'obsolete' Christian religion of their parents.**

The glittery promise of the Governor's School became a hellish nightmare — a monstrous course in occult mind control. And its curricula was *personally* planned and meticulously implemented by Bill and Hillary Clinton.

Nationalize His Arkansas School

Now, President Clinton wants to nationalize his Arkansas Governor's School. He wants to turn America's public schools into occult, black magic laboratories just like the one set up in Little Rock. Bill and Hillary Clinton want all of America's children to become part of the nightmare in Little Rock.[20]

John Dewey: "Progressive Education"

America 2000 Strategy for Education is the climax of a grandiose plan. It was begun in the 1880s by John Dewey, a member of the Skull and Bones Society of America, almost 100 years ago. He introduced his progressive education program at Columbia University and began training the cream of American educators. His agenda was designed to subvert the entire educational system of America and slant it toward a socialist New World Order (One World Government).

It spread like a cancer enveloping the entire structure of American education. It is now peaking out and cresting. And our generation is reaping some of its evil fruit — a generation that is being conditioned (brainwashed) to be Politically Correct for the new World Order.

Classrooms today, are becoming classrooms where the Bible has been banned and books on witchcraft and Satanism are acceptable; a society where nine year old boys are taught how to have anal sex, and where condoms are freely passed out to high school students; where Jr. High schoolers are taught how to have sex with beasts (Spokane School District in Washington).

W.A. John Johnson, editor of the *Daily News Digest* writes,

An educational mafia captured the high ground of American education in the late 1800s. They carefully orchestrated, with a hidden agenda, and deliberately steered the public schools, its teachers and children down a disaster road to socialism, secular humanism, radicalism, planned failure in reading, writing, suffocation of Christianity, the thrashing of basic values, and the establishment of one of the most powerful and dangerous unions, the National Education Association.[21]

Secular humanism is now king in the classrooms of America. (Secular humanism is simply the de-throning of God and the deifying of man.)

John Dumphy wrote a prize-winning essay in the *Humanist Magazine*:

> The battle for humankind must be waged in the public school classroom between the rotting corpse of Christianity and the new faith of humanism . . . humanism will emerge triumphant.[22]

How is this humanistic behavioral psychology affecting the school children of America?

In *Today's Journal*,

> "Student Suicide Epidemic"; add to that the devastating increase in student drug use, increased violence, venereal disease epidemic, pre-teen pregnancies, and the picture one gets of American education is one of tragedy and despair and ruin. Yet the N.E.A. wants more control of education.[23]

In his book *N.E.A. Trojan Horse in American Education* Samuel Blumenfeld writes:

> The simple truth is American classrooms have become places where intense psychological warfare is being waged against all traditional values. A child in America is little more than a guinea pig in a psych lab, manipulated by a change agent. All of this is being done with billions of federal dollars in the greatest scam in human history. If Americans put up with it much longer they will deserve the ruin they are paying for.[24]

What Should Christian Parents Be Doing?

What should we as parents and grandparents be doing at this time? What are our alternatives? Let's name some of the things that we can do to protect our children.

1) The Christian School Alternative

For a while (it will not always be there) we do have the alternative of a Christian school. But even then we must be careful and check it out. Even now Christian schools are being targeted for infiltration by the New Age religion. In the state of Washington, at an evangelical Christian school, parents made the discovery thatchildren were being required to sit cross-legged on the floor and go through Yoga exercises. This is a part of the New Age philosophy which is Hinduism.

2) We have the alternative of home schooling.

It has been proven over and over again that children in the home schooling program on their S.A.T. tests, in most instances, far surpass the grade level of the children in the public schools. However, there is strong evidence that the "Clintonista" educational program is moving rapidly to close the door for all home schooling.

3) Establish a close and intimate relationship with your children.

Let them know that they are your best friends in the whole world. Verbalize it to them. A daily hug around the neck will build self-esteem and self-image more than any other thing. If you go fishing with that little fellow now you won't have to go hunting for him later. If you mend broken dolls now, Dad and Mom, they'll bring their broken hearts to you later. One top educator said, "You can do anything on earth with that little fellow or girl if you love him, love her, and they know it."

In the Peninsula Gig Harbor area, out from Tacoma, Washington, as well as the Port Orchard area, I was ministering about two years ago. The new technique under the reading program called *Impressions* was sweeping the Peninsula and being required in the public schools. It was tantamount to occultism. I have the whole syllabus; I know whereof I speak. It was teaching New Age doctrine. One night a little mother came to me. She had to take her ten year old Christian boy out of the public schools because they were brainwashing him for the New Age. She was alert, and she loved that little boy. She had trained him in the Word of God, and he had invited Jesus into his life at an early age.

One day, that little fellow was in a store when one of the school board members that had brought the plan *Impressions* into the school saw the little fellow and knew who he was. He walked up to the little boy and said, "Why did your mother take you out of the public schools? We're training you in the New Age to be a citizen in the beautiful New Age that is coming. Why did your mom take you out?" The little fellow looked up at that school board member and he said, "My mother took me out, sir, because my mother loves God. **My mother loves the Bible. My mother is training me for eternity.**" That mom had gotten through to that boy, and he had a Biblical, moral fiber of courage stamped into his very personality.

4) Encourage your children to confide in you.

Encourage them to confide in you what they are being taught during that school day. In Michener's book *The Bridge Over Andou* he relates that when the Communists took over Hungary after World War II the Communists began to indoctrinate the school children in Marxism. The parents would keep the children sometimes until ten or eleven o'clock at night going over with their children what they learned that day in school and then reprogramming them into the truth. And they won! The entire nation won with that program of finding out night after night what their children had been taught and then counteracting it with the truth. We parents and grandparents have that extremely viable weapon.

5) Teach your children the Word of God.

It is the Word of God that will hold them in the midst of deception and delusion. In Deuteronomy 6 :5-9 Jehovah God encouraged every parent in the economy of Israel to do the following things:

> Thou shalt love the Lord thy God with all thy heart, and with all thy soul, and with all thy might. "And these words, which I have commanded this day, shall be in thy heart; and thou shalt teach them diligently unto thy children, and shall talk of them when thou sittest in thine house, and when thou walkest by the way, and when thou liest down, and when thou risest up. And thou shalt bind them for a sign upon thine hand, and they shall be as frontlets between thine eyes. And thou shalt write them upon the posts of thy house, and on thy gates.

In other words God knew that **by His precious Word,** moral character would be built into the very warp and woof of the lives of the children. They would be able to discern right and wrong. If delusion and deception is placed under the ultraviolet light of the Word of God, it will enable our children to detect error every time. It's the Word of God that will keep them from sin and impurity.

> Wherewithal shall a young man stay pure, by taking heed according to thy Word. Thy Word have I hid in my heart that I might not sin against Thee (Psalm 119:11).

Memorize the Word of God with them. Teach them the great principles of spiritual warfare in Ephesians 6, verses 10 through 18.

6) Surround them daily with a wall of intercessory prayer.

We as Christians have powerful spiritual weapons. The Bible reveals in 2 Corinthians 10:4-5,

> The weapons of our warfare are not carnal, but mighty through God to the pulling down of strongholds.

As you pray and claim over your children the all powerful blood of Jesus Christ, it will be their protection. We can, by prayer, place a hedge of thorns about our children that the serpent cannot penetrate. I love that verse in Zachariah 2:5 which says we can place a wall of fire about them. Jehovah says,

> I, Jehovah God, will be to her a wall of fire about her and the glory of the Lord in the midst of her.

Irene Parks, a few years ago, was the high Priestess of six hundred witches of the state of Florida. One day she was brought out of witchcraft by a confrontation with the Lord Jesus Christ. She was washed clean and pure and holy in His precious blood, redeemed by His grace, sealed by the Holy Spirit, and this was her confession to the Christians after she had met Jesus Christ. She said,

> When I was in witchcraft I ravished the little children in the schools. I ravished them with Satanism and sexual impurity. But those children who were from Christian homes whose families had prayed over them, and had claimed the blood of Jesus Christ over that child, I could not touch them.

There is power in the blood. Increasingly, I believe we have entered the awful days described in the Bible as perilous times. The Bible depicts this time as like unto the Days of Noah. Along with the widespread demonism, sexual and sensual impurity that is dominating our television screens, Christians will need to rely on spiritual weapons. For spiritual warfare Christians need the Sword of the Spirit, the Word of God, the power of prayer, and the blood of the Lamb. Revelation 12:11 is one of my favorite verses for spiritual warfare.

> We will overcome by the blood of the Lamb and the word of our testimony, and we will love not our lives unto the death.

7)   Lead that little lad or lassie to receive the Lord Jesus Christ.

When the living Redeemer is in their hearts, and they have been sealed by the blessed Holy Spirit of God and fortified in the Word of God, they will be able to stand as in no other way. When our physical influence cannot be with them, that spiritual power, that word that you built into their very lives, and the presence of the Holy Spirit will sustain them and keep them in the hour of temptation. God has given us a wonderful promise in 1 John 4:4, and we can claim that for our children. In the midst of awful deception John wrote in the first century, in the day of gnosticism when they were being taught godhood, denying the deity of our Lord Jesus Christ, he wrote by divine inspiration,

> Ye are of God, little children, and have overcome them because: greater is He that is in you than he that is in the world (1 John 4:4)..

8)   Do not be discouraged.

The battle is not yours but God's. If God be for us who can be against us? Remember Joshua 1:9,

> Have not I commanded thee? Be strong and of good courage; be not afraid, neither be thou dismayed; for the Lord thy God is with thee wherever thou goest.

God bless you and keep you and surround you with His power until He comes for His own.

EIGHT

The World's Last Dictator

There will be consummated one person, an Antichrist, who will come upon the scene, and again, you know what his message is — New World Order.
— Rev. Charles Stanley

And I saw a Beast rise up out of the sea (of the nations), and power was given unto him over all kindreds, and tongues, and nations.
— Revelation 13:1, 7

The world has a rendezvous with a super world dictator. He will be the last great dictator of history; he will be a man of fantastic brilliance and charisma — light years ahead of any man who ever lived.

God has given us, in the book of Daniel, a candid camera picture of this coming world ruler who is destined to appear on the world scene just prior to the second coming of Jesus Christ.

Through the miracle of Bible prophecy we can know the power block of nations out of which he will arise; what he will do in his infamous career; the exact time-frame that he will be allowed to reign; his fatal mistake; and his final doom.

At this junction point in history, the world's elite — kings, presidents, prime ministers and nobel prize-winning scientists — are calling for a leader. Walter Cronkite recently said, **"We are in a leaderless world."** Malachi Martin, the Roman priest, quoted Paul Mazur in *The Keys of This Blood:*

> In order to control the diverse bureaucracies (of our planet), a politburo will develop and over this group there is likely to arise the final and single arbitrator, **the master of the Order, the total dictator.**[1]

The president of the World Federalists (a powerful New Age organization), Thomas E. Erenzeller, called for a sort of **super being to preside over the earth.**[2] God's Word, the Bible, revealed in Daniel and in the book of the Revelation that a world president, a great chief executive, a total dictator, a truly super being will take the gavel of the United Nations. He will be the most powerful dictator of all time. He will be the Beast, the Antichrist, the man with the Satanic number 666.

God's Portrait of "Der Fuherer"

The Bible gives us a portrait of even the character traits of "Der Fuherer." In Daniel 7:8 he has "eyes like a man." Now, eyes always speak of intelligence. He will be endowed with super-human intelligence. He will be the most brilliant man who ever lived. Verse 8, "He'll have a mouth speaking great things." He'll be a spell-binding orator, the great communicator. He will be the greatest communicator of all time, using television to literally mesmerize his world-wide audience by Satanic, hypnotic power. He will be a man of great brilliance and charisma; he will be light years ahead of any man who has ever lived. He will be a skilled negotiator; but it will be by deception. He will speak lies. He will be a master strategist. Daniel 11:21 says he will obtain the kingdom by flatteries or by trickery, and Daniel 8:25 says, "By peace he shall destroy many."

Also in Daniel 8:25 he will cause craft to prosper in his hand. He will be a financial genius. He will inaugurate a "new international economic order," a perestroika, a restructuring of all the banking systems of the world. He will lead all nations to a world-wide financial system that will be beyond the wildest dreams of mankind. The affluence that he will bring, with his system of trade and international banking is described in Revelation, chapter 18, as Babylon's world-wide financial empire.

The Beast — the new Caesar of a revived Roman Empire — the coming Roman Prince of Daniel 9:26 will take the helm. That man will be the world's great Antichrist. The pieces are fitting into the puzzle with perfect precision.

Four Great World Empires

The prophecies in the book of Daniel reveal that he is destined to arise out of the nations of the old Roman Empire (Daniel 2:31-35). In these passages God revealed to Daniel that there would be four great world empires, covering a time span of almost twenty-six centuries. By divine inspiration Daniel saw the whole panorama of world history from the time of Babylon until the Jewish Messiah would set up His millennial kingdom.

Daniel was given the interpretation of Nebuchadnezzar's dream of the huge statue of the man who stood on the Plain of Dura:

- His head was of gold — the Empire of Babylon.
- His breast and arms of silver — the Medo-Persian Empire.
- His mid-section of brass — the Grecian Empire.
- His legs of iron — the Roman Empire.
- Then a gap (which we know now was approximately 1500 years).
- His feet and toes of iron and clay — This was to be the final empire of history.

As ten toes, the iron autocracy of Rome; the clay, democratic socialism.

The world has watched with amazement as the nations of the ancient Roman Empire have been forming into one of the great super powers of the 20th Century — the European Community (E.C.). Approximately 340 million peoples of Europe are fusing into the United States of Europe. It is emerging into the greatest political, economic confederacy of all time.

In Daniel 7 these same four world empires are portrayed as four wild beasts. The fourth beast was Rome. Look at verse 23:

> . . . It shall devour the whole earth, and shall tread it down, and break it in pieces.

Now watch very closely at verse 24:

> And the ten horns out of this kingdom are ten kings that shall arise: and another shall rise after them, and he shall be diverse from the first, and he shall subdue three kings.

A Revived Roman Empire

Here the Spirit of God is revealing that out of the old Roman Empire, at the end time shall arise ten nations, led by ten kings, and the other who shall arise after them is identified in verse 25. He is a man who shall speak great words against the Most High; he will be the leader of the ten nations of the revived Roman Empire in the last days — the Antichrist. Even though there are twelve nations in the E.C. now, the original goal of the Treaty of Rome, formed in 1957, was for exactly ten nations.

This same picture is given us in Revelation 13:1.

> . . . and I saw a beast coming up out of the sea (the sea of nations), having seven heads and ten horns . . .

The Modern Tower of Babel — and Eleven Stars

Recently the E.C. published its official poster entitled the Council of Europe. It portrayed the ancient Tower of Babel encircled by ten stars, each in the form of a pentagram with the points turned downward which is the symbol of Lucifer. Above the stars was a huge eleventh star (points turned down) thus indicating its headship over the ten stars. Though there are presently twelve nations in the E.C., yet the official poster portrayed only ten stars under the eleventh huge star.[3]

God's Word said there would be ten, and when the smoke all clears away there will be ten nations (ten toes, ten horns, ten kings in a revived Roman Empire).

This prophecy in Daniel 2 & 7 is being fulfilled before our eyes with breath-taking rapidity.

> The World Order of the power elite has already decreed that the United States of Europe (the E.C.) will become the seat of world government and it will be from its capital the supreme world ruler will reign.[4]

On August 4th, 1990, I watched a telecast on C-Span. What I saw that night almost overwhelmed me. The fortieth anniversary of the founding of the Aspen Institute for Humanistic Studies was being portrayed on the television screen. Barbara Walters of ABC was the M.C. Many of the great nations of earth were represented, i.e., European Community; United States; Japan; the United Nations; and Paul Volker represented the Federal Reserve Board.[5]

For the first time in media history, flashing across the T.V. screen, the words "The New World Order . . . World Community of Nations" (each was a code phrase for the One World Government). While it was not openly verbalized, I caught the undertone. Europe (the E.C.) was the proto-type for the coming New World Order. As the nations of the European Community surrender the sovereignty of their separate nations to become one (the United States of Europe) so the nation states of the world might surrender their separate sovereignty as we move toward the new World Order.

Official poster of the European Community (EC)

Following the telecast, on September, 1990, President George Bush addressed the United Nations general assembly. For the first time in American history a president spoke about the New World Order. He was given a thunderous applause.

Now enter Mr. Gary Kah, a high ranking member of the United States government liaison. He is listed in Who's Who in the emerging leaders of America. Mr. Kah is a Christian and knows the prophecies of the Bible. As he moved among the leaders in many countries of the world he began to pick up rumors of a new World Order. He put his ear to the ground and began to listen very carefully. He said that the things he began to hear literally astounded him. He describes it in his excellent book *En Route to Global Occupation.*

The World Constitution Parliament Association

He discovered that there is a powerful, secret, global organization that is planning and gearing up to lead all nations into a One World government. Its name is *The World Constitution Parliament Association.* He found the WCPA serves as a front for dozens of One World, New Age organizations, such as the World Federalists; Jesse Jackson's Rainbow Coalition; World Muslim Congress; the United Nations, Council on Foreign Relations, Club of Rome, Nobel Prize winning scientists, Members of the World Bank, UNESCO; etc.[6]

Yet, we have heard nothing of this powerful organization. There has been a complete media cover-up.

The World Constitution Parliament Association has actually drafted the Constitution of Federation (the constitution for the coming One World government).

The Ten Regions of Planet Earth

The Club of Rome and the Tri-lateral Commission have already divided the planet into **ten administrative regions.**

Their plan is to choose five cities as world capitals and one city to be the supreme capital of the world.

The ten regions are being referred to as *kingdoms*. Mr. Kah also discovered the plan — soon to be enacted — to change the name of the United Nations to Federation Earth.[7]

Gary Kah was asked to join the W.C.P.A. He reveals a letter dated December 12, 1990:

> To all Presidents, Prime Ministers, Kings, and Queens, and to all other heads of governments and national parliaments,
>
> We are convinced that to solve global problems peaceably and to administer human affairs on earth intelligently, a world federal government is required and we appeal to you to endorse a Federal One World Government.[8]

These global leaders are moving in such an amazing alignment and precision with the prophecies of Daniel and Revelation that it almost stuns you.

The World Federalists are calling for ten wise persons to govern the ten magna regions of earth. These global leaders are actually following the script that God the Holy Spirit wrote in His holy Word almost 2000 years ago:

> And the ten horns which thou sawest are ten kings which have received no kingdom, as yet, but receive power as kings, one hour with the Beast [the Antichrist] (Revelation 17:12).

The New Atlantis

Mr. Kah also revealed something else that astounded me. Some Masons and New Agers have spoken privately that the United States would be the world power to usher in the New Atlantis.

Occult tradition reveals that the world, prior to the flood, had a unified global government of ten regions called Atlantis.[9] Atlantis is the New Age secret code word for the advanced civilization before the flood. In the day of Noah it was a demonized society that God had to destroy. Remember the words of our Lord:

As it was in the days of Noah, so shall it be in the days of the coming of the Son of man (Matthew 24).

Could it be Christ's words were literal? Could we have come full cycle?

Gary Kah also learned that the United States has been chosen by the World Order to lead the nations of earth into the One World government. The name of the coming world government would be Federation Earth.

He also discovered the linkage between Free Masonry and the religion of the New Age, and that the World Council of Churches' hidden agenda was an ultimate merger with the church of Rome (the Roman Church is comprised of about one billion members). Make no mistake about it — the One World Church is forming rapidly. God's true servant Gary Kah discovered the linkage between the New Age religion and Free Masonry.[10]

In my research I have found that the order of Free Masonry (the Masonic Order) is the highest echelon of power, a secret, esoteric order of the Illuminati, whose goal is to establish on Planet Earth a One World government and at its core is a Luciferian connection.

Now, I want to address the order of Free Masonry. I have many dear friends that are Free Masons. I've led three 32nd degree Masons to come out of Masonry and receive the Lord Jesus Christ and trust His divine blood that was shed on Calvary for their eternal salvation. I want to be fair. Most Masons are totally unaware of the hidden agenda and the secret esoteric doctrines of Free Masonry. They sincerely believe that they are members of a fine fraternal organization. **What I reveal to you now is the truth.**

Free Masonry "The Deadly Deception"

As a minister of the Gospel I must give you the truth and let the chips fall where they will. I have incontrovertible proof and evidence of every word I am going to give to you now. Adam Wisehaupt, the apostle of Lucifer, was the founder of the Illuminati organization in 1776. He was deeply involved in the secret doctrines of Free Masonry. Alice Bailey, founder of the modern New Age movement wrote in her book *Externalization of the Hierarchy*, "Masonry is the way of salvation."[11] In her book *A World Problem* in 1950, she wrote, "A new world religion is on its way to externalize the earth. It is the Masonic ritual, the role of the solar angel." And later she revealed that the solar angel was the angel of light, whom the Bible calls Lucifer.

Now, enter Albert Pike. He was and is yet the most prominent figure in America in Free Masonry. His titles include: the Sovereign Grand Commander of the Supreme Council of the 33rd degree (the mother council of the world); and the Supreme Pontiff of Universal Free Masonry. He is the author of the book that all Masons count virtually as their "Bible" or their blue book, the ultimate word in Free Masonry, called *Morals and Dogma*. I have a copy of that book. His position in Masonry was, and is today, unparalleled in the entire world. The great Masonic temple in Washington, D.C. has a statue to Albert Pike, the Supreme Pontiff of Free Masonry. I quote from *Morals and Dogma:*

> Every Masonic temple is a temple of religion and its teachings are instruction in religion.

> Masonry is the divine, eternal, immutable religion.[12]

What is that religion? On July 13, 1889, Albert Pike issued his instructions to the 33rd Masonic Supreme Council of the world recorded in the French encyclopedia.

> To you Sovereign Grand Inspector Generals, we say that you may repeat it to the brethren of the 32nd degree. The Masonic religion should be by all of us initiates of the high degree maintained in the purity of the Luciferian doctrine. Lucifer is god . . . . Pure philosophic religion is the belief that Lucifer is the god of light and the god of good.[13]

Lucifer, the god of this world, and Satan, whose names are given in the Bible, is none other than the devil.

He wrote in the book the Masons count their blue book, *Morals and Dogma,*

> Lucifer, the *Light-bearer!* Strange and mysterious name to give to the Spirit of Darkness! Lucifer, the Son of the Morning! Is it *he* who bears the *Light,* and with its splendors intolerable blinds feeble, sensual, or selfish Souls? Doubt it not!.[14]

Albert Pike has been deceived by the god of this world and probably lost his immortal soul. God tells us in 2 Corinthians 4:4 that the god of this world will blind them who receive not the light of the gospel. Jesus said in John 8:12,

> I am the light of the world. He that followeth Me shall not walk in darkness but shall have the light of life.

In the book *Religion and Ethics,* Volume 12, page 204, it is revealed that Albert Pike was the head of the Paladian Society that worshiped Lucifer.[15]

The Bible reveals in Isaiah 14, that Lucifer was the most beautiful angel of light in all of God's creation.. But, he led one-third of all the angels of heaven in a rebellion against the triune God of glory, and he deceived them. Isaiah 14 says,

> How art thou fallen from heaven, O Lucifer?

> Jesus said, "I saw Satan fall like lightening from heaven."

Lucifer is identified in God's Word as Satan, the Prince of this World, the Prince of the Power of the Air, the Prince of Darkness, the false fallen Angel of Light, the devil.

Manly Hall is a Free Mason in the highest echelons of the order of Free Masonry. He is one of their peer writers and a 33rd degree Mason. He wrote:

> The seething energies of Lucifer are in his (the illumined Mason) hands.[16]

If you doubt what I am saying, please read the book by Jim Shaw, *The Deadly Deception.* Mr. Shaw was initiated into the 33rd degree of Masonry in the great Masonic temple in

Washington, D.C. He says, "I drank blood from a human skull."

Then he reveals that he had been inducted into an esoteric society that worshiped Lucifer. He said,

> When I discovered that, I broke my ties. I came out. I broke with Free Masonry. It was a doctrine of Lucifer. I opened my life to the Lord Jesus Christ and received Him as my Lord and Savior. I have left Masonic order forever and I will never return.[17]

Federation Earth

This is **awesome**. A ten-regionalized One World government is almost ready. Its name has already been chosen — FEDERATION EARTH. World leaders are calling for ten wise persons (kings) to head up each of these administrative regions (kingdoms) under the name FEDERATION EARTH. This will be the New World Order — the One World government. These global leaders are following the script that God the Holy Spirit wrote in His Word almost 2,000 years ago:

> And the ten horns which you saw are ten kings which have received no kingdom as yet, but receive power as kings, one hour with the Beast (Revelation 17:12).

The foundation has been laid. The super structure is about to be completed — a One World government led by the most powerful dictator mankind has ever known. The name of this leader? ANTICHRIST!

Dr. Spaak, former secretary general of NATO said that the peoples of Europe are looking for a man so powerful that he could hold the allegiance of all the peoples of Europe, and, "Be he man or devil," he stated, "we are ready to receive him now."

Satan's Counterfeit

Now his ominous shadow is beginning to fall across the nations of the planet. When he is revealed, Revelation 13:7 says, "Power will be given unto him over all kindreds and tongues, and nations." He will move with the speed of a leopard to galvanize all the nation states of earth into a New World Order, or a One World government. He is destined to become the Nimrod of the last days; the greatest political, economic, military, financial, ecclesiastical genius of all time.

The Bible gives us a clue to the source of his brilliance and genius. Daniel 8:24: "And his power shall be mighty, but not by his own power; and he shall destroy wonderfully." Did you catch that phrase — "Not by his own power"? He will operate by the genius of Satan, Lucifer, the god of this world. He will be endued with the power of the Prince of Darkness, none other than the devil. **He will be Lucifer, walking the earth as a man**, incarnate in that man of sin. The man that will pretend to be Christ will be a fake, a phony, a counterfeit. He will deceive the entire world except those whose names are written in the Book of Life of the Lamb, slain from the foundation of the world.

The Bible tells us that when the president (or chief executive) of the revived Roman Empire steps forth, he is going to pull off the greatest political coup of the century, if not the millennium. He is going to accomplish something that no political scientist or military strategist has ever been able to do in all modern times. He is going to solve the Middle East crisis. This is revealed in Daniel, chapter 9. When he accomplishes this feat, the whole world will marvel at his political acumen and it will propel him to global prominence.

I believe that soon after he takes the reins of power as the head of the revived Roman Empire, this Roman prince, a twentieth century Caesar, is going to offer the state of Israel a seven year security pact. He is going to offer the Knesset leaders a security of their borders for seven years. One can only fully understand and grasp the events of the last days if we understand the prophecy of the "seventy weeks of Daniel." This is a key pivotal prophecy and I'm surprised that it is not being addressed today.

The 70th Week of Daniel

If you want to know what time it is on God's prophetic time clock, keep your eye on the nation Israel. God reveals in Daniel 9:21 that the angel Gabriel, the mighty archangel who stands in the presence of God, was sent to reveal to Daniel all that would happen to his people, the holy covenant, earthly people — the Jewish race, the seed of Abraham, Isaac, and Jacob at the end time. In the prophetic domain, the nation of Israel (God's own earthly covenant people), is the key to all Bible prophecy.

Examine verse 25:

> Know, therefore, and understand, that from the going forth of the commandment to restore and to build Jerusalem unto the Messiah, the Prince, shall be seven weeks, and threescore and two weeks; the street shall be built again, and the wall, even in troublous times.

Daniel and his people were captives in faraway Babylon. Jerusalem had been captured by the Babylon armies almost seventy years before. Now, God reveals to Daniel, through the archangel Gabriel, that there will soon go forth a decree from Babylon to rebuild Jerusalem. Look closely at Daniel 9:24.

> Seventy weeks are determined upon thy holy city (that's the city of Jerusalem), to finish the transgression, and to make an end of sins, and to make reconciliation for iniquity, and to bring in everlasting righteousness, and to seal up the vision and prophecy, and to anoint the most holy.

What does all that mean?

In ancient Babylon at the time of Daniel, in the chronology of that day, one week was equivalent to seven years. Seventy weeks would be equivalent to 490 years and God reveals in verse 24 that six great world events would take place revolving around the state of Israel. We saw those six things as we read the 24th verse. Verse 25 tells us that from the going forth of the decree to rebuild Jerusalem (445 B.C.), until literally the Messiah would be anointed (set up His millennial kingdom) would be seventy weeks or 490 years. But this has not happened even after 2600 years.

Watch the marvelous, meticulous precision with which the Holy Spirit writes.

Sir Robert Anderson's Book
"The Coming Prince"

Now, enter Sir Robert Anderson. Sir Robert Anderson was the head of Scotland Yard to the end of the 19th century. He was one of the most brilliant detectives in all the British Empire. He was knighted by the Queen of England. He knew the Bible. He knew Bible prophecy. He was a humble believer in Jesus Christ. Today he would have held the position as Head of the CIA and the FBI of the United States. He was the Director of the Scotland Yard of the British Empire. He was an avid student of Bible prophecy. He read Daniel the 9th chapter, and was awed by this prophecy. He said, "Either this is an impostor or it is God-breathed." And, so, upon his retirement, after he stepped aside from the head of Scotland Yard, with his brilliant, analytical mind, he rolled up his sleeves and went to work with the skill and expertise of Sherlock Holmes.

First, he determined the exact date when the decree would go forth by Cyrus, King of Persia, to rebuild Jerusalem. Can we know for sure what that date is? We can. The archeologists have unearthed the archives of the Persian kings. **The date was March the 14th, 445 B.C.**

Now, watch closely. From that exact date until the Jewish Messiah would come to make reconciliation on Calvary (look at verse 24, right in the center, "to make reconciliation for iniquity"), through the blood of the everlasting covenant, would be 69 weeks. You pick this up again, in verse 26: "And after threescore and two weeks," and seven weeks in verse 25. In other words, "After 69 weeks shall Messiah be cut off, but not for Himself." The Hebrew says, "He shall have nothing." Messiah shall be "cut off." That word "himself" brings us to the time of Calvary (the cross). Verses 25 and 26 revealed it would be 69 weeks from the going forth of the decree to rebuild Jerusalem until Messiah would give Himself on Calvary to make reconciliation for the sins of His people. Multiply seven times sixty-nine and you will have 483 years.[18]

The Amazing Fulfillment of Bible Prophecy

That's exactly what was revealed to Daniel. Sir Robert Anderson meticulously checked out all the changes of the calendars over those 483 years, the Jewish calendar of 360 days, the change of the Roman calendar under Julius Caesar and Augustus, and then he made the greatest discovery of his lifetime. He says the day that the Lord Jesus Christ, the Jewish Messiah, rode into Jerusalem on Palm Sunday of Passion Week, to be crucified on Calvary, was Nisan 6, A.D. 32. The exact very day prophesied by Daniel in Daniel, chapter 9, verses 24, 25, and 26 — 483 years before. **No man could have ever done anything like this.** It could have only been done by the omniscient power of God, the Holy Spirit, through inspired Scripture. Sir Robert Anderson's final conclusion, and I quote him, "This is the God-breathed Word of the living God."[19] His book has been reprinted, called *The Coming Prince*. It's one of the most thrilling books you can get in the Christian bookstores.

God's Clock of Prophecy Stopped

But, the most holy (the Jewish Messiah) has not been anointed and He has yet to set up His everlasting kingdom. Now watch very closely. After the words, "to make reconciliation for iniquity," . . . Note the comma between the words "iniquity" and "to bring in everlasting righteousness." God's great clock of prophecy stopped, just as at a football game, the clock is stopped right there. This is the marvel of inspired Scripture. Please note Luke, chapter 4, verses 18 and 19. Between the last word in verse 18 and verse 19 there is a time frame of 2000 years. At exactly sixty-nine weeks, or 483 years, God's great clock of prophecy stopped and God stopped dealing with Israel as a nation. The Roman armies came under General Titus and destroyed the holy city and crucified over one million of the Jewish people, and the nation of Israel was scattered in 70 A.D. to all the nations of the earth.

The time frame of 2000 years since the cross until now, is known as the "grace age." The Holy Spirit has been accomplishing something that the Old Testament prophets did not see. It is revealed in Acts 15:14 that the supreme purpose in these 2000 years since Calvary is that "God has been taking out a people for His name." God has been building His church, "Drawing out a people for His name." Now all (Jew and Gentile) who heed the divine call of the Holy Spirit and receive the Lord Jesus Christ, the Lamb of Calvary as their Savior and Lord, become members of His church (the Ecclesia), **the called out ones.** In this Grace Age He is calling out a bride, a redeemed people to be His body, to be the bride of the Lamb. Is God finished with Israel? No! No! God is not finished with the Jew. God is not done with Israel.

Scores and scores of times in the Old Testament — in Jeremiah, Ezekiel, Isaiah, Amos — He tells us "In the latter years I will regather My people to their land. I will plant them in their land and they will never be rooted up again."

In Ezekiel 36:24: "For I will take you (that is His covenant people) from among the nations, and gather you out of all countries, and I will bring you into your own land."

God gave them the Abrahamic covenant in Genesis 12, and in Genesis 15, He gave them the land grant (the land of Palestine – Israel). That covenant will stand forever; it will never be abrogated. God's character is behind it. We saw the miracle of the restoration of the Jewish people to their land in 1948, and for the first time in 2600 years, Israel became a sovereign, independent nation again, and we've seen the miracle of the preservation of God's people in the land.

The Coming Roman Prince

Now there is one week left on God's prophetic time table. Remember, there were to be seventy weeks; sixty-nine weeks to the cross, and one week yet to be fulfilled. There is only one week remaining! Where is that week? Look at verse 26 of Daniel 9: ". . . And the people of the prince that shall come shall destroy the city." Put your finger on that verse. Analyze it for a moment. "The people of the prince that shall come shall destroy the city . . ."

Who destroyed the city of Jerusalem in 70 A.D.? Rome. Here God reveals to Daniel that there is coming at the close of this age, the time at the climax of history, a great prince that will be of the people of Rome, a coming Roman prince of the people that destroyed the city. He will be of the people of the "old" Roman Empire. He will be a Roman out of a "revived" Roman Empire. That's exactly what the Holy Spirit is saying in verse 26. He will be the leader of the revived Roman Empire for the "last days."

Next examine verse 27. When he appears on the world scene, "And he shall confirm the covenant with many." For how long? For one week. How long is a week in Daniel's chronology? Exactly seven years. And as you read through the verse it speaks about Israel. It pinpoints that a covenant will be made with God's people who had been returned to their land. He shall confirm the covenant for one week — seven years. We are almost at that critical moment on God's prophetic agenda. At this precise hour the stage is being set up for that very event to take place.

World events are moving in the Middle East with such electrifying acceleration and that soon, it would appear as though the state of Israel might be brought to that event. The Middle East is the powder keg of the world. Some of the top military men are saying World War III will be fought in the Middle East. The tiny state of Israel, with approximately 4.5 million people, is surrounded by an Arab world, an Islamic world of twenty-one nations, who have declared a "Jihad" (total war to the death).

Crisis in the Middle East

Behind every Arab attack, beginning in 1967 until now, there has been the military power of the Soviet Union. Every attack has been miraculously beaten back. All the world watched in amazement as **God has preserved this tiny nation!**

Now, the tiny nation of Israel, surrounded by one billion Islamic people, is in the most precarious situation of her entire existence. But, I remind you of Amos 9:14-15. God said, "In the latter years, I pledge you My promise, I will plant you My people in your land, and you will never be rooted up again."

At this time all Islam is demanding the state of Israel to give up some of its territory. They're demanding that the Israelis give up the Golan Heights; they're demanding the Israeli nation give up the West Bank, and yet the territory of the Arab world is 641 times the size of this tiny state of Israel. One late report from the *Intelligence Digest* from London recently asserts that the Soviets are now arming some of the Arab states with nuclear weapons. This same report, read by kings and prime ministers all over the world, predicted that unless there is a change in the situation, there would be a war in the Middle East by 1995. That is less than two years away. The balance of power is dangerously shifting toward Islam in the Middle East.

One Israeli told Hal Lindsey in Israel recently, "We Israelis are so desperate for peace, we would sign a peace pact with the devil himself if he would offer us peace."

That man did not realize how prophetically he spoke! For this is exactly what is going to take place. We will see that as we move into the future..

Signing of the Covenant

When the leader of the European confederacy appears on the world scene, the crisis in the Middle East could deepen. The scenario may not develop exactly like this, but it is shaping up and pointing in that direction; there comes a moment of critical instability. The Israeli people and the Arab world come to the brink of war. Perhaps the nations will come to the brink of World War III. Remember, oil will be involved in that territory. Israel desperate, her back to the wall, perhaps the United Nations condemning her again —. the leader of the greatest political, economic, military super-power in all history (backed by 360 million people), the president of the United States of Europe could seize that moment and offer the Knesset leaders a seven year security pact: "We will protect your borders for seven years."

The Israeli leaders (the Knesset) are going to buy that offer lock, stock, and barrel. The television cameras of the world will converge on this event, wherever that signing will take place, maybe the capital of the Beast in Europe, or perhaps the city of Jerusalem, the Knesset Building. The "great" television cameras of the world will be there — CNN, BBC, ABC, NBC, CBS — all the great television stations, carried by satellite to the billions of people of earth. They will watch the signing of the covenant. The Israeli people will have made the greatest mistake in their entire history. They will be signing a "peace" pact with hell.

God's Prophetic Time Clock Begins Again
T Minus 7 and Counting

At that precise instant of the signing of the covenant, God's clock of prophecy begins again. The world enters the 70th week of Daniel — the last seven years of this age. It is now T-minus 7 and counting until re-entry time — the return of the Jewish Messiah, Jesus Christ — and touch down on the Mount of Olives.

> And His feet shall stand in that day upon the Mount of Olives, which is before Jerusalem on the east (Zechariah 14:4).

That is also revealed in the book of Isaiah. The leader of the revived Roman Empire, posing as a man of peace, a flashing paragon of Satanic deception, will deceive the nation Israel, and they will actually receive him as their Messiah. Jesus said,

> I am come in My Father's name and you would not receive Me. One cometh in his own name and him ye will receive (John 5:43).

He was pointing ahead, some 2000 years, to the time of the false messiah. Recently Teddy Kollek, the popular Mayor of Jerusalem, said, "My toughest job is to prepare the people of Jerusalem for the coming of our Messiah."

Could it be that he is inadvertently preparing them for the false messiah? The Bible clearly reveals the nation Israel

will receive the false messiah first, and, but for divine
intervention and the return of their true Messiah — the Lamb
of Calvary, the Lord Jesus Christ — the state of Israel would
be totally and completely annihilated.

The entire world will hail this man, the Prince of Rome,
the leader of the revived Roman Empire, as the greatest man
of peace, the greatest peace negotiator that mankind has ever
known. Probably they will award him the "Prince of Peace"
medal. Perhaps some of the great religious leaders of
America will go to Europe to solemnize the giving of the
"Prince of Peace" award. Perhaps the world will give him
the Nobel Peace Prize.

But the Christian who knows his or her Bible will know
that "that" man is an impostor! In Daniel 8:25, we read, ". . .
and by peace shall destroy many." The signing of the
covenant will soon propel this man to the throne of the
world. This man will be given the throne of the entire planet.
Kings and prime ministers and presidents will surrender
sovereignty of their nations to him. The gavel of the United
Nations will be placed in his hands, and they will declare
him as secretary general of the "United States of the World,"
Prime Minister of Earth. He will be at the pinnacle of power,
a monolith of power such as no world ruler has ever
dreamed of possessing!

Antichrist — The Man Who Will Have It All

This man will have it all. He will become the solar man,
the master dictator, the chief executive, the president of
earth. Vested in his hands will be all the political power of
the entire world. He will be the president of the New World
Order, the One World government, the super world state.
All nations will surrender sovereignty under the New World
Order. He will wield full totalitarian power. He will
establish the super world bank, a giant federal reserve that
will give him power over all banking and the monetary
systems of the world. The Bible reveals he will restructure
the entire financial system of earth into a new "international
economic order," a perestroika of the monetary system of all

nations. We read about it in Revelation 13 as revealed by the Holy Spirit nearly 2000 years ago.

He will be the Commander in Chief of all the armies, Air Forces, and naval power of the entire planet. He will have awesome power over the world's arsenal of military weaponry. All nuclear warheads, under a global umbrella of Star War technology, giant particle beam weapons, platforms, satellites — under the control and command of one man! In Revelation 13:4, it is clearly foretold. The peoples of the world will cry, "Who is like unto the Beast? Who is able to make war with him?"

Then he will take control over all the religions of the world through his P.R. man, the false prophet. He will synthesize all the great religions of earth into a super world church called in Revelation 17, "Babylon, the Great Whore." He will revive the Satanic religion of ancient Babylon, the mysteries of ancient Babylon. The false prophet of Revelation 13 will become the Pontiff, the King Priest of this vast Satanic, religious empire. Men will again worship the sun and the moon and the stars as they did in ancient Babylon. It will be nature worship, witchcraft.

The Fatal Sword Wound

Then one day, as the world moves toward the half-way point of the seventieth week — 1260 days — the wheels of the industry will be whirling. Giant corporations will be transacting their global business. Thousands will be seeking pleasure on the golf courses, in their yachts, and before their television sets. When suddenly, without warning, all television programs will be interrupted. News will be instantly flashed around the world in seconds:

The President of the United States of the World has been assassinated!

The whole world will stand still. He will have received a fatal wound by an assassin's sword.

This is exactly what the Bible reveals in Revelation 13:14, "He will receive a wound by a sword." The Greek word is a "little hand sword," a wound by the sword. It will be fatal.

And then he will live again.

Three times this is spoken of in the 13th chapter. Now, some have symbolized this to mean that Rome was struck a death blow at the time of the Reformation and will be revived. Others have said that Naziism was struck a death blow in World War II — "Wounded Unto Death" — and will be revived. The Bible tells me it will not be a system. When the Bible is that specific, you can be **ABSOLUTELY** sure, with the hermeneutical laws of interpretation, the Holy Spirit means it will be a man! He tells us it will be a man, not a system. When the Bible is this specific, we dare not allegorize, spiritualize, or symbolize it away. In Revelation 13:12, we read the wound was fatal, the wound was unto death.

Satan's "Master Counterfeit"

Now Satan, the arch enemy of God, is a master deceiver, the greatest con-artist in the entire universe. He is going to pull off the slickest con job in the history of mankind — the ultimate counterfeit. He is going to stage a counterfeit resurrection. In Revelation 13:3 it says,

> And I saw one of his heads as though it were wounded to death; and his deadly wound was healed, and all the world wondered after the Beast.

God is going to allow Satan to accomplish this feat, and the whole world will marvel. Revelation 17:8 says,

> The Beast (the Antichrist) that thou sawest was, and is not, and shall ascend out of the bottomless pit, and go into perdition: and they that dwell on the earth shall wonder, whose names are not written in the "Book of Life" from the foundation of the world, when they behold the Beast that was, and is not, and yet is.

The Holy Spirit is saying here that this man — the Antichrist — lived. His wound was fatal unto death, after which he will live again.

Tal Brooke, in his book *When the World Will Be As One* analyzes this so vividly. Let me quote:

The soul of the Beast, the Antichrist, has another entity now. The Beast which comes up from the Abyss, the Abyss is that shaft of infinite darkness which is the gateway of demonic hierarchy, Lucifer himself, enters the body of the Beast. Satan, the false, fallen archangel of light, who is the god of this world, he will walk the earth as a man incarnate in the Antichrist. For only once in history a One World system with Lucifer at the helm, empowering and working through the Antichrist is allowed to take place. It is the crowning abomination of desolation. **Satan will be incarnate now in the man of sin.**[20]

The Abomination of Desolation

This is the goal for which he has schemed during the six millennia of time. It is now within his grasp. Perhaps on a sleek Air Force Jet I, traveling at Mach 3, he'll fly to the Holy City, touch down at the International Airport, walk into the new Jewish temple and actually enter the Holy of Holies. He has previously called for the television networks of the world to be ready. This is the day of his declaration. With the billions of the earth people watching on world-wide television, he declares, "I am God." This was pre-written by the Holy Spirit in II Thessalonians 2:3-4, nearly 2000 years ago. Verse 4 says,

> Who opposeth and exalteth himself above all that is called God, or that is worshiped, so that he, as God, sitteth in the Temple of God, showing Himself that He is God.

Jesus calls this in Matthew 24:15 "The Abomination of Desolation." The entire world by television will look upon the countenance, not only of the Antichrist, but reflected in him, they will gaze on the face of Lucifer.

1260 Days and Counting Until the Jewish Messiah Touches Down on the Mt. of Olives

Now, incarnated in the body of that man, the Beast is none other than Lucifer himself, who is Satan, the devil.

The day that he enters the Holy of Holies in the Jewish temple at Jerusalem and declares that he is god, the world will enter the last half of the seventieth week of Daniel. **It is now 1260 days** (3 1/2 years) and counting and soon Jesus Christ will return in power and great glory to take the millennial throne of the world.

This is the period of time the Bible calls the Great Tribulation.

EMPEROR WORSHIP OR DEATH

Let's go back to Jerusalem to the holy temple. The Antichrist makes his great declaration to all the world. One powerful New Ager wrote these words:

> When he does, a new One World religion will flood the souls of all mankind, and we will bring forth the New World Christ.

That day, as the great Caesar of Rome, he will mandate the entire world to worship him as the emperors did of old in the ancient Roman Empire. The new modern Caesar will declare and mandate world-wide Emperor worship under the capital punishment of death. Now deceived by the master con-artist Lucifer, their minds poisoned and traumatized by the lie, all the billions of earth will worship him as God unless their name is written in the "Book of Life" of the Lamb slain from the foundation of the world.

Satan will now have the billions of earth's citizens under total control. He will now reveal his true colors. He will turn into the most godless, ruthless, diabolical dictator the world has ever known — a Nimrod, a Genghis Khan, a Hitler, a Stalin — all in one man. He will be in total control of a New World Order, the One World government. He will unleash his hellish fury, not only against God's people, the blood-bought Saints, but against the covenant people, the Jewish race. Like Hitler, the "almost Antichrist," he will decree the final solution to the Jewish problem is genocide. We read about that in Daniel 8:24, "He will seek to destroy the holy and covenant people." At that time it will be the death penalty to be a believer in Jesus Christ or a member of the Jewish race.

At this point may I address one of the great themes of Bible prophecy — the return of our blessed Lord Jesus Christ. God's Word tells us that He is coming again. The apostle Paul wrote of this wonderful event in Titus 2:13, "Looking for that blessed hope and glorious appearing of our great God and Savior Jesus Christ."

About ten years ago, I went through an agonizing reappraisal. I took only the Word of God and, laying aside all my preconceived ideas, I began to search the Scriptures to see if these things were so.

I began with 2 Thessalonians 2:7.

> For the mystery of iniquity does already work; only He who now restraineth will continue to restrain until He be taken out of the way.

The Holy Spirit is very exacting. This verse is saying that there is a restraining power, a person (many Biblical passages indicate that this is the person of the Holy Spirit). He is the Restrainer; it is He who is holding back the wicked one (Antichrist) from being revealed.

"He will continue to restrain until He (the Holy Spirit) be taken out of the way." **This passage does not say that the Holy Spirit will be taken out of the world, but that "He will be taken out of the way."**

The Greek word here for *way* is *mesos* meaning *middle or between.*[21]

The inspired text is saying that, "He who restrains (the Holy Spirit) will continue to restrain until he be taken from between (or from the middle)." The meaning is clear. The restrainer will step back out of the way — from being in between. Then verse 8, "And then shall that wicked one be revealed (the man of sin, Antichrist)."

Now **Scripture can never contradict Scripture.** The prophet Joel clearly tells us in chapter 2, verses 28 and 29, "In those days, **I will pour out My Spirit upon all flesh . . .**"

"In those days" — in what days? In "the days when the sun shall be turned into darkness and the moon into blood, before the great and terrible day of the Lord" (vs. 31). **This is in the time of the Great Tribulation period.**

God's Word is crystal clear. **Instead of the Holy Spirit being taken out of the world, He is going to be poured out into the world.**

Joel reveals in verse 30 that there is going to be a moving of the Spirit of God that will cause the whole world to wonder.

> And I will show wonders in the heavens and in the earth: blood, and fire, and pillars of smoke.

Joel also reveals that this will be a time of salvation for a great multitude of people.

> And it shall come to pass that whosoever shall call on the name of the Lord shall be saved (Joel 2:32).

In that day, Joel saw a "great and strong people . . ." There has never been the like.

At this time known as the Great Tribulation, there will be a tremendous intensification of evil. All the forces of hell will be marshalled against God and His people. This is revealed to us in the book of Daniel.

> And there shall be a time of trouble, such as never was since there was a nation even to that same time; and at that time thy people shall be delivered, every one that shall be found written in the book. (Daniel 12:1).

Jesus spoke of this time that shall come upon the earth:

> For then shall be great tribulation, such as was not since the beginning of the world to this time, no, nor ever shall be (Matthew 24:21).

Satan is going to make war on the saints.

> And I beheld and the same horn (Antichrist) made war with the saints and prevailed against them (Daniel 7:21).

> And it was given unto him to make war with the saints and to overcome them (Revelation 13:7).

But also this will be a time of the intensification of righteousness! The Bible tells us in Revelation 12:9-12 that Satan is going to be cast down from the heavenlies, "to the earth having great wrath for he knoweth that he has but a short time." Verses 10 and 11 reveal that at that very time God is going to do a mighty work!

> Now is come salvation, and strength and the kingdom of God and the power of His Christ . . . and they (the saints) shall overcome him by the blood of the Lamb and the Word of their testimony and they loved not their lives unto the death.

Did you catch that? At the very time Satan and his demons are cast down from the heavens above for the final battle, verse ten says "Now is come salvation and strength and the power of his Christ." At that hour the commander of all the armies of heaven is going to do battle for His people, and then verse twelve, "And they shall overcome him by the blood of the Lamb and the word of their testimony and shall love not their lives unto death."

The Church will never be defeated. It will emerge a glorious church without spot or wrinkle, washed in the blood of the Lamb. Satan has never been able to defeat the Church in its 2000 year history. In the first centuries A.D. the Roman emperors sought to destroy the church — they failed. The blood of the martyrs became the seed of the Church. Three to five million were martyred for His name, but the Church emerged in 300 A.D. 25,000,000 strong!!

In our twentieth century, the Marxist regime sought to destroy the church behind the iron curtain. When that curtain was lifted, they found the underground church (believers in Jesus Christ) had grown to 90,000,000!

Mao Tse Tung sought to destroy the church in Red China. It is estimated that this tyrant had marked 30,000,000 Christian believers for extinction. Today, MAO is gone, but the underground church of Jesus Christ is nearly 100,000,000 strong and steadily growing!!

It is at this very hour that a great multitude will be saved out of every nation on the face of the earth.

This will be a time of the greatest ingathering the Church has ever known. This will be her greatest hour of triumph. Persecution has never defeated the Church (the true believers in Jesus Christ). God's people emerged victorious. **The blood of the martyrs became the seed of the church.**

Joel chapter 2 is an amazing Scripture. The God of heaven is going to raise up an army of His saints that will be invincible. The Lord will be at the head of that great army.

> . . . a strong people set in battle array . . . they shall run like mighty men . . . and the Lord shall utter His voice before His army; for His camp is very great; for He is strong who executeth His Word (vss. 5-11).

Daniel saw this strong people and wrote of them in Daniel 11:32.

> But the people that do know their God shall be strong, and do exploits.

John wrote of this time in Revelation:

> After this I beheld and, lo, a great multitude, which no man could number, of all nations, and kindreds, and peoples, and tongues, stood before the throne, and before the Lamb, clothed with white robes (Revelation 7:9).

> . . . They came out of great tribulation (the Greek reads "the great tribulation"), and have washed their robes, and made them white in the blood of the Lamb (Revelation 7:14).

This will be the church's greatest hour of triumph and victory. Hundreds of millions will refuse the Mark of the Beast and will follow Jesus the Lamb. I believe the Scripture is telling us here that this will be the time of the greatest ingathering to the kingdom of God that has ever taken place.

This great company of the redeemed is seen by Daniel 12:10, "Many shall be purified, and made white, and tried . . ."

In Revelation 15:2-3:

> And I saw . . . them that had gotten the victory over the Beast, and over his image, and over his mark, and over the number of his name, standing on the sea of glass . . . and they sing . . . the song of the Lamb, saying, "Great

and marvelous are Thy works, Lord God Almighty; just
and true are Thy ways, thou King of saints."

God's power will be mighty in the earth. Two witnesses
will be sent back from heaven to stand up against the
Antichrist — Elijah and Moses (or Enoch). No power on
earth can touch them, until their work is done.

And if any man shall hurt them, fire proceedeth out of
their mouth and devoureth their enemies (Revelation
11:5).

These shall prophesy for the entire time of the Great
Tribulation — 1260 days — forty and two months (Revelation
11:3).

Will Christian Believers Come Under the Wrath of God?

The true believers in Jesus Christ, those who have been
washed in the blood of the Lamb, will never come under the
wrath of God. The Scriptures make this crystal clear:

For God has not appointed us to wrath but to obtain
salvation by our Lord Jesus Christ (1 Thessalonians 5:9).

But there is a vast difference between the wrath of God
and the wrath of the Antichrist. Pastor Paul Wilde makes
this so clear in his splendid book *How Long, O Lord?*

It is plain that God has not appointed His children to
wrath, but it is just as plain that we are appointed to
tribulation. Tribulation is suffering that Christians must
endure: wrath is reserved for the ungodly who reject
God.[22]

We are given a perfect example of this in the book of
Exodus, chapters 7-12. The God of heaven poured out His
wrath in the form of ten terrible plagues upon a ruthless
dictator who was determined to crush the people of God.

But the entire nation of Israel was miraculously preserved in the land of Goshen. Not one plague could touch them.

> So there was hail, and fire mingled with the hail, very grievous, (see Revelation 8:7) such as there was none like it in all the land of Egypt since it became a nation . . . **Only in the land of Goshen, where the children of Israel were, was there no hail** (Exodus 9:24, 26).

And not one atom of God's wrath could touch them for they were over-shadowed by Jehovah in their land (Goshen).

The book of Revelation reveals that in the last days just before Jesus returns, there will be another Satanically-controlled world dictator, who will seek to destroy the people of God. We, too, will discover that,

> God is our refuge and strength, a very present help in trouble (Psalm 46:1).

> We may boldly say, "The Lord is my helper, and I will not fear what man shall do unto me" (Hebrews 13:6).

Isaiah wrote about how God will preserve His own in time of His wrath and judgment on the ungodly.

> Come, my people, enter thou into thy chambers . . . hide thyself as it were for a little moment, until the indignation is overpast. For behold the Lord cometh out of His place to punish the inhabitants of the earth for their iniquity (Isaiah 26:20-21).

The Tribulation Martyrs Under the Throne of God

The apostle John records in Revelation 6:9-11 that God will allow many Christian believers to be killed during the Great Tribulation.

> And when he had opened the fifth seal, I saw under the altar the souls of them that were slain for the Word of God, and for the testimony which they held.

> And they cried with a loud voice, saying, "How long, O Lord, holy and true, dost thou not judge and avenge our blood on them that dwell on the earth?"

> And white robes were given unto every one of them; and it was said unto them that they should rest yet for a little season, until their fellow servants also and their brethren, that should be killed as they were, should be fulfilled.

These are awaiting the return of Christ and the first resurrection that is described in 1 Thessalonians 4:16-17.

Through the centuries God has allowed His people to suffer persecution. Millions upon millions have loved not their lives, even unto death, but through the blood of the Lamb, they conquered and won the martyr's crown.

Israel Miraculously Preserved by the Hand of God

The God of Israel will preserve His covenant people during the Great Tribulation. He gave her his promise in Revelation 12:6, and 14:

> And the woman (this is the nation Israel) fled into the wilderness, where she has a place prepared by God.

> And to the woman (this is Israel) were given two wings of a great eagle (could this be a giant air lift) that she might fly into the wilderness, into her place, where she is nourished for a time, and times, and half a time (1260 days), from the face of the serpent.

At the time of the Great Tribulation, Satan and the Antichrist forces also will turn their wrath against the nation Israel. Jesus warned them of this very hour and gave instructions to the Jewish people:

> When you, therefore shall see the abomination of desolation . . . Let them who are in Judea flee into the mountains . . . Neither let him who is in the field return back to take his clothes (Matthew 24:15-22).

As the time of the Great Tribulation (the 1260 days) comes to a close, the Beast will have made war with the Saints, and he will have failed. He will have made war with Israel, and he will have failed. Now he will make his fatal mistake that will seal his doom forever. **He makes war with Jesus Christ the Lamb.** The Antichrist will gather all the great armies of the world with their awesome arsenals of nuclear weaponry. The land, sea, and air power of the planet will converge on Israel and the Middle East for the greatest battle of history — the Battle of Armageddon (Revelation 16:14-16).

> And I saw the Beast, and the kings of the earth, and their armies, gathered together to make war against him that sat on the horse (Jesus Christ the Lamb), and against his army (the Saints of the Most High) (Revelation 19:19).

Now the curtain is about to go up on the grand finale of the ages. Remember our Lord has given us His immutable promise that He will return for His bride, His Church, the redeemed of the ages. One of the most thrilling of all these promises is found in 1 Thessalonians, chapter 4.

> For the Lord Himself shall descend from heaven with a shout; with the voice of the archangel, and with the **trump of God**; and the dead in Christ shall rise first; then we who are alive and remain shall be caught up together with them in the clouds, to meet the Lord in the air, and so shall we ever be with the Lord (1 Thessalonians 4:16-17).

Now let's link these verses to 1 Corinthians 15.

> Behold, I show you a mystery: We shall not all sleep (die), but we shall all be changed, in a moment, in the twinkling of an eye, at the **last trump**; for **the trumpet** shall sound, and the dead shall be raised incorruptible, and we shall be changed (verses 51-52).

This is the first resurrection when all believers in Jesus Christ at the trump of God shall be caught up "in the clouds to meet the Lord in the air."

Revelation 20:4 tells us this event cannot take place until after the Great Tribulation.

. . . And I saw the souls of them that were beheaded
for the witness of Jesus, and for the Word of God, and
who had not worshiped the Beast, neither his image,
neither had received his mark upon their foreheads, or in
their hands; and they lived and reigned with Christ a
thousand years.

We are being told that the rapture will take place before
the Antichrist is revealed. But God's Word tells us plainly
that those who are martyred for Christ during the Great
Tribulation will take part in the first resurrection, **after the
tribulation is past.**

Jesus puts all these events into perfect perspective in
Matthew 24, in Mark 13, and in Luke 21. In these passages
our Lord gives us the exact sequence of these end-time
events.

These are the words of Jesus Christ, our Lord:

Immediately after the tribulation of those days shall
the sun be darkened, and the moon shall not give its light,
and the stars shall fall from heaven, and the powers of the
heavens shall be shaken.

And then shall appear the sign of the Son of man in
heaven; and then shall all the tribes of the earth mourn,
and they shall see the Son of man coming in the clouds of
heaven with power and great glory.

And He shall send His angels with a great sound of a
trumpet, **and they shall gather together His elect from
the four winds,** from one end of heaven to the other
(Matthew 24:29-31).

Mark records the words of Jesus Christ:

But in those days, after that tribulation, the sun shall
be darkened, and the moon shall not give its light.

And the stars of heaven shall fall, and the powers that
are in the heavens shall be shaken.

And then shall they see the Son of man coming in the
clouds, with great power and glory.

> And then shall He send His angels, and **shall gather together His elect** from the four winds, from the uttermost part of the earth to the uttermost part of heaven (Mark 13:24-27).

Luke records the words of Jesus Christ:

> And there shall be signs in the sun, and in the moon, and in the stars; and upon the earth distress of nations . . . for the powers of heaven shall be shaken.

> And then shall they see the Son of man coming in a cloud, with power and great glory . . . **then (when we see Jesus coming in the clouds) look up, and lift up your heads; for your redemption draweth nigh** (Luke 21:25-28)

This is the time of the **redemption of our bodies** at the first resurrection (the last trump) when we will be changed from mortal to immortal in a micro second (1 Corinthians 15:52).

This is the time when **Jesus will appear in the clouds** of heaven. This is the event of which Paul wrote in Titus 2:13, "Looking for that blessed hope, and the **glorious appearing** of our great God and Savior, Jesus Christ."

This is the time when **every believer in Jesus Christ will be gathered together from the four winds of heaven and caught up in the clouds to meet the Lord in the air** (1 Thessalonians 4:16-17) to return with King Jesus in His triumph, when He consumes "that wicked one (Antichrist) with the Spirit of His mouth and destroys with the brightness of His coming (2 Thessalonians 2:8).

This is the time when the saints of all the ages, the blood-bought bride will be brought to the marriage supper of the Lamb. This is the time of the consummation of the ages when the kingdoms of this world will become the kingdoms of our Lord and of His Christ and He shall reign forever and ever (Revelation 11:15).

The Final Victory of the Lamb

Ours is the final victory, because we have a champion and His name is Jesus, King of Kings and Lord of Lords. Daniel was given a glimpse of that moment 2,600 years ago in ancient Babylon.

> And there was given him (the Ancient of Days) dominion, and glory, and a kingdom, that all people, nations, and languages should serve him; his dominion is an everlasting dominion, which shall not pass away, and his kingdom that which shall not be destroyed (Dan. 7:14).

Almost 2000 years ago, John the Revelator, from the vantage point on the isle which is called Patmos, via his pen of divine inspiration, vividly describes that moment of the climax of history:

> And I saw heaven opened and, behold, a white horse; and he that sat upon him was called Faithful and True . . . He was clothed with a vesture dipped in blood; and his name is called The Word of God . . .And out of His mouth goeth a sharp sword, that with it He should smite the nations, and he shall rule them with a rod of iron . . . and he hath on his vesture and on his thigh a name written, King of Kings, and Lord of Lords (Revelation 19:11-16).

The rider on the white horse of Revelation 6 (Antichrist) will have a head-on collision with the rider on the white horse of heaven, the Lord Jesus Christ. The sword of Him who is the Word of God will flash, and in one micro second, the kingdom of the beast will disintegrate into a trillion smithers (Rev. 2:27). His Imperial Majesty, our Great Redeemer of Calvary will ascend to the millennial throne of the world. The gavel of the United Nations will rest in the nail-pierced hands of Him who is the Prince of Peace.

> And the Lamb shall overcome them, for He is Lord of Lords and King of Kings, and they that are with Him (the blood-bought saints of the most high) are called and chosen and faithful (Revelation 17:14).

This is our final destiny:

> To him that overcometh will I grant to sit with me in my throne, even as I also overcame, and am set down with my Father in His throne (Revelation 3:21).

NINE

The Beast
of Belgium

And he (the False Prophet) had power to give life unto the image of the Beast, that the image of the Beast should both speak, and cause that as many as would not worship the image of the Beast should be killed.

— *Revelation 13:15*

My friend, who is a bank manager in a Southern California Bank America, tells me that all their managers have been briefed on the advent of a total cashless economics . . . there is a mega-computer in Belgium — they call it THE BEAST.

— Dr. Larry Polland, Ph.D.
How to Prepare for the Coming Persecution

Larry Goshorn is a man who reached the top in scientific computerization and robotic engineering. His company is "Robotics International." This man is a computer genius and aligned with the worldwide program called SWIFT (Society for Worldwide Interbanking Financial Telecommunication). Its purpose is to link the

entire police departments and financial machinery of the
world to Europe and the Super Computer.

The following is taken from an audio cassette tape and
these are the exact words of Larry Goshorn.

As a young lad, he says,

> I went into heavy rebellion. I had seen the movie *The
> Devil and Daniel Webster*, where Webster gave his soul to
> Satan in exchange for the wealth and power of the world.
> I decided that that was what I was going to do.

> **I made a contract with Satan to exchange my soul for
> the wealth and power of this world.** Satan opened so
> many doors for me, but those doors always led to
> exchanging more of my soul for the wealth and power of
> the world.

> In my teens, I was traveling with the number two
> family of the Mafia of America. By the time I was in my
> early thirties, I had achieved all of the objectives that I had
> set out to achieve. The chairman of the Bank of America
> was on my board (of Robotics International). I would go
> to parties that would be attended by the most wealthy and
> most powerful people on earth. At that time, I learned
> that my mother had become a Christian and that she was
> praying for me.

> One night I saw the movie *Two Thousand and One.* It
> displayed infinity in the stars. I went home that night and
> went out into my front yard. I felt the power of the Holy
> Spirit of God. **God showed me pinnacles of power and
> spoke to me and said, "What would you do if you
> conquered the highest pinnacle of power on earth?"**

> I thought all that would be left in life for me would be
> to go for immortality. Suddenly, it was like someone
> pulled the house of cards out from under me and the
> whole thing crumbled. All of a sudden, my entire life
> started to crash and crumble about me. Everything
> started passing in front of me.

> I had this thing called "my cesspool" and all of the
> demonic activities of power were down there in that pool.

I always kept the lid on there. I could not let go. I had given so much of my soul for this power.

That night the lid flew off of that cesspool and I had to look down into it and see all of the demonic activities. I cried out to God, "Save me." And as I cried out, I opened my heart, and for almost twenty seconds I felt I'd rather die on a hand grenade than do what I was about to do. It would have been easier because my heart was so hardened, so controlled by Satan.

In about twenty seconds, a lightning bolt hit me right in the center of my heart, which was like a stainless steel watermelon. It was cracked open like a tree that had been hit by lightning. **Instantly I knew I was born anew.** There was a new P-O (a technical device in computer science) starting in my life that was going for infinity.

I felt the weight of the cesspool lift off of me, and I felt the love of God in my heart like I had never before experienced it in my whole life. God led me for the next four months, and He would teach me and answer every question that I had. And then God led me to a church where the pastor had the love of Jesus in his heart. After three months I went forward and was baptized.

In 1973, **we received the contract for the World Banking Organization to set up the super computer of Europe called SWIFT.** We started building the system in conjunction with Burroughs.

One day, two Christian men came into my office and said to me, "Do you know what you are doing? You are building the system that will be known as the Mark of the Beast. Are you going to build Satan's system to control every person on earth with the number 666 and the Mark of the Beast?"

I replied, "I didn't know that that was what I was doing."

They left, and I walked out on the floor of my factory where we were building these computer systems and I began to pray, and I said, "God, if this is not right, you'll have to tell me. I don't want to do Satan's work."

God spoke to me in such a reverberating volume, and this is what He told me deep within my heart. **"These are My prophecies in the Bible, and I can bring them to pass.** Satan does not want them to come to pass because he knows that when they do, his time is short. If you wouldn't do this, the rocks would do this in order for these prophecies to come to pass."

I said, "Lord, I don't understand this Mark of the Beast."

God spoke to me again and He said, **"The book of Revelation is a science book.** John did not understand it or have the vocabulary to describe what would take place in the last day. This is only understandable through the knowledge of modern computerization and scientific technology, and I will reveal it to you if you will seek Me."

Then God started speaking to me out of Revelation 13, where it speaks of the Mark of the Beast system, **which is actually this electronic funds transfer system.**

In 1977, we went over and inaugurated the system with the king and prince of Belgium and dignitaries from all over the world. They had the gold button which tied it all together. We invited Chuck Smith of the great church in Costa Mesa, California (Calvary Chapel) to come with cameras, and we wanted to photograph the entire system in Luxembourg called *The Beast*.

The authorities in charge said that we could not do this. **Do you know how God arranged it and made it possible?** They all got drunk one day, and we presented it again and they invited us into the bowels of the super computer of Europe called The Beast of Belgium three floors down, and Chuck Smith photographed the entire computer system.

Then the Lord took me from that world into the new computer world of artificial intelligence and supergraphics and robotics.

> And he (i.e., the false prophet) deceiveth them that dwell on the earth by the means of those miracles which he had power to do in the sight of the Beast (the world dictator, the Antichrist); saying to them that dwell on the earth, that they should make an image to the Beast which had the wound by a sword, and did live. And he had power to give life unto the image of the Beast, that the image of the Beast should both speak, and cause that as many as would not worship the image of the Beast should be killed (Revelation 13:14-15).

The Holy Spirit uses the Greek word for image four times in these two verses. Do you know what the Greek word is? The transliteration is *eikon*. **Icon is the modern computer word for a computer generated image of a person.** Icons are well known in Apple and MacIntosh computers. It is the word for computer-generated people. This image that he will build in the last days to which he will give life will have the kind of life designated in the Greek as *neuma*. This is the strangest word for life in all of the New Testament. It is not immortal life or eternal life. But it is a quasi form of life (what appears to be life). It is a ghost-form of life. God has reserved immortal life and eternal life for himself. But this is a ghost form of life comparable to artificial life.

Larry Goshorn continues:

> In the new "smart" programs you will have **three dimensional graphics.** What does this mean? They can bring an image through your television set (**an icon**), using graphic and holograms and **place a life-sized person in front of your television set by the bending of light beams,** and you could not tell if that person was alive unless you would place your hand in the light beam. "An image of the Beast . . ." It will have a ghost-form of life. The technology can take on spirit.

In Daniel 12, the Bible says that in the last days knowledge shall be increased. We now have knowledge-based engineering. These systems will have knowledge bases. This means that you can talk to it and ask it questions. It stores the knowledge of the experts. Soon you will buy knowledge in this decade. It will be a product. Knowledge is now doubling every three years.

It took two thousand years to double once, twenty years to double twice, and ten years to double three times. Now all world knowledge doubles every third year. There is no way that mankind can keep up with the doubling of knowledge like this. So they are building knowledge-base systems. You can buy the product for your home computer and eventually this image system can be plugged in and you can talk to this knowledge. **You will also be able to interact with it.**

James 3 tells us that there are two kinds of wisdom. There is the wisdom that is from above, and that is the wisdom of God. There is also wisdom that is from below. This is the wisdom that is demonic. The world will buy demonic knowledge and interact with it in this hi-tech world of science.

Larry Goshorn continues:

In January, an article appeared in *The Wall Street Journal.* The article revealed that the first product is now hitting the market. It is called "artificial reality." You put on gloves and glasses and interact with this system. You become a part of the system. Timothy O'Leary said, "This is further out than any LSD trip you can ever imagine." There is one that is porno where lust comes out of it so great that people could interact with these images in a lust activity.

Paul related that they who worship idols, worship demons. God revealed in the book of Revelation what men and women would be doing in the last days, and now we understand it as we could have never understood it before.

And the rest of the men which were not killed by these plagues yet repented not of the works of their hands, that they should not worship devils, and idols of gold, and silver, and brass, and stone, and of wood: which neither repented they of their murders, nor of their sorceries, nor of their fornication, nor of their thefts (Revelation 9:20-21).

The word *sorceries* is the Greek word *pharmakeia*, from which we get our word for the use of drugs. Now we know that through the use of drugs and LSD people can go on a trip and **actually be in contact with demonic beings.** Hi-tech science is showing us what God revealed to Larry Goshorn — that Revelation is God's science book of the ages. Larry Goshorn continues:

All they will be packaging up Satan's ways in a new form which will deceive all mankind. These world leaders do not realize that God has known their schemes from the foundation of the world. Their deluded minds have hatched the very plans that God will use in the end time for the salvation of millions of souls.

TEN

The Coming Cashless Society

And he had power to give life unto the image of the Beast, that the image of the Beast should both speak, and cause that as many as would not worship the image of the Beast should be killed.

And he causeth all, both small and great, rich and poor, free and bond, to receive a mark in their right hand, or in their foreheads, and that no man might buy or sell, save he that had the mark, or the name of the beast, or the number of his name.

— **Revelation 13:15-17**

A world without cash, currency, coin, checks or credit cards? All buying and selling on earth carried on by a mark or emblem implanted in the right hand or forehead of every person on earth? A total cashless society?

Impossible! Too Fantastic! Please Read On!!

"We, the members of the United Nations. . . Solemnly proclaim our united determination to work urgently for the establishment of a New International Economic Order."[1]

Almost thirty-five years ago, Willard Cantelon, a great Christian gentleman and monetary expert, revealed to the Christian world that he had sat in conference with the international bankers of the world and heard them planning for a total cashless society. He wrote the books *The Day the Dollar Died* and *New Money or None*. He revealed the elite international bankers had drawn up a plan which called for all money on earth – cash, currency, coin, and checks – to be declared obsolete and all commerce to be carried on by marks, codes, or numbers. We know it today as the electronic funds transfer system.

> Computer scientists are working on a master plan to assign numbers to every individual on earth. The number could be used for trading purposes – buying and selling. The report suggests that a digital number could be laser tattooed on the forehead or on the back of the hand. This international mark could do away with all currency. No member could buy or sell without having an assignment of a digital mark. (The article gives the source material, *New Money Or None*, by Willard Cantelon.)[2]

> The cashless society expected to become reality soon. The long talked about cashless society is almost here. Bank cards expected to go into nation-wide use soon.[3]

Would you be surprised to know that all of this was revealed to the Apostle John who had been banished by the Emperor of Rome to the lonely isle of Patmos in the Mediterranean Sea almost 2,000 years ago? In the days of ancient Rome, when a man was declared an enemy of the state he would be banished to the isle of Patmos. Here were located the salt mines of Rome. John had been charged with the crime of being a fundamental Bible believing Christian.

The year was about 95 A.D. It is believed that John was in his nineties, banished by the Emperor of Rome to a slave labor camp. One day, through the x-ray eyes of the Ancient of Days, he looked down the long vistas of time and he saw that time frame known as, "the last days." He describes minutely what he saw:

... and I saw a beast (a super world dictator) arising up out of the sea (the vast sea of the nations), having seven heads and ten horns (Revelation 13:1).

The Last Dictator of History

Almost six hundred years before John's revelation, God had revealed to the prophet Daniel this same last-days' world dictator (Daniel Chapter 2 and chapter 7).

A great dictator would take the helm of a ten-nation revived Roman empire and that man would be destined to become the final dictator of history. And when he takes the reigns of power, with that power block of ten nations behind him he, "will go forth conquering and to conquer" (Revelation 6:1).

Before he is done he will galvanize all nations of earth into one government and will emerge as the supreme commander of the New World Order — the total dictator. The state will then have become God. The illuminati-backed Skull and Bones Society will have fulfilled its ultimate goal:

A totalitarian, socialist, one world government where the Order has created a new synthesis along hegelian lines and where the state is all powerful and the individual can only find freedom in blind obedience to the state.[4]

The New World Order will be resplendent with a new world religion — the religion of the New Age — a universal world church described in the Bible (Revelation 17) as the Great Whore, the Satanic counterfeit church of the last days — Satan's counterfeit of the true blood-washed Church of Jesus Christ.

The super world dictator, the Antichrist, will take control of all the banking systems of the world. He will declare himself the head of the super world bank (the giant federal reserve) and for the first time in the history of man he will inaugurate a total cashless society.

John saw something that must have astounded him. He actually saw a super world dictator giving every person on earth a number, a strange mark in their right hand or in their forehead, and no one could buy or sell unless he or she had that mark.

Could we who are living in the last decade of the sixth millennium be closing in on that kind of a world . . . a George Orwellian world?

The *Senior Scholastics*, a secular magazine, in the issue dated September 20th, 1973, showed high school students in full color from all over the world with numbers tattooed on their foreheads. Then in an article entitled *Public Needs and Private Rights — Who is Watching You* it said:

> All buying and selling in the program will be done by computer; no currency, no change, no checks. In the program people will receive a number that has been assigned them tattooed in their wrist or forehead. The number is put on by a laser beam and cannot be felt. The number in the body is not seen with the naked eye and is as permanent as your finger prints. All items of consumer goods will be marked with a computer mark. The computer outlet in the store which picks up the number on the items at the check stand will also pick up the number in the person's body and automatically total their price and deduct the amount from the person's special drawing rights account.[5]

New Money System

Mr. Cantelon says in the book *New Money or None:*

> For over a decade bankers and technicians of Europe have been working feverishly to establish a new number system.

In 1977, Dr. Hanrick Eldeman, Chief Analyst for the E.C. announced that he was ready to begin assigning a number to everyone in the world and that he plans to use a three six digital unit — eighteen numbers.[6]

Dr. Eldeman has revealed that a computerized restoration plan is already under way to straighten out world chaos. A crisis meeting in 1974 brought together common market leaders, advisors and scientists at which time Dr. Eldeman unveiled The Beast.

> It is a gigantic, three-story, self-programming
> computer with the potential of numbering every human
> being on earth.[7]

Now enter Dr. Patrick Fisher. In the 1970's he was one of
the world's most prominent computer scientists, who is on
the staff of Magill University in Montreal, Canada. Speaking
with Dr. Emil Gaverluk, Ph.D., on the broadcast of the
Southwest Radio Church of Oklahoma, he revealed that
everyone in the industrial nations of the world is tied into the
super computer of Europe, and that there would be one more
step between now and the rise of a super world dictator who
would control the economy of the entire world. He also
revealed that the last step would be the issuance of a final
debit card. He said,

> That final card will be issued to over two billion
> peoples of earth. It has the potential of numbering every
> person in the world

"666" The Numbers

Your eighteen digit number is now in the giant computer
of Europe. Every person's number in the world begins with
the digits 666. How do I know this?

The Christian world is deeply indebted to Dr. Mary Relfe
and the two books which she had written, *When Your Money
Fails,* and, *The New Money System.* She reveals how, by the
divine wisdom of the spirit of God she was able to break the
secret of the bar code system (UPC). She made a breath-
taking discovery — the international bar code system and the
eighteen digit number in the computer called the Beast of
Belgium. She interviewed some of the international bankers
of the world (the U.S. News and World Report give her total
credibility). This number consists of three digits 666. The
number 666 is the international code which activates the
world computer in Brussels, Belgium; 110 is the national code
which will activate the central United States computer; your
local telephone area code; then your nine digit Social Security
number. Thus this construction makes your own personal
number to read, "666 - 110 - your area code - your 9 digit

social security number." Illustration:

666-110	205-540	101-147
6	6	6

The number 666 is the international code which activates the world computer! The first three digits of every person's number in the World is 666.[8]

> Here is wisdom. Let him that hath understanding count the number of the Beast (the Satanic world dictator) for it is the number of a man and his number is 666 (Revelation 13:18).

Could we be moving into a society where there will be world-wide usage of the number 666, the numerical entity characterizing the last day one world government? The answer is unequivocally yes! The Bible reveals that the final world government of history that will rule the entire planet, just before the return of Jesus Christ, will be a total cashless society epitomized by the usage of the number 666. And it is closer than you might think.

In 1985, I revealed this eighteen digit international number to an audience in a church in Oregon. At the close of the meeting a man handed me his VISA card which he had just received in the mail. There was his number on the front of the card, 666 110 509 540 210 316 (the last nine numbers changed to protect his privacy). Now the eighteen digit number is encoded on the metal strip on the back of each credit or debit card and is invisible to the naked eye.

Terry Galonay, former Director of Communications for VISA says:

> Protesting too loudly about it isn't going to help either, because the disturbance you kick up is going to end up in one of your files. And on the come-and-get-it-day when we are totally and completely dependent upon our card or whatever survival device might replace it, you might be left all alone without one.[9]

The Plot Thickens

The plot thickens as the New World Order crowd steps up the conditioning process (frog in the pot) to bring us into the cashless society. Could this be the system that a super world dictator will seize upon to place a mark in the right hand of forehead of all peoples of the earth? This was described by the Holy Spirit of God nearly 2000 years ago.

> And he causeth all, both small and great, rich and poor, free and bond, to receive a mark in the right hand or forehead, and that no man, might buy or sell save he had the Mark (Revelation 13:16-17).

This writer was on a jet airliner thirteen years ago. After we were airborne the stewardess announced that we would have a short fifteen minute film. What I heard and saw on that film awed me. I will condense what I heard that day into one sentence,

> We will soon be entering a total cashless society in which all currency, cash, and checks will be obsolete, and all buying and selling will be carried on by an electronic funds transfer system.

On November 7, 1989, *Good Morning America*, Charles Gibson and Joan Lunden spoke of the fast advancing debit card system, and then for the first time in television media history I heard this sentence, "This brings us closer to the cashless society."

The Beast of Belgium

The giant super computer of the world is in Luxemburg, just out of Brussels, the capitol of the European Community of Nations. It is now the financial capitol of the world. (Cray V has just been moved to Brussels from Stanford University). The super computer is called the Beast. This is a fact. We have documented evidence that the bank managers of Bank of America have recently been briefed that transactions will go through the super computer of Europe and its is named the Beast. It is an acronym:

B • Brussels
E • Electronic
A • Accounting
S • Surveillance
T • Terminal

There are now fourteen computerized terminals in the system. This system is not to be confused with the coming leader of the revived Roman Empire (the E.C.). In Revelation 13:1 he is called the Beast. This computer is not the Beast (Antichrist). The Beast will be a man — a Satanically controlled dictator. But this is the system that he will seize at the prophetic moment to control the economy of the world.

Now enter Larry Gosshorn, president of Robotics International. He is one of the World's most prominent robotics experts. He is a Christian and understands the prophecies of the Bible. He relates how his company in conjunction with the Burroughs Company set up the entire global system, tying in all FDIC banks on earth to the giant super computer in Europe. It is a thrilling story. We have his own voice on an audio cassette tape when he spoke to a group of Christian businessmen in South Carolina. (Please see the chapter on the Beast of Belgium.)

He reveals on that audio tape that he actually knew he was fulfilling Bible prophecy. He revealed, **"If you have a debit card now and would place it in any bank teller machine in the world, it would tie you in to the super computer of Europe and the first three digits that would activate your card would be 666."** (Please don't run out and ask your banker. Many of them simply do not realize this.)

Recently a personal friend of mine told me that he went into a bank here in America and asked if he might cash a foreign check. The bank teller said, "No problem, I'll pull it up on the computer." To his amazement she was able to pull up the signature of the check which was written in a foreign country, within a few seconds. The computer had accessed the Brussels terminal and the image of the person's signature had come up on the computer screen.

Is it coincidence that:

- The emblem of the E.C. (the United States of Europe) is 666?
- The symbol of the World Bank is 666?
- The symbol of the Tri-Lateral Commission is 666?
- The symbol of the New Age Religion is 666?
- That every person in the industrial world's number in the super computer of Europe is 666?

The Mark in the Right Hand or Forehead

The Bible tells us the Mark will be *in* the right hand or forehead not *on* them. The word *mark* is the greek word **CHARAGMA**: *a scratch or etching or cutting into*; a mark etched or cut into the hand or forehead.

> And he causeth all, both small and great, rich and poor, free and bond, to receive a **mark** in their right hand, or in their foreheads, and that no man might buy or sell, save he that had the **mark**, or the name of the beast, or the number of his name.

Future Shock Now

Implantable Bio-Chip Technology is Here

"A transponder I.D. bio chip in your right hand!"
According to Tim Willard, managing editor of the World

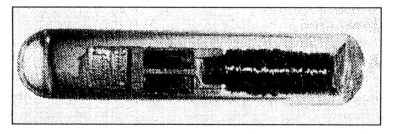

The injectable transponder –
a passive radio-frequency tag.

Future Societies' bi-monthly magazine *Futurist* . . . He says, "The technology behind such a human bio chip is fairly uncomplicated . . . conceivably a number could be assigned at birth and follow someone throughout life."

Willard said, "Most likely it would be implanted on the back of one's hand so it would be easy to scan at stores. It could be used as a universal identification card and would replace credit cards. At the super market checkout stand you would simply pass your hand over the scanner and your bank account would be debited automatically."

"It appears that the area of greatest economic impact in the next few years is likely to be telematics (the information of economy). Yes, the technological race is on to totally automate and computerize nearly every facet of our lives. These transponder chips are the perfect solution for positive identification of living creatures. Once the transponder has been injected under the skin and interrogated with an electronic scanner, it broadcasts back to the scanner a specific pre-assigned I.D. number that is unique to that creature. It is the same concept as the vehicle identification numbering (VIN) system for cars. It

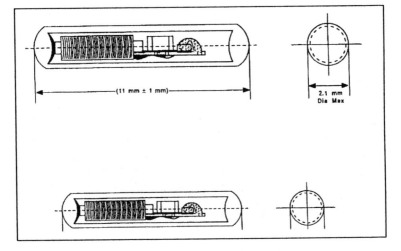

The implantable bio-chip — so small it
could be placed in the hand or forehead.

is the same use of the bio chip number that remains with the individual animals for life, allowing them to be traced, tracked, and controlled! The bio chip is the size of a grain of rice and has 250,000 component parts. The life of the transponder is about one hundred years."[10]

A Chilling Wind is Blowing Across the Horizon

Bible students know that a chilling wind is blowing across the horizon. Bible prophecy warns us in Revelation chapter thirteen that someday the global economic system of the world dictator, the Antichrist, a man whose number is 666, will call for just such an alphanumeric identification system.

Such a planetary network will enable the Illuminati's New World Order (United Nations controlled one world government) to assign a unique I.D. number for tracking and control.

This system will lead to a universal system of totalitarian enslavement under a computerized global economic network of electronic bondage. In this soon coming cashless electronic debit system no one will be able to buy or sell anything, anywhere, without the New World Order global bio chip mark in their right hand or forehead. This is what the Bible calls the Mark of the Beast. Without it no transactions of any kind will be permitted. There will be no income, no food, no shelter. No one will be excluded from having to take his Mark without facing the death penalty.

The Bible tells us that there is only one way out of this evil system. The way is Jesus Christ. He alone is the Way, the Truth, and the Life. If you do not know Him as your Savior please make that decision soon.

I have received reliable information that the pattern for the microchip transponder data is as follows:

1. Your name and picture.
2. Your social security number (international — remember that is the eighteen digit number whose first three digits are always 666, in every person's number in the world).
3. Fingerprint data.
4. Physical description.

5. Address.
6. Family history.
7. Occupation.
8. Tax information.
9. Criminal record.

All this information will be in the soon coming debit card (Smart Card) and will ultimately be replaced with a microchip in the hand or forehead. The Clinton-Gore team called for the Smart Card to be implemented soon.[11]

The *Christian Science Monitor* on January 25, 1993, revealed that there is a new Austin, Texas based government industry semi-conductor consortium, Sematech.

> Its goal is to this year make semi-conductors with a device the width of only 0.35 microns or 1/200th of a human hair. The 0.35 micron will be the standard for the subsequent generation of chips in the mid 90's. When put into use this technology will allow a single chip to store the equivalent of all the names and phone numbers of a **thousand page telephone directory**. Nearly 200 technologists met recently in Austin to help begin this planning effort.[12]

Undoubtedly this could be applied to the 666 bio-chips. This could be applied to the soon coming smart card. The Clinton-Gore team has already called for the issuance of the smart card to all citizens of America, to be implemented under Hillary's health care plan. With this fantastic scientific breakthrough, that smart card will have a person's personal financial profile with millions of pieces of information of everything you have ever done.

The smart card (final debit card) will soon be required. Remember Dr. Patrick Fisher, in 1979, on the broadcast of the Southwest Radio Church program, where he stated that the issuance of one more card would be the last step before a world dictator would require a number in the hand or forehead. We are almost there.

The *San Jose Mercury News* had this caption:

Avoid Being Caught in the Web of 666

Nearly 2000 years ago the Bible predicted the following: "He causes all to receive a mark in their right hand or in their foreheads, and that no man might buy or sell save he had the Mark."

The world leader (Antichrist) the head of a New World Order will do away with all cash and force one and all to succumb to a computerized system, it will begin with a card (such as a smart card), then eventually evolve to a very tiny microchip to be implanted in your right hand or forehead (hairline)."[13]

Many years ago I read a part of the book *Tragedy and Hope* by Carrol Quigley, professor at Georgetown University. He was a powerful member of the council on foreign relations and a strong advocate of the New World Order. He wrote the following words:

The individual's freedom and choices will be controlled within very narrow alternatives by the fact that he will be numbered from birth and followed as a number (Note: he or she will be a number) through his educational training, his required military or other service (no draft dodging then), his tax contributions, his health and medical requirements and his final retirement and his death benefits.[14]

"A number from birth to death" — from the womb to the tomb. Professor Carrol Quigley was Bill Clinton's mentor and role model at Georgetown University. He was the one man to whom the President referred at his inaugural address on January 20, 1993.

The *Marin Independent Journal* had this headline:

Future Shocker — Bio Chip
Science Fiction Technology Here

Conceivably a number could be assigned at birth and go with a person throughout life. Most likely it would be implanted on the back of the right or left hand (the Bible says it will be the right hand) for convenience, so that it would be easy to scan. It could be used as a universal identification card that would replace credit cards, passports, etc. At the checkout stand at a supermarket you would pass your hand over a scanner and your bank account would automatically be debited. Most importantly it could be programmed to replace a medical alert bracelet.[15]

I'm not paranoid; I don't see 666 under every bed. But I do see a massive media conditioning of people for the acceptance of the coming debit card (Clinton's smart card) which will be the final precursor of the Mark! The *Arizona Republic*:

Eye In the Sky to Track Kids

Each child whose parents sign up would get a computer chip planted under the skin and an identification number. The chip would transmit a signal that would bounce off a satellite and be picked up by the police on a computer screen map. A parent with a missing child could call the police, give the kid's scan number and have the child traced.[16]

Microtechnology — could this be the forerunner of the Mark of the Beast?

Prophecy in the News:

The race is on. Several companies are now competing in a new market that has practically unlimited potential. The implantation of electronic identification transponders in animals. When electronically interrogated they broadcast a specific number. Using a hypodermic needle the unit is placed just beneath the skin of an animal.[17]

The news was flashed on television in August, 1993, that all animals in the European community must have the microchip implant. It is estimated world-wide there are millions of animals with the microchip embedded. With the use of cellular towers and satellite surveillance the microchip implant can triangulate the position of the animal anywhere in the world within ten feet.

The economic system of the Antichrist will some day call for just such a numeric identification system. An individual so numbered could be traced and all of his movements.

Tim Willard in the *Futurist* magazine states,

"A human microchip identification system would work best with a highly centralized computer system (remember the Beast of Belgium?). Conceivably a number could be assigned at birth and go with a person throughout life. Most likely," he added, "it could be implanted on the back of the hand . . . so it would be easy to scan."[18]

In August, 1991, *20/20* showed how it is now being implanted in babies. Are we almost there?

The 666

Here is wisdom, let him that hath understanding count the number of the Beast (Antichrist) for it is the number of a man and his number is six hundred, three score and six — 600 60 6 or 666 (Revelation 13:18).

The Number That Seals

What does it all mean? Do you know that 666 is actually a Greek word? (See *Strong's Concordance* #5516: CHI XI STIGMA.) CHI XI STIGMA used as numbers, denoting *600 60 6 (666)*.[19]

STIGMA: stick or prick — "a mark punched or incised for recognition of ownership" (Strong's #4742).[20] WAIT! STOP RIGHT THERE. 666 — **"Recognition of ownership."**

Alice Bailey, the "Titular modern day founder" of the New Age Religion, in her massive satanic writing, *Externalization of the Hierarchy*, etc., revealed that the number 666 stands for Shamballa (Hell), Satan's hierarchy or kingdom: **"You are sealed to his kingdom by the number 666."**[21]

Here in the inspired scripture, the blessed Holy Spirit is warning us, that all who take that Mark in the last days will be sealed to Satan forever. That is why you must never take that Mark in your hand or forehead. For all who do, will be lost forever. You can never go back.

The world has reached that point in time, via hi-tech super-computerization, cellular towers, satellite surveillance, and implantable micro technology, whereby one man, a world dictator, could sit in front of the fourteen computer terminals in Brussels known now as the Beast of Belgium, the financial center of the world, and scan the billions of people who have taken his Mark in one half billionth of a second. He would know those who are his. He would be able to say,

These are mine. They have taken my Mark of ownership. They belong to me. They are sealed to my kingdom forever.

What an awesome hour in which to be alive. How close are we?

A Storm Warning Voice

When the body of Christ is in danger God always raises up a warning voice. Now enter pastor Barry Smith, an evangelical pastor in Australia. He has been monitoring the plan of the New World Order crowd for twenty-five years. They chose the little continent down under for a "trial run", a massive conditioning of the peoples of Australia and New Zealand toward a cashless society.

The following headlines appeared in an Australian newspaper.

Picture of a man with the universal
product code on his forehead.[22]

Bar code on forehead of a lady in the supermarket.[23]

After years of conditioning, in September, 1987, the government, under the direction of the Prime Minister Bob Hawk, announced the debit card system (the final step before the cashless society). Hundreds of thousands of alert Christians took to the streets in protest. Forty thousand people were marching to protest in the city of Perth. Our son was there at that time and sent us the pictures in the West Australian newspaper dated Thursday, September 24, 1987. This stunned the government. They had to back off. But the Prime Minister said later that they would bring it in. Did you hear about this in the newspaper or television media in America? No, you didn't because the Rockefeller-controlled media didn't want you to know.

Below is a reproduction of a letter I received from a Christian lady in a southern Oregon City. I have protected their privacy by not revealing their names:

My father holds a key position in a large steel corporation. Recently a young lady who had just come from Australia applied for a job in the company. My father hired her. She was not a Christian. She told my father, "They in Australia have been on the debit card system for two years now, but they still have their twenties, tens, fives, and ones."

But, she volunteered this information with hostility that they would not put a computer chip the size of a grain of rice in her hand or forehead.

"My father also warned her," and she said, "I must warn my parents."

The Mark — How Close Are We?

Pastor Barry Smith came to America two years ago and gave us this warning via an audio cassette tape series. I quote verbatim:

> The United States and Canada are on the verge of the greatest economic crisis mankind has ever known. Currency will soon be recalled and eventually all cash will be done away with completely and the electronic funds transfer system will be facilitated with a plastic card (debit card) but will eventually be replaced by a surgically implanted computer chip in the right hand or in the forehead. By the research material of the Global 2000 report he projects that the Mark will begin in Europe in 1993, and after that it will be implemented in America.[24]

Could it be that we Christians in America have heard these things for so long that somehow we have been traumatized and desensitized into thinking that it is a long way down the road and it could not be happening in our day? This may be our greatest danger. It is not a long ways down the road!! It's almost upon us and we need to remember the warning of our Lord that He gave to us who would live in the Last Days:

> And take heed unto yourselves lest at any time your hearts be overcharged **with the cares of this life** and so that day come upon you unawares for like a snare shall it come upon all them that dwell on the face of the whole earth (Luke 21:34-35).

Early in 1993, a pastor of an evangelical church called me. He said,

> One of my parishioners was in a supermarket in the greater Portland area. The lady at the checkout stand told her, 'We have just installed new electronic units. We will soon be entering into the debit card system in which cash and currency will be phased out.' Then she also revealed that the new unit (scanner) was designed to pick up a mark in the hand or forehead and eventually all transactions will be via that EFTS.

From another letter I received in January 1993,

> A friend of mine was in the Fred Meyer store before Christmas, and the man in line in front of him was from Europe. To pay for his items, he raised his shirt sleeve and had the checker scan above his wrist. He told her a few more numbers that would tie him into the world bank.

This is not wolf-wolf. This is not science fiction. **These things are real and they are here!**

The Mark of the Beast

The word *mark* (in conjunction with the Antichrist) is used exactly eight times in the book of Revelation. But only twice does the Spirit of God use the phrase, "The Mark of the Beast," per sé, once in Revelation 16:2, and once in Revelation 19:20. Only once is the phrase "the Mark of his (Antichrist) name" used. At this point in time on the prophetic agenda, can we possibly know what the Mark of the Beast is? I believe that we can. Let's explore this together.

The microchip, with the number of the Beast, 666, is a part of the Mark, but there seems to be another facet. For twelve years, I "have had my ear to the ground," and I have been monitoring the leaders of the New Age Religion. I have spent 3000 hours of intense study of this satanic religion which carries every "ear mark" of being the religion of the Antichrist.

The following is one of David Spangler's chilling, if not blasphemous, statements:

> Lucifer is the agent of God's love . . . and we move into a New Age . . . each of us in some way is brought to that point which I term the Luciferic Initiation.[25]

Albert Pike, the Supreme Pontiff of all Free Masonry wrote:

> Yes, Lucifer is God . . . the true and pure philosophic religion is the belief in Lucifer . . . Lucifer God of Light and God of good.[27]

Alice Bailey spoke highly of Free Masonry as being the precursor of the New Age World Religion.

The Mark and the New Age Religion

The following exact quotations are taken from David Spangler's book *The Reflections of the Christ*.

> The light that reveals to us the path to Christ comes from Lucifer . . . the great initiator . . . Lucifer comes to give us the final initiation . . . that many people in the days ahead will be facing for it is **an initiation into the New Age**.[28]

How false! In John 8:12, our Lord Jesus said,

> I am the light of the world; he that followeth me shall not walk in darkness, but shall have the light of life.

David Spangler has made it clear that no one will be allowed to enter the New Age unless he or she will take a Luciferic initiation. He means a pledge to worship Lucifer.

The only reference to the name of Lucifer in the Bible is in Isaiah 14:12 Lucifer was the great arch angel, the annointed cherub who led one-third of the angels of Heaven in rebellion against the Triune God.

> How art thou fallen from Heaven, O Lucifer, son of
> the morning! How art thou cut down to the ground, who
> didst weaken the nations!

Jesus said in Luke 10:18, "I beheld Satan, as lightning falling from Heaven."

The Bible identifies him as the fallen, false arch angel, the "God of this world," Satan, the Devil, "the Prince of Darkness," the arch foe of the Triune God of glory. David Spangler has been deceived!

Luciferic Initiation —
A Pledge to Worship Lucifer

Now, we cannot be absolutely positive, but from our present vantage point, it would seem strongly possible that the Mark of the Beast could be the implanted microchip in the right hand or forehead, in which is the number 666; this is also the Satanic number of the Beast — Revelation 13:18, "And his number is 666."

With that and the pledge to worship Lucifer (the Luciferic Initiation), this could add up to be the coming Mark of the Beast. The Bible clearly reveals that all who take that Mark will lose their immortal soul. This is the great counterfeit seal of the master deceiver of the universe. But for every counterfeit there is a genuine. The true seal of God is revealed again and again in His holy word, the Bible.

> Nevertheless the foundation of God standeth sure,
> having this seal, the Lord knoweth them that are His
> (2 Timothy 2:19).

> And grieve not the Holy Spirit of God whereby ye
> were sealed unto the Day of Redemption (Ephesians 4:30).

When we come with a broken and contrite heart to the cross where the Lord Jesus Christ shed His own precious blood to reconcile us to God, and there repent of our sins and ask God to forgive us, we can then by faith, receive Him into our lives as our Lord and Saviour. The Bible tells us, in that instant, we are cleansed in the Savior's precious blood. We are translated out of the kingdom of darkness into the kingdom of His dear Son, and we are sealed unto the Day of Redemption!

But Satan, the god of this world is about to reveal his master counterfeit seal through which he will deceive the billions of earth's people. The Bible reveals that counterfeit seal will be the Mark of the Beast. All who take it will never have another opportunity to be saved.

All the signs of the times seem to indicate that we are in the last days on God's prophetic time clock. We are rushing toward the grand finale — the second coming of the Lord Jesus Christ and the dawning of the seventh millennium.

Satan sits at the roulette wheel. He knows he has but "a short time". The stakes are high. He is playing for "all the marbles". The prize — nearly six billion immortal souls. The lines are being closely drawn. Soon it will be the worship of Jesus Christ the Lamb of Calvary or the worship of Lucifer the god of this world.

Have you made that eternal choice to surrender your life to Jesus Christ? That choice will determine your eternal destiny.

What Should We Be Doing Now?

If you are a Christian, a believer in Jesus Christ, the Son of the Living God, if you follow Him as Lord and Master, then there are some things which we should be doing as we approach these closing days of this Grace Age:

1) You have not one atom to fear.

Our God is the Commander of all the armies of heaven.

> If God be for us, who can be against us? (Romans 8:31).

> **I will not be afraid of ten thousands of people, who have set themselves against me round about** (Psalm 3:6).

The angel of the Lord encamps round about those who fear Him, and delivereth them (Psalm 34:7).

The Lord is on my side; I will not fear. What can man do unto me? (Psalm 118:6).

You are of God, Little Children, and have overcome them, because **greater is He that is in you than he that is in the world** (1 John 4:4).

2) Determine, by His grace, to never take that Mark in your hand or forehead.

Your forehead has been reserved for the name of Him who is the King of Kings and Lord of Lords, "And they shall see His face and His name shall be in their foreheads" (Revelation 22:4).

3) Warn your loved ones, friends, and neighbors, to never take that Mark.

If they do they will forfeit forever all opportunity of salvation.

4) Fortify your heart in the Word of God!

This will make you "strong in the Lord and the power of His might." "And they overcame him (Satan) by the blood of the Lamb and the Word of their testimony . . ." (Revelation 12:11). "Take the helmet of salvation and the sword of the spirit which is the Word of God" (Ephesians 6:17). Saturate your heart and mind in God's Word. Hide the precious promises in your heart. In this day of deception and counterfeit, it is the Word that will reveal that which is true and that which is false. Test everything you see and hear on television by the Word of God. Ask, "Does it stack up with the Word of God?"

5) Begin a close walk with the Lord.

In the ante-deluvian world (Genesis 6) a sex-crazed, demonized world of violence, rebellion and terrible sensuality, there was a man — his name was Enoch, "And he walked with God, and he was translated that he should not see death. For before his translation he had this testimony, that he pleased God" (Genesis 5:22; Hebrews 11:5).

Jesus warned the generation that would live in the last days that it would be exactly like that in those days before the flood. God is looking for men and women who will walk with Him in godliness, righteousness, and purity. Only as we judge known sin in our lives and put it away can we experience the joy of intimacy and fellowship with Him.

> If we walk in the light as He is in the light we have fellowship one with another and the blood of Jesus Christ cleanses us from all sin (1 John 1:7).

6) Maintain a deep commitment to the Lord Jesus.

It is my conviction that unless we have a total commitment to Him now we may not be able to withstand the pressure in the coming crisis as described in Ephesians 6:13, "Take unto you the whole armor of God that you may be able to withstand in the evil day."

Drive down a stake at Calvary's altar: "By the divine enablement of the Holy Spirit, I now make a full and total commitment of my life to follow the Lord Jesus Christ, no matter what others may say and no matter what it may cost me!"

Remember the song:

> I have decided to follow Jesus
> No turning back, no turning back.
> The world behind me, the cross before me,
> No turning back, no turning back.
> Though none go with me, yet I will follow
> No turning back, no turning back.

This was the commitment of the Apostle Paul. He reflects this in Acts 20:24, "But none of these things move me neither count I my life dear unto myself, that I might finish my course with joy . . ."

7) Above all else make sure your name is in the Book of Life.

There are two verses in 2 Thessalonians that would frighten me if I were not a Christian:

> And with all deceivableness of unrighteousness in them that perish, because they received not the love of the truth, that they might be saved. And for this cause God shall send them strong delusion, that they should believe the lie (2 Thessalonians 2:10-11).

Here the Holy Spirit warns us that the "fall-out" of Satanic deception will be so great, that everyone who turns away from the truth of the Word of God will be deceived and follow the false christ.

Do You Know If Your Name is in the Book of Life?

Do you have that joyous assurance that your name is in the Book of Life? You can be sure!!!

Personal salvation is not found in a creed, a religion, a denomination or a system, but it is found in a person. His name is Jesus Christ, who loved you, died for your sins on Calvary's cross and rose again for your justification. Jesus said in John 14:6, **"I am the Way, the Truth and the Life, no man cometh unto the Father but by Me."**

Come to the cross where Jesus shed His own divine blood to reconcile you to God. Ask Him to cleanse your heart of all the guilt, failure, and sin. Then by faith, as a little child, open the door of your heart to Him; invite Him to come into your life, and receive Him to be your Savior and your Lord. His promise is sure!

> And him (or her) that cometh to me I will in no wise cast out (John 6:37).

Jesus said, "Behold I stand at the door (of your heart) and knock, if any man (or woman) will hear My voice and open the door, I will come in and fellowship with him and he with Me" (Revelation 3:20).

In that moment the miracle will take place! You will have an encounter with the Lord Jesus Christ that will not only change your life but your eternal destiny. You will be able to say with glad assurance and joy, "I am forgiven, my name has been inscribed in the Lamb's Book of Life!"

When I was a lad of twelve years, I invited the Lord Jesus Christ into my heart. That was the greatest moment I have ever known. I remember a song we used to sing in our little church in California. The words of that song voices the deep commitment of my life through the years:

I have made my choice forever
'Twixt the world and God's dear son,
Naught can change my mind, no never,
He my heart has fully won.

Take this world with all its pleasures,
Take them, take them great and small
Give me Christ, my precious Savior,
He is sweeter than them all.

Make that eternal choice today and you will never regret it for eternity.

Don't Take The Mark

Words and Music by
Louise Kinman

Harmonization by
Bonnie Bruechert

For a list of songs by the above author write to:
Louise Kinman
P.O. Box 386 • Canby, Oregon 97013

Author's Note

As I close the book, I am writing this note to you in order that you might know the deep, personal motivation in my heart in these pages. I seek only to exalt and magnify the name of my Savior, Jesus Christ, and to so present the message of His grace that men and women might come to know Him as their Lord and Savior. Also, it is my earnest desire to alert the people of God, so that they might know where we are on God's prophetic time clock.

Truly the barometer of His Word strongly indicates that we may soon be entering crisis days; days that will test the metal of our souls.

I am not an alarmist: only a watchman on the wall. As I observe the rapid, moral decline of the nation that I love so well; the incredible rise of a new world religion (New Age) which is deceiving tens of millions of people across our land; the U.S. government coming under the control of secret organizations, comprised of men and women in the highest echelons of power, who lust to bring our nation into the New World Order (their code for a One World government), then as a minister of the gospel I must be a true watchman on the wall and give a clear, clarion sound of the trumpet. We who know our Bibles, realize that "their New World Order," may soon be controlled by the most ruthless, Satanic tyrant this planet has ever known.

I fully realize that I am placing my life in jeopardy, and perhaps the lives of my family whom I dearly love, but I know the Lord will be with me and preserve me until my work is done.

He has deeply implanted the words of Acts 20:24 in my heart,

> But none of these things move me, neither count I my life dear unto myself, so that I might finish my course with joy, and the ministry, which I have received of the Lord Jesus, to testify the gospel of the grace of God.

May I ask one personal request? If you have information which you deem pertinent to this alert, I would be so deeply appreciative if you would send it to me. Many of you dear folk have information that would be of immense help to God's people. My address is:

Dwight L. Kinman
P.O. Box 386
Canby, Oregon 97013

I will count it a personal privilege to read your letters, and I will answer them just as soon as I possibly can.

God bless you and keep you ever in His love,

Sincerely yours in Christ Jesus our Lord

Dwight L. Kinman

APPENDIX A

Waco Tragedy

"ATF Lied About Waco Raid: Report Shows Bungling and Coverup by Agents"

Federal agents bungled the raid on the Branch Davidian sect near Waco, Texas, and then lied to cover their mistakes, says a sharply critical Treasury Department report.

Jack Zimmermann, a Branch Davidian lawyer, said the report "vindicates" the sect. "I don't think the ATF should even be a law enforcement agency," he said (*USA Today*, Friday, October 1, 1993).

A Part of the American Heart and Soul Died There; America Will Never be the Same

(Reprinted from the Heritage Baptist Church Paper, Sharpsburg, Georgia, May 25, 1993.)

A Time for Weeping

The government massacre of nearly 100 men, women and children in Waco is the worst and most grievous event ever to take place in America.

It is somethng that never should have happened. It is something that never could have happened if God-fearing Americans had been better guardians of the freedoms our founding father envisioned and structured in our founding documents.

It is something that never would have happened if government servants had been bound by the chains of the constitution. We must understand that there was more than human suffering and carnage at Waco.

There is a monthly report entitled *McAlvany Intelligence Advisor* edited by Don McAlvany, whose alert goes into fifty-seven nations of the world and is read by Senators, Representatives, Prime Ministers and many heads of state. It is a monthly analysis of global and monetary and geo-political trends. Mr. McAlvany is a Christian and a loyal American patriot who is desperately seeking to alert the American people concerning the danger of the New World Order (One World Government).

The McAlvany office has given me its approval to reprint a part of the MIA for July, 1993.

This is Must Reading for Every American Citizen

When the righteous are in authority, the people rejoice; but when the wicked beareth rule, the people mourn (Proverbs 29:2).

There is a black cloud rolling across America. The great majority of Americans cannot even see it as they live on in a contented, complacent comfort zone that sees no evil, hears no evil, and feels no evil. There are powerful forces at work in America today which have a well-strategized design to move America into a socialist police state and a globalist New World Order.

These forces have been accelerating tremendously over the past five years and especially over the past six months. They believe that there is virtually **no resistance** to their plan to control and subjugate the American people into their globalist vision of "a world that will be as one," by the year 2000.

Certainly there is no resistance from a Congress on judiciary which is going along with 98% of the agenda which the Establishment has for America. There is **no resistance** from the churches of America which are also in a very complacent comfort zone –– the mainliners supporting the Establishment's goals; the fundamental evangelicals too busy "loving the brethren" and striving "to feel good about themselves" to notice the evil sweeping across America (or lift a finger to oppose it); and most Christians (real, nominal or pseudo) in a complacent comfort zone that is presently very difficult to disturb. **It is as if a spirit of blindness or delusion has settled over Americans in general and the Christian Church in America in particular,** and as the affronts, the insults and attacks against our traditional, Constitutional, and Biblical values in America grow every day, almost geometrically, the average Christian in America goes even more deeply to sleep.

And there is **no resistance** from the general American population which continues in its comfort zone of prosperity and affluence as the government and media hypnotize, mesmerize, and pacify them, even as America descends into an economic, social, political, moral and spiritual free fall. **America is much like Nazi Germany in the late 1920s and early '30s — in moral, spiritual and political decline, and psychologically ripe to accept the new World Order.**

The Waco Massacre: Trial by Fire
(A Case Study in Police State Tactics in America)

The devices of power and its minions are the same in all countries and in all ages. It marks its victim, denounces it; and excites the public hatred, to conceal its own abuses and encroachments.

Senator Henry Clay, March 14, 1834

On Monday, April 19, 1993, the U.S. government in an act of mass murder unrivaled in U.S. history (intended to send a warning to gun owners and so-called "religious nuts" across the country), burned 86 people, including 24

children to death in the Branch Davidian compound in
Waco, Texas — climaxing a 51 day siege launched by the
Bureau of Alcohol, Tobacco, and Firearms (BATF) on
February 28, 1993. As editorialist Charley Reese recently
wrote: "When you start with an 'allegation' that a gun
control law has been violated, and you end up with nearly
100 people including 25 children, killed, and millions of
taxpayer's dollars down the drain, that's bad law
enforcement no matter how you slice it."

On February 28, the U.S. government (led by BATF)
launched an assault with 100 militarized warriors and
large amounts of military equipment against the Branch
Davidian religious commune, their church and their
home, in its Mt. Carmel compound near Waco, Texas.
The original attack left four BATF agents dead and 16
wounded and somewhere between five and ten Branch
Davidians dead. The attack had been planned for nearly a
year, using an almost identical replica compound in
Arkansas built for training by the BATF.   Photographs
taken by aircraft provided the exact dimensions of all
structures as well as the locations of the windows and
doors.

The BATF botched the original raid in every way
possible, maintaining that they were simply trying to
serve a search warrant to look for illegal weapons inside
the compound (i.e., with 100 troops, stun grenades,
helicopter gunships, etc.).   There seems a strong
possibility that at least some of the BATF agents were
killed or wounded by "friendly" fire from their own men,
or from the helicopter gunships overhead. Several
unarmed Branch Davidians not in the compound, but on
or near the grounds were shot and killed by BATF snipers
at the time of the raid (or that evening). Military
helicopters shot at the compound from above and killed a
young girl sitting on her bed nursing her baby.

The final raid involved the FBI (who took over after
the BATF botched the operation) and the U.S. Marines
attacking the compound with tanks, punching holes in the
walls, pumping in a battlefield chemical warfare agent
(CS gas) for six hours, and igniting fires that killed all
eighty-six inhabitants (i.e., sixty-two adults and twenty-
four children, including seventeen under ten years of age).

As the Los Angeles Times wrote: "Almost as many Americans died in the two assaults as died in the entire Gulf War." In the aftermath of the massacre, President Clinton, Attorney General Reno, and officials of the FBI defended their action, claiming the Branch Davidians (a bunch of religious nuts and child abusers) set fire to their own compound, committing a massive, pre-planned suicide.

Koresh and his followers held no hostages, had committed no violent crimes, were not threatening to kill or harm anyone. They were minding their own business on their own property. Everyone in the compound was there of their own free will. Texas social workers had been in the compound and found no indication that any outsider who visited the compound would be in any danger. One of the children living in the compound told her father, according to him, that, "it was a joy to live there."

A massive cover-up by the Clintonistas, the FBI, the BATF and the Establishment-controlled media has pacified the great majority of the American public in spite of the worst massacre of men, women and children by our government in U.S. history. President Clinton and the Establishment's message in the aftermath was clear: Let this be a warning to religious misfits, dissidents, gun regulations violators, Constitutionalists, and traditionalists: get in our way, oppose us, or thumb your nose at us and we will destroy you — by fire if necessary.

What a horror to watch men, women and children burned to death for no other crime than resisting the omnipotent state. **It is a chilling example of the police state that is emerging in America with ominous parallels to Nazi Germany, which "coincidentally" massacred hundreds of Jews in the Warsaw ghetto exactly 50 years earlier on April 19, 1943. Gun control, people control, persecution of religious minorities, and incredible ruthlessness and wickedness were all part of the Third Reich in Germany and are part of the Fourth Reich emerging in America today.**

The Branch Davidians were not the first (nor will they be the last) group the BATF has attacked for "alleged" gun control violations. **Last year alone, the BATFs raided over 2,000 homes or businesses with a number of innocent victims killed, and tens of millions in assets seized and hundreds of Americans jailed, in their quest for the Holy Grail called gun control.** And it should be realized that this gestapo-like organization did not just arrive with Bill Clinton. It came on stream in 1968 with the Gun Control Act of 1968 and has been growing in power and in its attacks on the American people ever since.

It is obvious that the government (and the BATF) wanted a highly publicized "victory" over gun owners and "religious nuts" and thanks to the whitewashing and coverup by the Administration and the media, the American people have by-and-large slept through the most unspeakable slaughter of innocents in U.S. history. In spite of all the mess-ups, the government has its victory; **gun owners and religious groups across America now live in fear of similar treatment at the hands of Clinton's Gestapo, and the momentum toward gun control, toward persecution of Christians and other minority religious groups, traditionalists, and Constitutionalists, and towards a socialist America; and the New World Order continues to accelerate.**

After the initial attack (2/28/93), former McClennon County Texas District Attorney Vic Feazell blamed the BATF for the deadly confrontation, accusing them of "a vulgar display of power."

In 1987, Feazell helped lead an investigation of the Davidians and their firearms, in which they were completely exonerated from any illegal activity. "We treated them like human beings rather than stormtrooping the place."

Likewise, Jack Harwell, the McClennon County Sheriff, called Koresh on the telephone and informed him of the charges, and asked him to turn himself in, along with six others and to surrender their weapons. When deputies arrived at the church grounds, Koresh and the other Davidian members peacefully complied. Feazell said of the Davidians, "They're protective of what's theirs. They're protective of their land. They view their land as

Muslims to Mecca and Jews view Jerusalem . . . **if they'd (the BATF) called and talked to them, the Davidians would've given what they wanted."**

Subsequent to the first BATF attack, Feazell predicted that the government would kill all the Davidians, and after the massacre (the second attack) he said that **they intended to kill these people from the beginning to cover their tracks of their own crimes they committed by raiding the compound to begin with.**

USING GAS ON CHILDREN – President Clinton, Janet Reno, and their FBI/BATF employees have described CS gas as a "harmless tear gas, an irritant, designed to cause the mothers to grab their children and run out of the building." No one in the police or military who has ever used CS gas believes this. CS gas (O-chlorobenzylidene malonitrite) has been **banned as a chemical warfare battlefield agent by the Chemical Weapons Convention signed in Paris in January by the U.S. and 130 other nations.** Used during the Vietnam War to flush Vietcong from hidden tunnels, the **gas causes dizziness, disorientation, shortness of breath, chest tightness, nausea, burning of the skin, intense tearing, temporary blindness, coughing and vomiting — in short it is designed to blind and disable (very different from "relatively harmless").** **CS gas is a battlefield incapacitating gas!**

On March 10, the *Houston Chronicle* reported that former Houston police SWAT commander Lt. Jim Gunn said that "CS gas can get into a child's lungs and cause congestion and kill them."

Benjamin C. Garrett, executive director of the Chemical and Biological Arms Control Institute in Alexandria, VA, said in the *Washington Times* (4/23/93) that "the CS would have most harshly affected the children in the compound. The reaction would have intensified for the children since the smaller you are, the sooner you would feel response. **It is important to note that the children did not have gas masks (they were too small to wear them)."**

Beth Stephens, a lawyer with the Center for Constitutional Rights, a public interest law firm based in New York, said "**Tests have documented at least eighty deaths caused by exposure to CS gas.** Tests have found that CS is a toxic substance which is highly dangerous to people who inhale its fumes, particularly when in confined areas."

CS was pumped into the Mt. Carmel Compound (an enclosed area) for six hours before the facility caught fire and burned to the ground.

The Washington Times (4/22/93) wrote: "The powerful chemical the FBI used at the Branch Davidian compound would have turned the cult childrens' last moments into a final hell," chemical experts said yesterday. "It would have panicked the children whose eyes would have involuntarily shut. Their throats and lungs would have been burning. They would have been coughing wildly," said Benjamin Garrett. "Eventually they would have been vomiting in a **final hell.**" (This is the gas Clinton, Reno, and their underlings described as a "harmless irritant.")

Neal Knox, head of the Firearms Coalition, said recently: "CS gas is classified as an irritant only in very low concentrations. In higher concentrations such as in a building, it immobilizes by nausea, vomiting and vertigo."

Thomas C. Swearenger, in his authoritative reference work Tear Gas Munitions states that: "In **outdoor situations** where it is desired to drive a mob from an area, the use of CS may hamper the movement of the rioters **because of the rapid onslaught of immobilization symptoms**. In indoor situations, a victim could be immobilized and could possibly receive a lethal dose through his own helplessness." Amnesty International calls CS "particularly dangerous when used in **massive quantities** in heavily built up and populous area . . . or when launched into homes or other buildings."

"Bo" Gritz told this writer that "CS gas is not just an irritant, it is designed to knock you down and makes you incapable of any practical functions." **That our**

government would use it on women and children
(thereby immobilizing them and preventing them from
running from the building) is cruel, inhuman, and
unspeakably evil, and is the kind of thing the Nazis and
Communists would have relished in.

[ED NOTE: For this reason alone Clinton should be
impeached, and Reno, Wm. Sessions and Stephen
Higgins (head of the FBI and BATF) should be fired and
all four tried for criminal child abuse. Isn't it ironic that
Clinton and Company are pushing criminal child abuse
laws for spanking children, refusing to get forced
government inoculations, etc. and then helped
perpetrate this crime (the greatest example of
government child abuse in U.S. history) on twenty-four
innocent children. Ignore what they say, but watch
what they do!]

CS Gas is Highly Flammable in Enclosed Areas

U.S. Army Special Forces retired Lt. Col. "Bo" Gritz
has said that the use of CS gas in an enclosed space set the
stage for a total inferno. When the buildings exploded
into flames, it was like they were filled with natural gas.
Flames exploded everywhere almost all at once. Gritz has
said on several national radio talk shows (including one
with this writer) that "the dispersanta used in CS gas,
known in military assault circles as 'CAP' is a highly
flammable dust initiator. **Just a small spark would cause
CS gas to explode into an uncontrollable and engulfing
fire."** Gritz told of one survivor, thirty-seven year old
Derek Lovestock, who said, "Government tanks rammed
and smashed through the walls of the Branch Davidian
Church buildings, knocking over a kerosene lamp which
started the fire."

CS gas, dispersed in a fine white particulant (powder)
called CAP is therefore highly flammable and explosive.
It acts like coal in a coal mine or dust in a grain elevator
that can be ignited into a conflagration by just one spar.
This writer has talked to a half dozen active duty or
retired military personnel, police, and government agents

who have had hands-on experience with CS gas. **All acknowledged that it is highly flammable and explosive in an enclosed area and that is common knowledge in the military and the police.**

If that is true (and it is!) then the FBI and the Clinton people must have known that by pumping the CS gas into the enclosed (tinderbox) compound, that they were signing the Branch Davidians' collective death warrant. **Therefore, the strong possibility needs to be considered that the Waco conflagration was not an accident, that it wasn't mass suicide (which will be discussed below) but premeditated, cold blooded, murder of eighty-six people — in order to burn up the evidence of BATFs illegal/unconstitutional attack on the compound on February 28** — just as former McClennon County District Attorney, Vic Feazell suggested.

One survivor said, "The black smoke was so thick that within seconds he couldn't see where he was. People were trapped. The building was falling down. The damn tanks had just destroyed the structure and nobody knew where they were because the ceiling had just fallen in. Everyone was disoriented and blinded by the CS gas."

Isn't it incredible! The American government has agreed not to use CS gas against Iraqi (or any other) enemy soldiers but used it against helpless women and children. What has our government come to? And most Americans don't even see anything wrong with their actions!

[ED NOTE: The burn units at local hospitals and hospitals as far away as Dallas were warned hours before the final attack that they could expect a large number of burn patients. The FBI must have "expected" (or planned?) a fire!]

Was the Waco Holocaust a Mass Suicide?

All of the survivors said that there was **no** plan for a mass suicide or even individual suicides. The Branch Davidian religion (an offshoot of Seventh Day Adventist and totally different from that of Jim Jones) forbade and taught against suicide. It should also be remembered that no one commits suicide (except for a few Monks during the Vietnam War) by burning themselves. **There has never been a mass suicide by burning.**

And yet, Clinton, Reno, and the FBI justified their attack on the compound by saying that they feared a mass suicide. Then after the gas, which they pumped into the compound for six hours, ignited a raging inferno that killed the eighty-six, they said, "See, we told you we feared a mass suicide." Could this have been a very Machiavellian government strategy to get rid of the incriminating evidence of their botched, unconstitutional 2/28 raid by burning all the evidence and embarrassing court testimony, and calling it mass suicide?

Koresh was found with a bullet hole in his **forehead**. Police friends tell this writer that people don't commit suicide by shooting themselves in the forehead. Koresh's first lieutenant, Steve Schneider, was found with a bullet hole in the **back** of his head. People don't commit suicide by shooting themselves in the back of the head. Were the bullets fired later by government agents to make it look like suicide? We will never know!

Government justification of the massacre: Operation Cover Their Backsides — President Clinton gave a Rose Garden press conference on 4/20/93 in which he defended and sought to justify Reno's, the FBI's and BATF's actions in Waco. The lies and distortions which Clinton told in that press conference were incredible:

1) "The Branch Davidians had illegally stockpiled weapons and ammunition." [ED. NOTE: That was only suspected, but never proven. Shouldn't the government have proven that before they killed almost 100 people? Is it now lawful to kill people during investigations of

wrong doing? Lawful or not, it is now commonplace in America!]

2) Koresh "placed innocent children at risk." [ED. NOTE: There was no risk until the government attacked the compound. Wasn't it Clinton, Reno, the BATF, and FBI that put the innocent children at risk?]

3) "The Bureau's efforts were ultimately unavailing because the individual with whom they were dealing, David Koresh, was dangerous, irrational, and probably insane." [ED. NOTE: None of the townspeople who knew Koresh observed this, nor did the former District Attorney of McClannon County, nor the sheriff's deputies who knew him. He did have strange religious views, but most of the townspeople who knew him liked him.]

4) Clinton said the April 19 FBI attack on the Branch Davidians was "an effort to protect the young **hostages.**" [ED. NOTE: The government didn't protect them, they killed them. And, the children were **not** hostages. They were there of their own free will. **The Waco siege was never a hostage crisis.**]

5) Clinton said, "The [FBI] plan included a decision to withhold the use of ammunition, even in the face of fire, and instead use tear gas that would not cause permanent damage." [ED. NOTE: No one knows who fired at who during the final siege, because the press were kept two miles away, unless one wants to accept Clinton's word, and the government **did not** use tear gas. It was highly lethal, flammable CS gas (as discussed above).]

6) Clinton said, **"I hope very much that others who will be tempted to join cults and to become involved with people like David Koresh will be deterred by the horrible scenes they have seen over the last seven weeks."** [ED. NOTE: Is this a **not so veiled threat** that if you belong to an unpopular, misfit, non-mainstream religious group, the same thing could happen to you? **The intimidation value from the Waco inferno for the government against small religious groups, conservative, patriotic, pro-life, or non-mainstream groups is incredible. Conform or we'll destroy you!**]

7) When asked by a reporter, "Why now," Clinton replied: "There was a limit to how long the federal authorities could maintain with their limited resources the quality and intensity of coverage by experts there. They might be needed in other parts of the country." [ED. NOTE: Limited resources? This is the government which is giving billions of dollars to Russia in aid and requesting billions more for 1001 boondoggles. And as far as spreading the "experts" too thin, there were only a few hundred troops and agents there. The government has tens of thousands of federal agents and allegedly over a million military personnel.]

8) Clinton said: "The danger of them (the Branch Davidians) doing something to themselves or to others was likely to increase, not decrease, with the passage of time." [ED. NOTE: Quite to the contrary, as time went by, the likelihood that they would come out increased, according to experts who have dealt with many of these types of crises.]

9) Clinton said: "They (the FBI) had reason to believe that the children inside the compound were being abused significantly, as well as being forced to live in unsanitary and unsafe conditions." [ED. NOTE: There was no evidence of child abuse according to several Texas social workers who had visited the compound. However, the gassing (with CS gas) and burning of the children by the Clintonistas does seem to this writer to qualify as child abuse. And if the conditions were unsanitary and unsafe in the compound it was because the government had turned off the water, heat and electricity, fifty days earlier. Government gunfire into the building might also qualify as "an unsafe condition."]

10) Clinton said: "I was frankly surprised to see that anyone would suggest that the Attorney General should resign because some **religious fanatics** murdered themselves." [ED. NOTE: But what if the Attorney General and her subordinates murdered these people? Will **your** religious group be the next one to be labeled by Mr. Clinton or Ms. Reno as "dangerous religious fanatics"?]

11) Clinton said, "There is unfortunately a rise in this sort of fanaticism all over the world. **And we may have to confront it again."** [ED. NOTE: Is that a veiled threat against other religious non-conformist groups?]

12) Clinton said, "I do think it is important to recognize that the wrong doers in this case were the people who killed others and then killed themselves." [ED. NOTE: This is like declaring the Jews of the Nazi holocaust as the "wrongdoers" for killing German military officers and then killing themselves by rushing headlong into the gas chambers.]

To hear how over twenty children endured a nightmare of torture by CS gas, and then see the Attorney General praised in Congress and hear the President ruthlessly dismiss their deaths in a tone of voice as devoid of humanity as Lenin's, has for the first time in my life made me ashamed of being an American.

The Child Abuse Accusation

The Clinton administration has tried to justify their Waco massacre by accusing the Branch Davidians of being child abusers. [It is very important Constitutionally to note that child abuse is a local or state crime and therefore does not fall under the authority of the federal government (i.e., the FBI, BATF, etc.).]

President Clinton, Janet Reno, and other officials, through their spokesman George Stephanopoulos said on 4/21/93: "There is absolutely no question that there's overwhelming evidence of child abuse in the Waco compound."

George Stephanopoulos said, "The children were being abused, even to the instruction on how to clamp down on cyanide pills."

The FBI has conceded that there was no truth to this claim. [ED. NOTE: Incredible! It was supposedly "concern for the children, their sexual and physical well-being" that caused Reno and her associates to pump in lethal CS gas for six hours when those children had no gas masks, an act that probably killed them with the fire that followed! Ron Paul recently remarked: "How dare the Clinton Administration talk about sexual deviance! Its officials could have had their own float in the Gay, Lesbian, and Bisexual parade."]

The facts seem to vary from the Clintonista version. **The Texas Child Welfare Department, which had visited Mt. Carmel several times, said that they found no evidence of child abuse at the compound and they interrogated children and mothers and other adults extensively.** Dr. Bruce Perry, the psychiatrist heading the team treating the twenty-one children who left the compound, said after intensive psychological as well as physical examinations that "none of the twenty-one children had been sexually abused or molested."

The Texas Department of Human Services had on three occasions extensively investigated the Branch Davidians regarding allegations of child abuse at the compound, interviewing both children and adults, and found no signs of physical or sexual abuse. Janice Caldwell, executive director of the Texas Department of Protective and Regulatory Services, told reporters on March 5: "They (the twenty-one children) are in remarkably good shape considering what they have been through. No signs of physical abuse have been found."

The March 6 *Houston Post* reported that authorities had found that all the youths appear to be in good condition psychologically and physically. Social worker Joyce Sparks said, according to the *Post*, that "the children (who were home-schooled) were remarkably well-educated and they're fascinated by books." [ED. NOTE: Compare those opinions by Texas medical, social, and welfare experts with accusations by Clinton and Reno. Who's lying and who's telling the truth? Who's trying to protect themselves? It's called CYA. As Alexander Cockburn wrote in the *Los Angeles Times* (4/21/93): "Incredibly, today when the government calls someone a 'child abuser', it's like calling someone a communist in the 1950s or a witch in the 17th century. Normal standards of evidence or reason don't apply."]

Silencing BATF and FBI Agents

Shortly after the original BATF attack, two agents came forward on TV in New York (though their faces were not shown) and said they were afraid of a coverup. All BATF agents have already been threatened by the Washington office of BATF with the possibility of being punished, dismissed, or prosecuted for speaking publicly about the raid. The agency is struggling to keep these agents silent. Four of their comrades died because of bungling, malfeasance, and mendacity at the top of the BATF.

The So-Called "Independent" Arson Team had Close Ties with the BATF

The Clintonistas, immediately after the fire, suggested an "independent" investigation of the burned out Branch Davidian compound site to confirm the "truth." That "independent" investigator, who claimed the fire had been set by the Davidians (based, he said, on infrared photos taken from a helicopter) was revealed on ABC Nightline to be a former BATF employee (who had been on a joint BATF task force for ten years) and long time contractor for the FBI, **whose wife is personal secretary to the head of the Houston BATF** — where the whole raid was planned. **The FBI controlled the crime scene for three weeks following the holocaust, letting no Texas Rangers, local police or truly independent arson investigators in, and then bulldozed the entire site on May 12. (So, now, no one else can investigate the burnt out compound.)**

The Justice Department Will Not Investigate the Decisions for the Final Assault

Although Bill Clinton promised a "vigorous and thorough" investigation of the handling of the entire

Waco affair, **on May 15 the Justice Department said it would not investigate the decision making process associated with the final assault.** (This is like saying in a murder case we will not investigate who pulled the trigger or who gave the order to pull the trigger, or in Watergate, not investigating who gave the order for the Watergate break-in.)

As the *New York Times* (5/16/93) said: "Clinton officials said that since Ms. Reno has been widely supported in Congress, and since polls show that the majority of Americans supported her decision to use tear gas, and blame the cult members themselves for the final deadly fire, department officials concluded that nothing could be gained by looking more closely at her order to carry out the assault."

Lies the Government Told During and After Operation Waco

"Governments are constituted to lie to the greatest number of people the greater part of the time," Machiavelli, in *The Prince*. BATF, FBI, and Clinton Administration officials have consistently lied and contradicted themselves since the siege of Mt. Carmel began. Just a few of a growing list of the lies include:

1) The BATF said that Koresh had to be arrested at the compound because he had not left it for several months. Numerous people in the area said that was a lie and that they had frequently seen him out jogging, at the store, and in town until shortly before the attack. The BATF finally admitted they knew nothing about Koresh's movement because they NEVER even put him under surveillance, let alone did they try to arrest him.

2) The BATF originally said that they had an arrest warrant for Koresh and a search warrant for the compound. Later it was shown that they only had a search warrant and no arrest warrant.

3)   The BATF said that the element of surprise was the key to success and that they wouldn't have attacked if they had known that the Branch Davidians were expecting them. This was a lie. Everyone in town, including the Branch Davidians, knew about the coming attack. They moved a whole army of men and equipment up to the compound. Later BATF director Higgins admitted that they knew they had lost the element of surprise and went ahead with the attack anyway. That decision caused the death of four BATF agents.

4)   The BATF told the Texas National Guard (in order to obtain use of their helicopters), that there was an illegal drug lab at the compound. There was no evidence of this before, during, or after the raid according to the *Waco Tribune-Herald* (3/28/93).

5)   On March 6, FBI officers denied that they had any plans to use psychological warfare techniques against the Branch Davidians (i.e., such as loud rock music, bright lights, weird sounds). The FBI used them constantly throughout the siege.

6)   In his press conference the evening of the fire, Bill Clinton said Janet Reno had acted because of the children "who were being abused." Later, officials admitted that there was no evidence of child abuse.

7)   On March 2, the FBI's Bob Ricks told reporters that when the FBI approached Koresh, he was going to go outside with grenades (in front of the TV cameras), pull the pin, commit suicide and take as many agents with him as he could. On 4/20 on *MacNeil/Lehrer Newshour* FBI Director William Sessions said that all of the FBI analysis of Koresh indicated that he would never commit suicide.

8)   BATF Director Stephen Higgins testified before a Senate subcommittee (4/2/93) that the BATF mission failed only "because the Branch Davidians ambushed the BATF." What a lie. The BATF attacked the Branch Davidians and not the other way around.

9)   The FBI and Janet Reno stated repeatedly that the reason they attacked the compound on April 19 was

"concern for the safety and well being of the children."
This was a lie! You don't ram into buildings with military
tanks and pump CS gas (a gas so deadly and debilitating
that it has been banned by international treaty for use in
warfare) into a building filled with women and children,
and call it "a concern for the safety of the children."

10) CS gas was described by Clinton, Reno and FBI
officials as a harmless (irritant) tear gas. **This is a lie!** It is
eighty times stronger than tear gas, immobilizes its
victims and throws them into violent, coughing and
convulsions (i.e., the "perfect" weapon for a police state to
use against young children and women!)

11) Clinton said on 4/20/93 that CS was a "tear gas
which had been tested not to cause permanent damage to
adults or children." **That is a lie!**

12) The government said they had exhausted all
avenues to resolve the standoff. **This is a lie!** They
refused to let **any** of the family members speak with the
Branch Davidians even though this has helped to resolve
many such former standoffs. They refused to let "Bo"
Gritz and Jack McLamb, who negotiated Randy Weaver
and his family out last August, assist, although they
volunteered numerous times.

13) The BATF said after the February 28 fiasco that
"we were outgunned." **That was a lie!** They had
helicopter gunships, armored vehicles, and fully
automatic weapons to use against the Branch Davidians
not to mention stun grenades and the military's most high
tech equipment.

14) George Stephanopoulos said, "The children were
being abused, even to instruction on how to clamp down
on cyanide pills." Though this makes for chilling
headlines, the FBI has denied that this was true.

15) On April 19, FBI spokesman Bob Ricks quoted
Branch Davidian survivor Renos Avraam as saying: "The
fire's been lit. The fire's been lit." But when questioned
on camera by reporters, Avraam said: "One of the tanks
knocked over a gas lantern, and it started a fire under

some bales of hay that were laying around. The fire wasn't started by us."

16) Attorney General Janet Reno branded him a "dangerous, irrational criminal" and Bill Clinton called Koresh "dangerous, irrational and probably insane." Then the media repeated these unsubstantiated (and largely untrue) allegations thousands of times and to the average American they became "truth." [ED. NOTE: The dynamic duo of government and media have the ability to create "reality," or the "appearance of reality" out of thin air!]

[ED. NOTE: It has occurred to this writer that he has seen no pictures of the people killed at Waco, including the children. After a plane crash or other tragedy, pictures of the victims (while alive) are usually shown. Not so with Operation Waco. The picture might elicit public sympathy (e.g., **these were real people, real children, real babies which were slaughtered.** No pictures are likely to be forthcoming).]

Before the last bodies were removed from the rubble in Waco an NBC film crew was already recording the re-enactment scenes at the reconstruction of the actual site in Oklahoma.

CONCLUSION: Does anyone really think that a Justice Department investigation of its own FBI, or a Treasury Department investigation of its own BATF will be anything besides a total whitewash? And as far as a Congressional investigation, Senator Dennis DeConcini (D-AZ), a member of the Senate Judiciary Committee, has already said, regarding a congressional investigation: "I'm not looking for them to blame anyone or anything like that." The fix is already in! They must cover up and bury the biggest potential political scandal in U.S. history. If Watergate could sink the Nixon Administration, Wacogate, which is 100 times bigger, could certainly sink a Clinton Administration. But it won't — it will be completely covered up!

There is another parallel between Nazi Germany in the 1930s and America in the 1990s. **The Third Reich** declared "open season" on non-mainstream (i.e., those not controlled by the government) religious minorities which were considered "dangerous misfits." These included Jews, fundamental evangelical Christians, gypsies and others. In America today, the Fourth Reich (i.e., the Establishment, the Clintonistas, the New World Order, New Age, environmentalist, pro-gay, pro-choice crowds) have declared "open season" on non-mainstream (non-government approved) religious minorities, sects, etc. — now defined as the smoke clears from Waco as "dangerous religious cults." Many small Christian churches, communities, and groups are about to be so re-classified.

This writer believes that among other things, Operation Waco was the beginning of religious persecution of unpopular, non-mainstream religious groups in America. Since the American people (including Christians) did not protest one peep over the destruction of the Branch Davidian sect, the attacks will now begin to accelerate.

The Waco incident is a clear example of how little respect the U.S. government has for its own Constitution. The BATF not only trampled the politically incorrect Second Amendment, they also made a mockery of the First and Fourth Amendments as well. They also trampled one of our most sacred Constitutional rights — freedom of belief (i.e., freedom of religion).

Almost fifty years have passed since the Allied forces crushed the Nazis, but their totalitarian philosophy of Ordnung is now beginning to reappear in the New World Order with all of its police state manifestations. Fifty years have passed, but little has changed.

President Reagan referred to the BATF as "that rogue agency." Senator James McClure (R-ID) has described the BATF as "an agency that has gone wild."

Pastor Martin Niemoeller, a Lutheran pastor who was sent to a concentration camp (DACHAU) in 1938 wrote these words: "In Germany the Nazis first came for the communists, and I didn't speak up because I wasn't a communist; then they came for the Jews and I didn't speak up because I wasn't a Jew; then they came for the trade unionists and I didn't speak up because I wasn't a trade unionist; they came for the Catholics and I didn't speak up because I was a protestant; finally they came for me, but there was no one left to speak up."

Friends, unless we speak up now and quickly we will lose our freedoms and they will never be returned.

One of the founding fathers said:

When the government fears the people there is liberty.
When the people fear the government, there is tyranny.

Mt. Carmel Waco Alert[1]

The government has arranged to further desecrate the Mt. Carmel building site and the surrounding seven acres. A contractor has been authorized by the Texas Natural Resource Conservation Committee and the Texas Water Commission to excavate from 6" to 18" of top soil which is advertised to be contaminated with lead and human waste.

Noted private investigator from Force 1, Gordon Novel, has secured at least forty-eight Branch Davidian death certificates indicating lethal blood levels of Cyanide, while none was found in the digestive system. In addition, from the manufacturers of CS gas, the technical data indicates that it will ignite at 327° F and produces heat up to 4,200° F while burning, functioning as a high temperature fire excellerant. Further, when water is added to a CS fire, it will explode. Thus explaining why the fire trucks were not allowed to the Mt. Carmel fire.

It is now clear that the government is in their last phase of the massive cover-up by hauling away evidence of the Cyanide poisoning deposited in the remains of Mt. Carmel.

The bull dozing was halted last Friday when Waco attorney Brian Pollard secured a "stay" in the digging operations until the merits of a temporary restraining order (TRO) are presented in the State District Court; visiting Judge Frank McDonald presiding. The hearing will be held Thursday morning, June 23, 1994, at the McClennon County Court House. Former U.S. Attorney General Ramsy Clark is scheduled to argue the case of Gordon Novel to enter the property and to secure necessary samples from the remains of the Mt. Carmel building and soil for an independent analysis.

Seventeen Little Children[2]

Just in case you don't remember
Let me jog your memory:
In a Church they called the Waco compound
Back in April '93,
Seventeen Little Children,
All so helpless and so small,
Died a Senseless death of gas and flame —
How many names can you recall?

Seventeen Little Children
Don't it make you wonder why?
Seventeen Little Children,
How could **they** deserve to die?
Maybe we should stop and ask ourselves —
If we've become so blind —
Will Seventeen Little Children
Finally open up your mind?

How did you sleep last night, Bill Clinton?
Tell me, did you feel their pain,
As Seventeen Little Children
Cried out and perished in the flames?

by Carl Klang

Chanel Andrade, 3	Crystal Martinez, 3
Dayland Lord Gent, 3	Isaiah Martinez, 3
Palges Gent, 2	Joseph Martinez, 7
Bobie Lane Koresh, 2	Starile Summers, 1
Cyrus Howell, 6	Hollywood Sylvia, 2
Starr Howell, 5	Mayanah Schnider, 3
Serenity Jones, 4	Mellissa Morrison, 4
Chica and Little One Jones, twins, 1	Newborn Gyarfas

APPENDIX B

The Great Seal

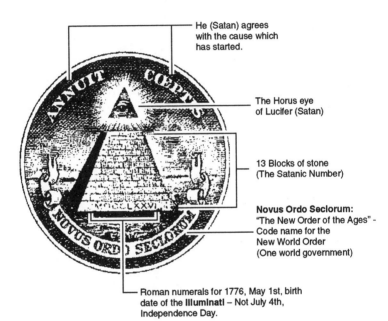

He (Satan) agrees with the cause which has started.

The Horus eye of Lucifer (Satan)

13 Blocks of stone (The Satanic Number)

Novus Ordo Seclorum: "The New Order of the Ages" - Code name for the New World Order (One world government)

Roman numerals for 1776, May 1st, birth date of the **Illuminati** – Not July 4th, Independence Day.

The Illuminati was founded by Adam Weishaupt, a professor of Cannon Law in Inglestodt, Germany, on May 1, 1776. He was an ex-Jesuit Roman priest, a Free Mason, and a man deeply involved in witchcraft (an apostle of Lucifer). Its major goals were five-fold:

- The destruction of all democratic governments.
- The abolition of all rights to private property.
- The destruction of Christianity.
- The establishment of a one world government.
- The elevation of Lucifer to the throne of the world.

257

The Triangle

The triangle within the circle is the supreme symbol of Lucifer, Satan, the devil, the Prince of Darkness, "the god of this world."

The triangle represents (in occultic secret code) the three Satanic deities in ancient Babylon. The citizens of Babylon worshiped the sun god Lucifer; their world dictator Nimrod; and the sun and the moon and stars and their Mother Goddess Earth (witchcraft) whose Satanic number was "666." This was Satan's counterfeit — the blasphemous, unholy trinity — a mockery of the blessed triune God of heaven, the Father, the Son and the Holy Spirit.

Benjamin Creme, director of the New Age movement of North America **links the triangle with the coming world ruler "the Christ."** This is the one whom the BIble identifies as Antichrist. He states, "The Christ will be known as the point **within the triangle."**[1]

The triangle is the symbol of the Lucis Trust. This has its fountain head in the United Nations. Its logo is **the triangle** with a representation of the unholy trinity inside.

Triangle — Supreme Symbol of Environmentalists

The triangle is the supreme symbol of the global environmental movement. The United Nations endorsed *The Great Invocation* as the official prayer of Earth Day, April 1990. It is the occultic, Satanic prayer invoking Lucifer to return and set up his hierarchal kingdom upon the earth. Earth Day linked 2.5 billion people together in the greatest extravaganza of all time. Flashing across the television screens of the world were the **white and green triangles.**

The New Age authors of The Rainbow Bridge describe Planet Earth "as a network of light composed of inter-linking triangle energy force fields. Link up with these universal force fields and you will be one with God." When enough people on earth link up to this network, they claim the New Age Christ and all his hierarchy of spirits (demons) will appear to establish their New Age Kingdom. Then the "sons of men" will be one.[2]

Texe Marrs writes in Mystery Mark of the New Age, "Djwal Khul, the demonic Tibetan master reveals that the triangle, through *The Great Invocation*, represents the combined energies of the Solar Father 'the Christ,' the hierarchy and humanity. In Christian terms this means the triangle represents the combined energies of Satan, his false New Age Christ, and the demonic angels (demons) of hell and mankind."[3] The Great Invocation is prayed by hundreds of millions of people around the entire globe.

The All Seeing Eye of Lucifer

The all seeing eye, at the apex of the triangle, in the great seal was known in ancient Egypt as the *Horus Eye of Ra*, the Egyptian sun god. The **Horus eye was the eye of Lucifer** (Satan).

Barbara Walker, in the *New Age Encyclopedia*, writes, "The triangle is the universal symbol of the 'Mother Goddess.' "

Robert Muller describes the emerging One World Order "as a glorious aphrodite emerging from the sea."[4] Aphrodite is the ancient Greek version of Babylon's Mother Goddess. This polluted the entire world with Satanism. India has the Mother Goddess and worships her today as the Great Serpent. Revelation 18 describes her as the Great Whore, the Bride of Satan, the False Counterfeit Church of Satan. Babylon will re-surface in the last days. She is the woman of Revelation 17:3; Satan's master counterfeit of the true, pure, blood-washed bride, the true church, "the Lamb's Wife."

Mr. Environmentalist Al Gore writes in his book *Earth in the Balance*,

> We can understand our religious heritage based on a single earth goddess who is assumed to be the fountain of all life.[5]

Could modern homosapiens, the most enlightened generation which ever lived, be going back to witchcraft, the worship of the sun and the moon and the stars and the worship of the earth (the Mother Goddess religion of ancient Babylon) whose Satanic number in Babylon was "666"?

U.S. News and World Report portrayed the All Seeing Eye of Lucifer centered within the pyramid with an arrow pointing toward the future. The title of the article was "Points in Time 1990 to 1999."[6] Could they have been signalling to their world-wide network of New Agers and Luciferians, "This is our time table for the New World Order?"

The Goal 2000 A.D.

Robert Muller, former Ass't Secretary General of the U.N. has repeatedly stated the goal is to usher in the New World Order and have "their New World (cosmic) Christ on the millennial throne of the world by the year 2000 A.D.

This writer believes that all the signs are pointing to one inescapable truth — we are in the last days of the Grace Age and we are watching the final rebellion of fallen man against the God of heaven. Remember, the Bible tells us, "Rebellion is as the sin of witchcraft" 1 Samuel 15:23.

The Masonic Connection

Free Masonry has its roots in the religions of ancient Babylon and Egypt. The following is taken from an authorized publication of Free Masonry, *Encyclopedia of Free Masonry and Its Kindred Sciences.*

> In all the old manuscripts, records which contain the legend of The Craft, mention is made of Hermes as one of the founders of Masonry.[7]

Hermes was the son of Ham (Cush). Cush was the father of Nimrod "who became a mighty hunter before (literally against) the Lord" Genesis 10:8-9. This was the beginning of his kingdom of Babel (Genesis 10:10).

According to Albert G. Mackey,

> Nimrod, the legend of the craft in the old constitutions refer to Nimrod as one of the founders of Masonry.[8]

The most prominent Free Mason in American history is Albert Pike, the author of the book *Morals and Dogma*. He states:

> The Masonic religion should by all of us initiates of the highest degrees be maintained in the purity of the Luciferian Doctrine.[9]

Manley Hall, a 33rd degree Mason, wrote in the book *Lost Keys of Free Masonry*:

> When the Mason learns that the key to the warrior on the block is the proper application of the dynamo of living power, he has learned the mystery of the craft: **the seething energies of Lucifer is in his hands.**[10]

Albert Pike wrote:

> Lucifer, the light bearer! Lucifer, Son of the Morning! It is he who bears the light![11]

The U.N. Meditation Room and The Great Black Stone

There is a meditation room in the United Nations building in New York City. It is designed in the form of a laying down pyramid with the capstone missing (see the pyramid on the reverse side of the $1.00 bill). The Illuminati believe when that capstone comes down, then their God Lucifer will come to reign over the earth. They believe they are illumined by the great Sun God whom they worship.

There is also in the Meditation Room a **great black stone**. Some day all the world will worship the great black stone who is none other than Satan. He basically is the great capstone of the pyramid, the "Son of Perdition." He will come and no doubt address the United Nations and then kneel before the great black stone.

The Meditation Room has a Hindu Guru. He teaches that the number *666 is a holy number*. The Bible reveals in Revelation 13:18 that the number *666* will be the unholy number of the beast, the world's great Antichrist, Satan, Lucifer, incarnate in "the Man of Sin."

The Black Stone Altar in the U.N. Meditation Room.

The Masonic "House of The Temple" in Washington, D.C.

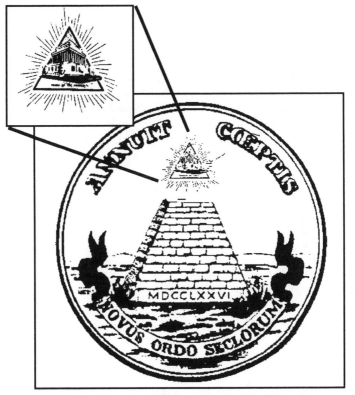

Unveiling of the Great Light. . . Lucifer! Building the "Temple of RA" – the Universal Temple of the Masons!

Exactly thirteen blocks from the White House in Washington, D.C., is the great Masonic Temple of the Scottish rites. It, too, houses the great black stone. The temple is the 33rd degree Masonic temple.

Albert Pike wrote, "The ancients adored the sun under the form of a great black stone."[12]

That great black stone is the symbol of their god, Lucifer.

The Stone Cut out of the Mountain

The Bible, God's holy Word, reveals that **there is another stone.** That stone is destined to become the "head of the corner." The stone which the builders rejected has become the Head of the corner. **That stone is Jesus Christ** (1 Peter 2:6-7).

"For other foundation can no man lay than that which is laid, which is Jesus Christ" 1 Corinthians 3:11.

Twenty-six hundred years ago, the eternal triune God of heaven revealed to Daniel (Daniel 2:44-45) "the stone, cut out of the mountain without hands." It smote the empire of the world's last dictator, the beast son of perdition, Antichrist. That stone is the Lord Jesus Christ, Lord of Lords, and King of Kings.

This same scene is described in Revelation 2:27, "And He shall rule the nations with a rod of iron; as the vessels of a potter shall they be broken to shivers."

> And in the days of these kings shall the God of heaven set up a kingdom, which shall never be destroyed . . . it shall break in pieces and consume all these kingdoms, and it shall stand forever (Daniel 2:44-45).

> But the saints of the Most High shall take the kingdom, and possess the kingdom forever, even forever and ever (Daniel 7:18).

> The kingdom of this world is become the kingdom of our Lord, and of his Christ, and He shall reign for ever and ever (Revelation 11:15).

APPENDIX C

Notes

Chapter One

1. George Bush in an address to the U.S. Congress, September 11, 1990.

2. General Brent Skowcroft, from a taped radio broadcast on the eve of the Gulf War.

3. Pope John Paul II, as quoted by Malachi Martin in *The Keys of This Blood* (New York: Simon & Schuster, 1990).

4. ibid.

5. *The Oregonian*, January 17, 1991.

6. Norman Cousins, *Human Events*, August 1985.

7. *Institute 666*, pp.177.

8. Texe Marrs, *Millennium* (Living Truth Ministries Publisher, Austin, TX), p.21.

9. Catherine B. Dalton, *Constitutional Money and Banking Procedure*, p. 4.

10. *Foreign Affairs*, April 1974.

11. Rear Admiral Chester Ward, as quoted by Anthony Sutton in *The Skull and Bones, America's Secret Establishment* (Liberty House, Billings, MT), pp.144-148.

12. Senator Barry Goldwater, *With No Apologies* (New York: Morrow, 1979), p.203.

13. Sutton, p.123.

14. Texe Marrs, *Flash Point*, July 1992.

15. Al Gore, *Earth in the Balance* (Boston: Houghton Mifflin, 1992).

16. Don McAlvany, *Toward a New World Order* (Hearthstone Publishing Co., a division of Southwest Radio Church of the Air, 1985).

17. Dennis Cuddy, Ph.D., "Elitist Insiders Dominate Clinton's Appointees," April 2, 1993, No. 9, p.1.

18. Marrs, *Flash Point*, September 1993, p. 4.

19. *The Spotlight*, April 2, 1992.

20. John Foster Dulles, quoted from the *William Jenner Congressional Record*, February 23, 1954.

21. *Congressional Record*, April 2, 1992.

22. "White House Gets Cult Fever," from *Line by Line*, an Evans–Pritchard Report, Washington, D.C., *Sunday Telegraph*, June 20, 1993.

Chapter Two

1. Dennis Cuddy, Ph.D., *Dawning of the New World Order* (Hearthstone Publishing Co.), p.316.

2. McAlvany, p.224.

3. *Microelectronics and Society*, a report to the Club of Rome, as quoted in McAlvany's *Toward a New World Order*, p. 224.

4. *Calgary Albertan*, April 18, 1980.

5. "Ten Kingdoms With the Beast," *Newswatch Magazine*, March-April 1984, pp.12-15.

6. Des Griffin, *Fourth Reich of the Rich* (Emmisary Publications).

7. James Perloff, *Shadows*, pp.23-24.

8. Dalton, p.4.

9. *The Rockefeller File*, Congressional Record, Vol. 51, Part 2, December 22, 1913, p. 1446.

10. Marrs, *Millenium*, p.158.

11. William R. Goetz, *The Economy to Come* (Horizon House Publishers, 1983), p. 69.

12. Marrs, p.184.

13. Salem Kirban, *The Coming World Currency* (Huntington Valley, Penn; Second Coming, 1989), pp. 19-22.

Chapter Four

1. Woodrow Wilson, *The New Freedom*, as quoted by Dr. Dennis Cuddy, Ph.D. in the Introduction of *Now is the Dawning of the New Age, New World Order*.

2. *London Sunday Illustrated Herald*, February 8, 1920.
3. Marrs, *Millennium*, pp. 75-76.
4. *Oregonian*, January 3, 1987.
5. Richard Gardiner, former Deputy Assistant Secretary of State, *Foreign Affairs*, April 1974.
6. Harvey Watchman as quoted in *Flash Point*.
7. *Ron Paul Report*, January 15, 1993.
8. *McAlvany Intelligence Advisory Report*, July 1993.
9. *The Washington Times*, April 4, 1993.
10. Martin Anderson, Howard News Service, *Stanford Bulletin*, October 1, 1993.
11. Barbara Walker, *Woman's Encyclopedia of Myths and Secrets* (Harper & Row, 1983), p. 798.
12. Dr. Roy Anderson, D.D., ed., *The New Age Movement, The Illuminati "666,"* p. 70.
13. Bill Clinton and Al Gore, *Putting People First* (New York: Times Books, 1992), p. 109.
14. *Daily Mail* (England), June 24, 1993.

Chapter Five

1. *U.S. News and World Report*, August 13, 1990.
2. *Time*, October 11, 1992.
3. Peter Grace, as quoted in *Time Magazine*, October 1992.
4. John ZaJack, *The Coming Catastrophic Changes on Planet Earth*.
5. Larry Burkett, *The Coming Financial Earthquake*.
6. McAlvany, *Toward a New World Order*, p. 136.

Chapter Six

1. Alice Bailey, *Externalization of the Hierarchy* (Lucis Publishing Co., New York City, N.Y., 1957).
2. Kurt Koch, quoted in "Operation Vampire," *The American Citizens and Lawmen Association* (P.O. Box 8712, Phoenix, AZ 85066), 1992.
3. David Spangler, *Reflections of the Christ* (Findhorn Lecture Series), pp. 36-39.
4. David Spangler as quoted by Malachi Martin in *The Keys of this Blood*.
5. Constance Cumbey, *Hidden Dangers of the Rainbow* (Shreveport, LA: Huntington House Publishers, 1983), p. 140.
6. Robert Muller, *The New Genesis* (New Genesis Image Books, a division of Doubleday & Co., Inc., 1984), p. 29.
7. Alexander Hislop, *The Two Babylons* (Hearthstone

Publishers, Oklahoma City, OK), p. 288.
8. Martin.
9. Hislop, pp. 285-287.
10. ibid.
11. Cardinal Alphonsus de Liguori, *The Glories of Mary*, p. 94.
12. ibid., pp. 180-181.
13. Dr. John Walvoord, *The Bible Knowledge*, p. 971.
14. ibid.
15. Barry Smith, *The Second Warning*, p. 121.
16. *Oregonian*, September 22, 1992.
17. Marrs, *Millennium*, pp. 95-96.
18. Martin.
19. Matthew Fox, *The Coming of the Cosmic Christ* (San Francisco: Harper & Row, 1988).
20. Carl Sagan, *Cosmos* (New York: Ballantine Books, 1985).
21. Mary Daley as quoted by Dr. Dennis Cuddy, Ph.D., in *Dawning of the New World Order and New Age Religion*.
22. *Reader's Digest*, July 1991.
23. *The Los Angeles Times*, October 25, 1989.
24. John Randolph Price, *Planetary Commission*.
25. Marrs, *The Mystery Mark* (Westchester, IL: Crossway Books, 1988), pp. 176-177.
26. Benjamin Creme, *Maitreya Amsterdam* (Mission Share International Foundation, 1986), p. 46.
27. From the manuscript on the "Fourth World Wilderness Congress," 1987, *Bacca, Ashrams, and Institutions*, by George Hunt.
28. *Two Disciples, the Rainbow Bridge*, p. 73.
29. Barbara Marx Hubbard, *Co-Creation*, 1980.
30. Benjamin Creme on radio Q107, Toronto, Canada, May 30, 1984.
31. Willis Harmon, *Journal of Humanistic Psychology* (Stanford University, Winter 1981).
32. Vera Alder, *When Humanity Comes Alive*, pp. 20-24.
33. From the symposium "Toward a Global Brain, Our Next Evolutionary Step," November 9-11, 1984.
34. Robert Muller as quoted by Dr. Dennis Cuddy, Ph.D. in *Dawning of the New Age*.
35. Muller in an address to the National Catholic Education Association, St. Louis, Missouri, April 8-12, 1985, from the *Catholic Fidelity Report*.
36. Muller, *The New Genesis*, p. 191.
37. Thomas P. Erenzeller, *Solar Man*.
38. Sutton, pp. 104-105.

39. Muller as quoted by Cuddy in *Now is the Dawning of the New Age, New World Order*, pp. 271-272.
40. The John Ankerberg T.V. Program.
41. Jacques Vallee, *Messengers of Deception* (Berkeley, CA: And/Or Press, 1979), pp. 19, 21.
42. John Randolph Price, *Planetary Commission* (Quartus Foundation, Texas).
43. Dr. M. Scott Peck as quoted by Cuddy, p. 282.
44. Ed Decker, *The Question of Masonry*, p. 9.
45. *The Lost Keys of Free Masonry*, p. 92.
46. Bernadette Roberts, *Experience of No Self*, Yoga Journal, Nov.-Dec., 1986, p. 35.
47. Swami Muktananda as quoted by David Hunt in *Cult Explosion* (Eugene, OR: Harvest House Publishers, 1982).
48. Kenneth Copeland as quoted by David Hunt in *The Seduction of Christianity* (Eugene, OR: Harvest House Publishers, 1984).
49. Earl Paulk, *Satan Unmasked* (Atlanta, GA: K Dimension Publishers, 1984), pp. 96-97.
50. *The Lost Keys of Free Masonry*, p. 48.
51. Randall Baer, *Inside the New Age Nightmare*, pp. 55-64, 75.
52. Alice Bailey, *Educating for the New Age* (Lucis Publishing, 1954), pp. 111-112.
53. Dr. M. Scott Peck, *Marching to a Different Drum Beat*
54. Barbara Marx Hubbard, *The Apple of Eden's Eye*, 1958.
55. *The Keys of Enoch*, p. 332.

Chapter Seven

1. Kathi Simonds, *A Critique of America 2000, Citizens for Excellence*.
2. Lamar Alexander as quoted by Cuddy, p. 358.
3. René DuBos as quoted by Cuddy, p. 358.
4. Mirandola as quoted by René DuBos in *A God Within* (New York: Scribner, 1972), p. 358.
5. Alexander as quoted by Marilyn Ferguson in *The Aquarian Conspiracy* (Los Angeles: J.P. Tarcher, 1980).
6. ibid.
7. Alexander in a speech in Witchita, Kansas, on November 1, 1989.
8. Cuddy, p. 353.
9. Maria Augusta Trapp, *The Story of the Trapp Family Singers* (Philadelphia: Lippincott, 1949).
10. "Project Ten," *No Special Rights Committee Bulletin*,

May 12, 1992.
    11. Sandy Ogle, "Find Out What Our Schools Teach," *Spokane Newspaper.*
    12. ibid.
    13. School Bulletin, "Celebrate the Return of the Light."
    14. Sheila Schwartz, *Humanist Magazine*, Jan.-Feb. 1976.
    15. Betina Dobbs as quoted by Simonds, pp. 30-31.
    16. ibid.
    17. Dr. Pierce, Harvard University, 1973.
    18. *The Teacher and World Government National Education Association Journal*, January 1946.
    19. Des Griffin, *The Midnight Messenger*, March-April 1993.
    20. Texe Marrs, *Flash Point*, June 1993.
    21. *Daily News Digest.*
    22. John Dumphy, *Humanist Magazine*, Jan.-Feb. 1983.
    23. *Today's Journal*, Sept.-Oct. 1977.
    24. Samuel Blumenfeld, *N.E.A. Trojan Horse in American Education* (Boise, ID: Paradigm Co., 1984).

Chapter Eight

    1. Paul Mazur as quoted by Malachi Martin in *The Keys of This Blood*, p. 343.
    2. Erenzeller.
    3. The Official Poster, Council of Europe.
    4. Marrs, *Millennium*, p. 82.
    5. "40th Anniversary of the Aspen Institute for Humanistic Studies," C-Span television, August 4, 1990.
    6. Gary Kah, *En Route to Global Occupation*, pp. 85-86.
    7. ibid., p. 40.
    8. ibid., pp. 174-175.
    9. ibid., p. 116.
    10. ibid., p. 88.
    11. Alice Bailey, *Externalization of the Hierarchy*, p. 511.
    12. Albert Pike, *Morals and Dogma* (L.H. Jenkins, Inc., 1930), pp. 213, 219.
    13. A.C. La Rive as recorded in the French Encyclopedia *La Femme et Enfant dans La Franc Maconnerie Universal*, p. 588.
    14. Pike, p. 321.
    15. *Religion and Ethics*, Vol. 12, p. 204.
    16. Manley P. Hall, *The Lost Keys of Free Masonry*, p. 48.
    17. Jim Shaw & Tom McKenny, *The Deadly Deception* (Huntington House), p. 109.
    18. Sir Robert Anderson, *The Coming Prince* (Kregel Publications; reprint 1984), pp. 127-128.

19. ibid.
20. Tal Brooke, *When the World Will Be As One* (Eugene, OR: Harvest House Publishers, 1989), p. 226.
21. *Strong's Concordance*, #3319.
22. Paul Wilde, *How Long, O Lord?* (Woodburn, OR: Solid Rock Books, Inc., 1993), p. 30.

Chapter Ten

1. *United Nations Monthly Chronicle*, May 1974.
2. Willard Cantelon, *New Money or None*, as quoted in the *San Jose Mercury*, August 8, 1975.
3. *The Daily Oklahoma*, September 21, 1976.
4. Sutton, p. 122.
5. *Senior Scholastics* (Scholastic, Inc.), September 20, 1973.
6. Dr. David Webber, *The Point of No Return* (Southwest Radio Church, Oklahoma City, OK).
7. CFN Information Network, Jerusalem Bureau, February 1975.
8. Dr. Mary Relfe, Ph.D., *When Your Money Fails*.
9. Terry Galonay, former director of communications for VISA.
10. *Futurist Magazine*.
11. Clinton and Gore, p. 109.
12. *The Christian Science Monitor*, January 25, 1993.
13. *San Jose Mercury News*.
14. Carrol Quigley, *Tragedy and Hope* (Hollywood, CA: Angriff Press, 1974).
15. *Marin Independent Journal*, April 2, 1989.
16. *Arizona Republic*, July 20, 1989.
17. *Prophecy in the News*, November 1990, p. 4.
18. *Futurist Magazine*.
19. *Strong's Concordance* #5516.
20. ibid., #4742.
21. Bailey.
22. *Sydney Morning Herald* (Australia), October 11, 1993.
23. ibid., February 15, 1984.
24. Barry Smith in a taped message, 1991.
25. David Spangler as quoted by Martin in *Keys of this Blood*.
26. Spangler as quoted by Manly P. Hall in *The Lost Keys of Free Masonry*, p. 48.
27. Albert Pike, *Queensborough Theocracy*, pp. 220-221.
28. David Spangler, *The Reflections of the Christ* (Scotland Findhorn, 1977), pp. 36-44.

Appendix A

1. *Mt. Carmel Waco Alert* from Dewey Millay, N.D., Energyologist, 3416 N. 3rd St., Waco, TX 76706.
2. Words and music by Carl Klang, P.O. Box 217, Colton, OR 97017, (503)824-3371. Used by permission.

Appendix B

1. Creme, *Maitreya's Mission* (Amsterdam: Share International Publications, 1986), p. 46.
2. The Two Disciples, *Rainbow Bridge*, p. 196-200.
3. Marrs, *Mystery Mark of the New Age*, p. 83.
4. Muller, *The New Genesis*, p. 29.
5. Gore, from *The Christian American*, April 1994, p. 6.
6. *U.S. News and World Report*, "Points in Time 1990 to 1999," December 25th/January 1, 1990.
7. Albert G. Mackey, *Encyclopedia of Free Masonry and its Kindred Sciences*, p. 322.
8. Mackey, Vol. 2, p. 518.
9. Pike, pp. 220-221.
10. Hall, p. 48.
11. Albert Pike, *Morals and Dogma*, p. 321.
12. Pike, p. 775.

Reference Books

America's Secret Establishment of Skull and Bones
   by Anthony Sutton
America, the Sorcerer's New Apprentice
   by David Hunt
America 2000 Critique
   by Kathi Simonds
Bible Commentary
   by Dr. John Walvoord
Coming Persecution
   by Dr. Larry Polland, Ph.D.
Count Down to Armaggedon
   by Hal Lindsey
Church in Crisis
   by Hank Hanegraaff
Cult Explosion
   by David Hunt
Dark Secrets of the New Age
   by Texe Marrs
Dark Majesty
   by Texe Marrs
Deadly Deception
   by Jim Shaw and Tom McKenney
Descent into Slavery
   by Des Griffin
En Route to Global Occupation
   by Gary Kah
Educating for the New World Order
   by B.K. Eakman
First and Second Warning and Final Warning
   by Pastor Barry Smith

Fourth Reich of the Rich
   by Des Griffin
Hidden Dangers of the Rainbow
   by Constance Cumbey
How Long, O Lord
   by Rev. Paul Wilde
Inside the New Age Nightmare
   by Randall Baer
Mystery Mark
   by Texe Marrs
Millennium
   by Texe Marrs
N.E.A. Trojan Horse in American Education
   by Samuel Blumenfeld
New Age Lies to Women
   by Wanda Marrs
New Covenant, The
   by John Barella
New Money or None
   by Willard Cantelon
New Money System, The
   by Dr. Mary Relfe, Ph.D.
New World Order
   by William Still
Now is the Dawning of the New Age —
New World Order
   by Dennis Cuddy, Ph.D.
Trojan Horse: How the New Age Movement
Infiltrates the Church
   by Brenda Scott and Samantha Smith
Two Babylons, The
   by Rev. Alexander Hislop
When the World Will Be As One
   by Tal Brooke
When Your Money Fails
   by Dr. Mary Relfe, Ph.D.

How Long, O Lord?
by Paul and Carolyn Wilde
ISBN 187-911-2167

How Long, O Lord? is an easy to read book packed with Scriptures that deal with the following subjects:

- Jesus is coming! Can we know when?
- The Thief in the night!
  Is it phase one of Christ's coming?
- Why is Christ coming as a thief?
- What is Tribulation?
- What is its purpose?
- God has not appointed us to wrath!
  But are tribulation and wrath the same thing?
- The end-day pharaoh!
- Portrait of the Antichrist!
- The Mark of the Beast
- God's end-day people
- The Day of Wrath
- Do the Scriptures confirm that Christ is coming after the Tribulation?
- The surprising origin of the teaching of a pre-trib rapture
- Should this message be preached?
- Will people be saved after Christ returns?

"In his new book, *How Long, O Lord*, Pastor Wilde has superbly laid out the rapture of the Church — not the time of the rapture for no man knows the day or the hour. But he shows where the rapture fits into the sequence of prophetic events. I highly recommend this book."

Dwight L. Kinman
Author, *The World's Last Dictator*

Available at
fine Christian Booksellers everywhere

Lord Give Me A Repentant Heart

by Thomas LeBlanc

ISBN 187-911-2221

Can revival come to America?
Only if a wave of true repentance comes first. For God has promised to revive those with repentant hearts.

"If my people, who are called by my name, shall humble themselves, and pray, and seek my face, and turn from their wicked ways, then will I hear from heaven, and will forgive their sin, and will heal their land." 2 Chronicles 7:14

God's people are clearly the ones who have within their grasp the power to change this nation. But are we willing to pay the price for a fresh move of God?

In this booklet, Mr. LeBlanc has placed in microcosm the most vital message that could possibly be given to the church of Jesus Christ in America.

Mr. LeBlanc portrays the spark that ignited the church in America during the days of Jonathan Edwards in the seventeen hundreds – a time when revival flames swept all of New England and brought our young nation back to God. He presents the catalyst that again brought the fires of revival to America in the eighteen hundreds, at the time of Charles Finney, when hundreds of thousands were swept into the kingdom of God.

Mr. LeBlanc has captured that same message that is so urgently needed at this crisis hour. It is a message that will bless you and thrill your heart and could become the key to lift your life to a new dimension of power and victory. I highly recommend this splendid booklet to you!

Dwight L. Kinman
Author, *The World's Last Dictator*

Available at
fine Christian Booksellers everywhere

Seven Biblical Principles for Financial Peace of Mind

by Paul and Carolyn Wilde

ISBN 187-911-2094

How many people do you know who have financial peace of mind? Do you have it?

The number one cause of divorce today is fighting about money! **MONEY!**

Worrying about it causes ulcers, migraines, divorces, murders, thefts, prostitution, suicides . . . the list could go on and on, but God's Word sums it all up by saying our love for it is the root of all evil.

Did you know there are seven principles we must follow if we want the blessing of God upon our lives?

You may follow two or three of them – but do you know and follow all seven?

We, as Christians, especially in the coming days of financial turmoil and economic collapse of the monetary system as we know it, need to know and put into practice every single one of these principles. Then, and only then, will you have financial peace of mind.

This book will show you what these seven principles are and how to practice them!

**Available at
fine Christian Booksellers everywhere**

We've Come This Far By Faith
by Carolyn Wilde

ISBN 187-911-206X

Paul and Carolyn were deeply in debt when an automobile accident led Paul to make a life-changing commitment to put God first in his life, and their extraordinary, living-by-faith adventure began.

We've Come This Far By Faith is a heart-warming book, not just about a family who learned to trust their God for their needs, but about a living, faithful, loving God who cares for His children.

We've Come This Far By Faith will challenge and inspire you to trust God to guide and take care of you as you put His principles into action in your life. The comment most often heard from readers of **We've Come This Far By Faith** is, *"I stayed up all night reading this book! I just couldn't put it down!"*

We've Come This Far By Faith will give you that extra faith you need to step out on the sea of life with your eyes and faith firmly fixed on Jesus Christ! He will not let His followers sink, no matter how the storms around us rage!

**Available at
fine Christian Booksellers everywhere**

Personal Relationship
by Thomas LeBlanc

Christianity is not a religion, but a relationship – a living personal relationship with God. He desires to be a real part of our lives. He longs to develop a personal relationship with each of us.

In this book, you will read about many examples of how Jesus can touch and influence a person's life. You will see that only He can eliminate our guilt and fill our emptiness. Learn how through Him, we can overcome fear. You will understand that He offers a peace that surpasses human comprehension.

In this book you will:
- Learn how "emptiness" is filled
- See how to combat fear
- Understand God's peace
- Recognize God's faithfulness
- Discover the ingredients for a miracle

New Discovery:
- Learn how our thoughts and words affect our physical bodies.

Thomas LeBlanc is a Christian businessman, a registered physical therapist and a publisher. He has authored Christian tracts, a physical therapy article, and an electronic communications text that is used in technical colleges across the country. He lives with his wife, Karen, and three children, in Oregon.

**Available at
fine Christian Booksellers everywhere**

Please write for a FREE listing
of all audio and video tapes that are
now available.

Dwight L. Kinman
P.O. Box 386
Canby, Oregon 97013

Other products from
Solid Rock Books, Inc.
include:

☑ **Books**

☑ **Audio Tapes**

☑ **Video Tapes**

For a *FREE* catalog, please write to:

Solid Rock Books, Inc.
979 Young Street, Suite E
Woodburn, Oregon 97071
(503) 981-0705   FAX (503) 981-4742